AESTHETIC IMPROPRIETY

Aesthetic Impropriety

PROPERTY LAW AND POSTCOLONIAL STYLE

Rose Casey

FORDHAM UNIVERSITY PRESS   NEW YORK   2025

This book was a recipient of the American Comparative Literature Association's Helen Tartar First Book Subvention Award. Fordham University Press is grateful for the funding from this prize that helped facilitate publication.

This book has been made possible through a grant from the West Virginia Humanities Council, a state affiliate of the National Endowment for the Humanities.

Copyright © 2025 Fordham University Press

All rights reserved. No part of this publication may be reproduced, stored in a retrieval system, or transmitted in any form or by any means — electronic, mechanical, photocopy, recording, or any other — except for brief quotations in printed reviews, without the prior permission of the publisher.

Fordham University Press has no responsibility for the persistence or accuracy of URLs for external or third-party Internet websites referred to in this publication and does not guarantee that any content on such websites is, or will remain, accurate or appropriate.

Fordham University Press also publishes its books in a variety of electronic formats. Some content that appears in print may not be available in electronic books.

Visit us online at www.fordhampress.com.

For EU safety / GPSR concerns: Mare Nostrum Group B.V., Mauritskade 21D, 1091 GC Amsterdam, The Netherlands, gpsr@mare-nostrum.co.uk

Library of Congress Cataloging-in-Publication Data available online at https://catalog.loc.gov.

Printed in the United States of America

27 26 25   5 4 3 2 1

First edition

Contents

Introduction: An Aesthetic Theory of Law and Literature   1

1. Symbiosis: Oil Extraction in the Racial Capitalocene   29

2. Reciprocity: Female Dispossession in Inheritance and Divorce   62

3. Accretion: Decolonizing Intellectual Property Law   90

4. Dispersal: Admiralty Law and Raising the Dead   120

Conclusion: Hope's Impropriety   154

Acknowledgments   161

Notes   165

Works Cited   201

Index   219

AESTHETIC IMPROPRIETY

Introduction
An Aesthetic Theory of Law and Literature

When the bronze statue of slave trader Edward Colston (1636–1721) was toppled on June 7, 2020 in Bristol, England, then hauled toward the city's harbor and cast into a watery grave, protestors rejected the public monumentalizing of a major beneficiary of chattel slavery—a man whose role as deputy governor of the Royal African Company meant that he not only profited from the slave trade but was also responsible for ordering the forced transportation of enslaved Africans across the Atlantic Ocean into which the Bristol Channel flows. The statue's spectacular removal, at one of the many Black Lives Matter protests that spread across the world in summer 2020, led to the prosecution of the so-called Colston Four under the Criminal Damage Act 1971; prosecutors alleged that by tying rope around the statue, pulling it down, and launching it into Bristol Harbour, the defendants had committed violent acts against public property.[1] On January 5, 2022, the Colston Four were acquitted at Bristol Crown Court, with jurors agreeing by an 11–1 majority that the accused activists had a lawful excuse for damaging the property of Bristol City Council.[2]

Yet the verdict was sufficiently controversial that Attorney General Suella Braverman referred the case to the Court of Appeal to address one of the arguments heard at trial: that conviction would pose "a disproportionate interference with the defendants' right to protest" under articles 9, 10, and 11 of the European Convention of Human Rights.[3] On September 28, 2022, appeal court judges upheld Braverman's concerns, ruling as a point of law that damage to public property that is "inflicted in a violent or non-peaceful manner attracts no Convention protection against prosecution and conviction."[4] Addressing the Colston case specifically, judges found that because "[t]he toppling of the statue was violent" and "the damage to the statue was significant," the defendants qualified for conviction under the Criminal Damage Act.[5] While the Court of Appeal's ruling could not overturn the acquittals of Rhian Graham, Milo Ponsford, Sage Willoughby, and Jake Skuse, it has dampened rights to protest in the UK,[6] especially given its announcement mere months after the implementation of the draconian Police, Crime, Sentencing and Courts Act of 2022 and not long before the Public Order Act of 2023. Taken together, the removal of Colston's statue and the Crown Prosecution Service's subsequent legal actions evoke pressing political questions about parliamentary overreach, the right to protest in a democratic society, and racial justice in contemporary Britain, not to mention the widely discussed issue of how best to deal with monuments that inspire white supremacist hagiography.[7]

But the controversy surrounding the Colston sculpture also raises less obvious, or at least, less widely considered questions: about property law's extensive and varied role in British colonial domination; about how art not only registers but also produces epistemological change; and about the transformative capacities of both aesthetics and the law. Fittingly, this monument to a white man who had legally treated Black people as property—and who had built his wealth upon the brutal system of racialized ownership that Britain employed to populate its colonized territories and produce vast amounts of raw goods—had itself become a site of property contestation. And yet, Colston's statue, this piece of public art, could not have been so poetically deposed, nor the protestors so convincingly acquitted, had substantial groundwork not been laid in advance. The conditions of possibility for toppling Colston's statue had been established slowly and patiently, over the course of several decades, through the sustained work of Bristol's Black community and the city's vibrant arts scene.

In 2006, in an early aesthetic engagement with Colston's legacy, British-Guyanese artist Hew Locke was commissioned by Bristol's Spike Island arts center to produce a series of mixed-media sculptures that would show how displaying statues of certain historical figures, including Colston, effectively glorified colonial plunder and racial violence.[8] The question of Colston's legacy remained contentious, with local opinion divided between those who admired a man who had brought significant wealth to Bristol, his name adorning multiple streets, schools, pubs, and other civic buildings to honor his philanthropic activities and cultural status,[9] and those who recognized him as a major figure in Britain's slave trade. In a public climate that was not yet ready to see the toppling of monuments to revered historical figures as anything other than criminal acts, Locke engaged with his selected pieces of public property in ways that fell within the law.

In what he describes as acts of "mindful vandalism," Locke produced modified versions of the statues by photographing them, printing their likenesses on aluminum, and adorning the reproductions with an abundance of primarily gold-colored objects that signify colonial violence.[10] In the piece titled *Colston*, the photographed monument is draped with necklaces made of cowrie shells, which were used by British slave traders to purchase enslaved Africans, along with crystal studded skulls, pound coins, silver lions rampant, and copious ceremonial gold chains, together illuminating the source of Colston's wealth: namely, Britain's deadly and dehumanizing practice of enslaving West Africans for profit.[11] While the sheer mass of glitzy objects that are carefully arrayed on Colston's reworked statue signals the extent of his wealth, their cheap, plastic materiality playfully undermines Edward Colston's value as a historical figure. Locke's deployment of lighthearted irony, in his aesthetic strategies as well as in naming this series of substantively altered monuments *Restoration*, at once produces deeply sincere critiques of British colonialism and participates in a broader project of changing the terms of public debate. Given his preference for irony, it is appropriate that, unlike his more famous Lockean namesake, John — who similarly theorized property in relation to-capitalist colonialism, and who was, like Colston, a shareholder in the Royal African Company — Hew Locke rejects British colonialism's racially privative property regime.

If Locke's *Restoration* series played an early and significant role in establishing the discursive environment in which protestors could feel confident dislodging a heavy and valuable piece of public property without legal consequences, it did so in large part because of its ornate, stylized aesthetics. The Colston Four's very public act of protest, which involved physically removing a heavy block of metal and disposing of it at sea, was widely reported not simply because it occurred at the height of the Black Lives Matter movement but also because it so clearly established the relationship between act and meaning: between the act of damaging public property and the system of racial ownership that the statue represented and its protestors renounced. Locke's work, by contrast, is more obviously aesthetic, in the sense that it draws attention to itself as art, employs a relatively abstracted and conceptual style, and makes claims that are somewhat indirect. As with most aesthetic works, Locke's stylistic intricacies and conceptual complexities reward attention: the viewer is initially drawn in by the boldness of his colors and textures, only subsequently proceeding to identify elaborate details, such as tiny objects that are carefully arrayed upon a figure's neck and body, that challenge British colonialism's system of proprietary, racialized ownership. By rewarding sustained engagement, aesthetically experimental works like Locke's *Colston* piece or his *Restoration* series bear significant impact on collective sensibilities even if, unlike the Colston Four's own act of critical reframing, their effects are less immediate and more difficult to measure. Indeed, it is through their very indirectness that aesthetic works are capable of participating in social transformation. By only indirectly registering changing social beliefs and cultural commitments, works of visual art, literature, or performance can viscerally produce new structures of value.

In using stylized, publicly engaged art to reject British colonialism's property regime and contribute to forming a society that values racial justice, Locke's *Restoration* series recognizes the aesthetic's role in both registering and producing new ways of being in the world. By recontextualizing existing materials, like a public monument and some cheap plastic skulls, *Restoration* draws out submerged histories, providing new meaning to old conventions. Similarly, it plays with scale, appearing to bear one signification from a distance—a mass of golden objects upon a statue might seem to celebrate accumulation—and another when looked at more closely, thereby staging the process through which public perceptions of shared national history are remade. In transforming the historical narrative from honoring Colston's philanthropy to rejecting him as a slave trader, *Restoration* reframes our relationship to existing forms of knowledge. Importantly, Locke's work offers more than simply a changed perspective on Colston; it also alters how we think about colonial history, public art, and ongoing racial inequality as a result of capitalist-colonial racial violence. Locke's engagement with contested monuments has participated in transforming publicly shared ideas about Bristol's—and Britain's—relationship to the past. In both encoding and producing new forms of thought, works like *Restoration* can help to change the legal realities of our present.

My opening trifold example of Colston's monumental toppling, Hew Locke's *Restoration* series, and Britain's legal response exemplifies this book's own trifold concern with property, justice, and aesthetics. While *Aesthetic Impropriety: Property Law and Postcolonial Style* primarily analyzes various forms of property law in relation to literary works rather than visual art, the Locke-Colston-Crown event usefully encapsulates this book's analytic focus. The compound term "Locke-Colston-Crown" signals what I take to be, in the circumstances that this book examines, an inextricable relationship between aesthetics, advocacy, and the law: between, in this case, the contemporary visual artist Hew Locke; the activists that the Colston statue metonymically invokes; and the United Kingdom's legal system, the Crown Prosecution Service. In bringing together three events across time, Locke-Colston-Crown also acknowledges that aesthetically encoded structures of thought can contribute to the process whereby social commitments begin to change, much as Locke's experimental aesthetics bore a slow but discernable impact on public perceptions of Edward Colston over the course of sixteen years: from 2006, when Locke's *Restoration* series was first exhibited; to 2020, when Colston's statue was deposed; to 2022, when the Crown Prosecution Service returned its final verdict. Signaling an even longer period of temporal elongation, the neologism Locke-Colston-Crown also aurally evokes a much earlier moment in Britain's imperial history, calling to mind three significant figures of the seventeenth and eighteenth centuries: the philosopher John Locke, whose theory of property influentially shaped colonial English thought and law; his peer Edward Colston, whose means of wealth generation, in trafficking enslaved Africans, exemplifies the source of England's own wealth; and the early modern English state, synecdochically the Crown, as a sovereign political entity that was entering a period of world domination. Above all, my opening assessment of the Locke-Colston-Crown event encapsulates the four main claims subtending this book: that English-derived property law began, in the sixteenth century, to take the proprietary form that made mass colonial dispossession thinkable and achievable; that experimental postcolonial aesthetics frequently reveal structures of thought that reject proprietary colonial logics and instead theorize more just modes of being in common; that artists, activists, and progressive legal actors across the anglophone world are involved in reforming proprietary forms of property law; and that aesthetic processes of creation, circulation, and appreciation frequently contribute to changing unjust laws, their protracted temporality not negating their material impact.

Aesthetic Impropriety argues that an anti-colonial model of property relation is emerging across the postcolonial anglophone world, in both legal instruments and literary works, in response to colonial English property laws that continue to shape the legal systems of former colonies. I reveal the existence and extent of anti-colonial reforms to property law by analyzing a set of legal reforms and literary innovations in four sites that are geographically and culturally distinct yet joined by their shared colonial history: Nigeria, India, South Africa, and the Black Atlantic.[12] In modifications that are being made to a wide range of property laws as well as in aesthetically experimental literary works that interrogate existing property regimes, a logic of equitable relation is emerging that defies and counteracts English-derived property law's proprietary logic and its formal structuring upon the topos of enclosure. This emergent, anti-colonial property relation, which appears only by analyzing legal reforms and literary innovations together, illuminates a global practice of continued resistance to, and rejection of, British colonialism and its ongoing consequences. These legal reforms and aesthetic innovations also usefully reveal the importance of analyzing property law as an expansive category, one that includes, in this book's formulation, tort law, energy law, environmental law, inheritance law, divorce law, and intellectual property law. As a strictly legal category, property law encompasses only immoveable property (land) and moveable property (personal belongings), yet the logic of property also structures many other areas of jurisprudence whose typical omission from property law practice occludes proprietary ownership's formative influence across many areas of social and political life. By attending to property law's expansive scope, *Aesthetic Impropriety* registers the pervasive extent and privative consequences of English-derived property law.[13]

In the jurisdictions that this book examines, extensive efforts have been made to amend proprietary formulations of property law that shape modes of permissible collective being, including laws that regulate land ownership but also those that extend well beyond property's typical purview. These distinct but related movements address all manner of injustices, including the land laws that govern petroleum extraction in contemporary Nigeria, discussed in Chapter 1; gendered inheritance and divorce laws in postcolonial India, examined in Chapter 2; intellectual property law's dispossession of Indigenous and racially marginalized people, especially women, in South Africa, analyzed in Chapter 3; and English admiralty law's doctrine of racialized legal personality, identified in Chapter 4. These reforms, or attempts at reform, at times arise from collective suits that seek damages after harms caused by existing statutes (Chapters 1 and 2); at times take the guise of statutory reform after public and activist pressure (Chapters 2 and 3); and at times preempt reform even as they build on legal precedent (Chapter 4). While "reform" is frequently understood in liberalism's ameliorative mode, it also bears a more radical signification, like in the formulation "nonreformist reform" that has been articulated recently by scholars in the socialist and Marxist Law and Political Economy (LPE) movement.[14] In these terms, reform operates to advance radical critique, engage anti-colonial commitments, and build local power.

Alongside these positive changes to anglophone property laws, writers of poetry and prose have been similarly reworking those proprietary formulations of ownership that made colonial domination thinkable and enforceable. From Nigeria to India, South Africa to the Americas, writers of all forms and genres are critiquing and aesthetically reworking colonial property law's proprietary tenets. Employing a set of aesthetic characteristics that this book identifies as improper, many writers are theorizing anti-colonial modes of property relation: modes that are exemplified in this book's five core literary works. Chapter 1 theorizes symbiotic ecological relation in Nigeria through analyses of

Ben Okri's 1986 short story "What the Tapster Saw" and Chigozie Obioma's 2015 novel *The Fishermen*; Chapter 2 examines gender reciprocal access to land and housing in India as theorized by Arundhati Roy's 2007 novel *The God of Small Things*; Chapter 3 analyzes the accretive process of collective, inherited, and oral Indigenous works of art in South Africa that Zoë Wicomb's 2000 novel *David's Story* constructs; and Chapter 4 shows how M. NourbeSe Philip's 2008 poetry collection *Zong!* disperses erstwhile English admiralty law to restore legal personality to the African victims of the 1781 Zong massacre. Together, these aesthetically similar literary works from distinct global regions share both their engagement with the afterlives of colonial British property law and their involvement in producing anti-colonial legal regimes.

Above all, this book advances twinned claims: that aesthetics can be a site of radical possibility and that postcolonial legal systems can play a significant role in producing more just societies. I build my argument by coining the term "aesthetic impropriety," a concept that reckons with historic and enduring forms of colonial dispossession, names a literary style, theorizes literature's involvement in producing legal change, and allows for new ways of theorizing property relations. The category of aesthetic impropriety functions analytically to name patterns that are simultaneously legal and literary: at once a commitment, in works of literature as well as in legal venues, to confronting English property law's role in colonial and postcolonial dispossession; and, at the same time, a set of stylistic modalities and conceptual logics that are aesthetically produced in both postcolonial anglophone literary texts and coterminous legal endeavors. As well as an analytic category, aesthetic impropriety operates politically to bring together cultural, methodological, and disciplinary domains that are not self-evidently connected in order to identify existing and potential nodes of solidarity.[15] Over the course of this book, one of the functions of "aesthetic impropriety" as a category is to make existing literary, legal, and activist coalitions visible, facilitating future interjurisdictional work that can continue to build toward anti-colonial, racially just futures.

The remainder of this Introduction provides the grounds for understanding that which I am arguing is an emergent anti-colonial challenge to proprietary property law across diverse postcolonial anglophone regions by expanding on three areas: first, offering an account of English property law's capitalist-colonial history, especially its proprietary function and contours; second, identifying aesthetic theory's complex historical connection to postcolonial studies and arguing for its persistent relevance, especially in relation to the production of new structures of thought that bear material impact; and third, developing a fuller explanation of the concept of aesthetic impropriety, thereby setting out this book's argument and stakes.

English Property Law's Proprietary Form

As a concept, category, and motivating logic, property bears fundamental significance to the world-expanding, world-destroying project of European colonialism. European empires were built through land theft, resource extraction, and racialized dispossession and as such, they have always involved property acquisition and have always been shaped by culturally specific conceptions of property ownership. Given that the European colonial enterprise involved multiple nation-states and has lasted for five hundred years and counting,[16] the motivating factors for and consequences of colonial domination have fluctuated according to time and context,[17] involving an admixture of politics, culture, religion, and economics, including anxiety over neighboring states' territorial expansion, perceived cultural superiority and racial supremacy, and a sensed opportunity for wealth generation. Yet, despite the many distinct causes and consequences of colonial domination across its diverse instantiations, property remains a constant feature, if not the most distinguishing feature of all, especially in the anglophone contexts that this book examines.

The period of capitalist-colonial expansion that took hold in the sixteenth century was made possible by extending property's purview: by intensifying immoveable property's capacity for alienation under English law; by imposing European philosophies of land as property upon Indigenous peoples who largely understand land as relation; by broadening the scope of what could count as property to encompass knowledge, cultural production, and people; and by racializing not just property ownership but property itself. In other words, capitalist-colonial modernity is predicated not simply on racially and territorially exploitative ideas about property but on a globalized legal system and its vastly expanded definition of property law. Substantial scholarship already exists on property's significance for European colonialism in general and British colonialism in particular, primarily in Black studies and Native studies, and my own thinking has been shaped by this extensive and vital body of work. Broadly, analyses of colonialism as a system that can be understood in relation to property employ one or more of the following explanatory frameworks: capitalism, particularly in Marxist scholarship;[18] race and slavery, especially in Black studies;[19] land dispossession, primarily in Native studies;[20] state formation, typically in the social sciences;[21] and jurisprudence, especially in legal studies.[22] Much of the most compelling and convincing scholarship draws on multiple explanatory frameworks and disciplinary commitments in order to parse European colonialism's vast sweep and long duration, an approach that this book likewise follows.

In the most obvious sense, property is an inextricable feature of colonial domination because territorial expansion entails acquiring new land through coercion or force. As feminist theorist Aileen Moreton-Robinson (Geonpul) argues in her incisive account of Indigenous sovereignty in the face of colonial occupation, particularly in Australia, "The British imperial project was predicated on taking possession of other people's lands and resources for the benefit of Empire."[23] Brenna Bhandar's analysis of what she terms "racial regimes of ownership" in settler-colonial societies similarly identifies land as the most significant feature of colonial domination; she writes, "If the possession of land was (and remains) the ultimate objective of colonial power, then property law is the primary means of realizing this desire."[24] In a more localized site of analysis, Edward Said's *The Question of Palestine* identifies Israel as a settler-colonial power, examining economic, legal, and political mechanisms which show that "the Zionist goal was to acquire land in order to put settlers on it."[25] In African settler-colonies, too, land functions as both the primary mechanism of domination and the site of anti-colonial liberation. In Frantz Fanon's *The Wretched of the Earth*, revolutionary sensibilities emerge as a response to material and ontological dispossession: "For a colonized people," Fanon avers, "the most essential value, because it is the most meaningful, is first and foremost the land: the land, which must provide bread and, naturally, dignity."[26] Both psychologically and materially, land is usually colonialism's most significant asset, for colonizers and colonized alike. The exception to this rule is in colonial societies that employed the institution of chattel slavery, in which case, enslaved people and their forced labor served as that society's most valuable resource.

In the colonial context, land ownership is always racialized, an analytic precept that has become widely accepted following critical race scholar Cheryl Harris's argument in "Whiteness as Property."[27] In her formative essay, Harris charts the co-constitutive development in US legal history of race and ownership as discursive and legal categories. As Harris explains, not only is the system of property rights in the United States "rooted in racial domination,"[28] both of Native Americans through land dispossession and Black Americans through enslavement, but its historical development also shapes its operations in the present. In seizing Native American land, colonial America and the neocolonial United States established European formulations of property ownership as the only viable mode of understanding human relationships to place. The act of land seizure, or settlement, was facilitated by colonizers' inability to recognize that Indigenous peoples hold significant relationships to land that are comparable to Anglo-American formulations of property, even as the former operate within a radically different epistemological framework. For white colonizers, Harris explains, "the 'race' of the Native Americans rendered their first possession rights invisible and justified conquest."²⁹ As Robert Nichols argues in his account of Indigenous dispossession and colonial property relations, this paradoxical epistemological maneuver "combines two processes typically thought distinct: it transforms nonproprietary relations into proprietary ones while, at the same time, systematically transferring control and title of this (new formed) property."³⁰ Put another way, theorizing Indigenous dispossession and stolen land entails employing colonial ideas about land as property even as those very ideas are the ones that had made dispossession thinkable in the first place.

Recognizing in a wholly new way the extent to which property shaped every aspect of colonial domination and continues to shape the present, Harris's argument is significant not because she recognizes, like others before her, that "slavery made human beings market-alienable" but because she explains how the process whereby Blackness came to signify commodification simultaneously produced whiteness as a property itself.³¹ While not every Black person was necessarily enslaved, as Harris points out, Black people could be legally subject to enslavement whereas white people could not. Consequently, "[b]ecause the system of slavery was contingent on and conflated with racial identity, it became crucial to be 'white,' to be identified as white, to have the property of being white. Whiteness was the characteristic, the attribute, the property of free human beings."³² Over time, whiteness came to be associated with the right to own property; what's more, it became a property in itself that operates according to the principles of US property law, established through statute and precedent.

The monograph that most closely shares *Aesthetic Impropriety*'s legal and geographic purview, Brenna Bhandar's *Colonial Lives of Property: Law, Land, and Racial Regimes*, transposes Harris's analysis to contemporary settler-colonial polities, arguing that "racial subjects and modern property laws are produced through one another in the colonial context."³³ Concordant with Harris, Bhandar contends that it is property, not land appropriation or racism, that "subtend[s] racial formations in the settler colony."³⁴ Bhandar similarly demonstrates that "property ownership was central to the formation of the proper legal subject in the political sphere":³⁵ that both political sovereignty and legal subjectivity are racially demarcated in British settler colonies. Bhandar is particularly interested in how modern settler-colonial societies deploy property as a legal instrument and ideological framework to justify their founding and continued existence; to this end, she examines specific legal mechanisms along with statutory and case law across Australia, Israel-Palestine, and Canada to theorize what she terms "the recombinant and fractured nature of how legal rationales for ownership are used to dispossess indigenous peoples of their land."[36] By analyzing the logics of property ownership as evidenced in archival materials and legal opinions, Bhandar shows how English-derived property law employs racialized logics of use and improvement to appropriate Indigenous land.

Whereas Bhandar conceptualizes property as naming a legislated relationship to land and territory to expose the processes of ongoing territorial and sovereign dispossession, *Aesthetic Impropriety* significantly expands property's purview to include environmental law, mineral law, inheritance law, divorce law, intellectual property law, admiralty law, and legal personhood. Extending property's scope in this way reveals that English property law and its underlying logics structure the political operations and epistemological tenets of all colonial possessions, not solely the settler-colonial sites of Bhandar's analysis, and almost all aspects of legal life, not just the relationship between people and land. In some ways, I am recognizing what many scholars have identified as modernity's possessive logic, following the argument made by political economist C. B. Macpherson that the "possessive market economy" of eighteenth-century England and its colonies was "read back into the nature of the individual" to produce what he named the possessive individual of capitalist modernity.[37] More recently, Judith Butler and Athena Athanasiou have attempted to think outside the logic of possession that they identify as a "key construct of capitalism," aiming to "articulate aspirations to self-determination without seeking recourse to the grand narrative of the self-contained, self-sufficient individual."[38] Similarly to Butler and Athanasiou but in an expressly anti-colonial context, Moreton-Robinson argues that capitalist-colonial modernity has been shaped, above all, by a structure of thought that developed in Europe and characterizes settler-colonial and colonized polities alike:

> At an ontological level, the structure of subjective possession occurs through the imposition of one's will-to-be on the thing that is perceived to lack will.... For [Captain] Cook to be able to take possession of the east coast of Australia without the consent of the "natives" means that he had to position Aboriginal people as willless things.[39]

For Moreton-Robinson, land dispossession and racial domination were made possible by the primacy of possession within colonial British thought, rather than the other way around.

Extending this robust intellectual history of capitalist-colonialism's possessive features, this book favors the term "proprietary" to refer to the logics of appropriation, extraction, possession, dispossession, ownership, and exclusion that have long shaped the legal suppositions of what Susan Koshy et al. describe as colonial racial capitalism.[40] The *proprietary* is, I propose, at once more accurate for describing the extent to which English-derived property law has shaped jurisprudence and juridical practice across much of the world and, at the same time, more analytically generative for recognizing emerging anticolonial reforms to existing property laws. The *Oxford English Dictionary* confirms that, as an adjective, *proprietary* simultaneously denotes the following: the state of property ownership or of being propertied; the state of being owned by a single owner or small group of owners; an item whose manufacture or use is restrictively owned, particularly through patent; and relating to property or proprietorship.[41] Grounded etymologically in property and its ownership, *proprietariness* productively turns critical assessments of capitalist-colonialist modernity toward the law, illuminating the extent to which property law has been used to conceptualize, implement, and justify colonial regimes as well as recognizing how colonial legal systems continue to shape the postcolonial present. At the same time, the framework of proprietariness retains the core insight that possession necessarily entails exclusion and privation, as countless other theorists have recognized.[42]

While the very process of colonial expansion was prompted, in part, by philosophies of ownership that served to enclose land, labor, and resources in order to extract and accumulate wealth, English formulations of property were also advanced through legal mechanisms. When Britain established sovereignty over a given region, it broadly imposed a globalized model of property ownership that remains entrenched in many legal systems to this day—notwithstanding Lauren Benton's characterization of colonial legal regimes' development as always plural and complex.[43] In the Northern and Southern Protectorates of what is now Nigeria, as my first chapter reveals, Britain reformed customary systems of land tenure in order to build extractive industries, including coal and petroleum, that would yield the greatest profits for the colonial government, short-circuiting existing landowners' claims.[44] In India, as Chapter 2 demonstrates, Britain codified customary laws that regulated property ownership upon marriage and divorce, inadvertently eliminating many of the existing property protections for Indian women and writing newly restrictive regulations into statute.[45] In South Africa, British copyright and intellectual property law were superimposed onto the existing colonial Dutch system to produce a mode of property protection that undermined Black and Indigenous cultural production, as Chapter 3 discusses. And the colonial and neocolonial system of racialized legal nonpersonhood that legitimated and strengthened the system of chattel slavery has continued to shape Black life long since abolition, as Chapter 4 acknowledges. Given the legal system's deep involvement in granting legitimacy to the colonial state and perpetuating injustice in the postcolonial present, it is not surprising that historians and literary critics alike have widely condemned the law for what is often understood to be its constitutive violence.[46] Postcolonial scholarship remains typically deeply suspicious of the law's capacity to function as a tool for justice in the present, not least because the legal systems that Britain had imposed remained largely in place at independence and often formed the basis for the newly independent nation's own laws.

Yet, as part of the ongoing process of claiming postcolonial sovereignty, and in response to pressure from citizens, jurists, and activists, colonial-era laws are, in many locations, gradually being rewritten.[47] *Aesthetic Impropriety* identifies vanguard legal actions across the anglophone world that suggest the potential for law to be a vital component of achieving justice. These actions include two lawsuits in London and the Hague that would force multinational company Royal Dutch Shell to rectify environmental and human harms in the Niger Delta, as addressed in my first chapter; India's progress in granting equal inheritance rights to women along with activists' ongoing efforts to introduce equal property rights upon divorce, described in Chapter 2; and South Africa's recent steps toward decolonizing intellectual property law, uncovered in Chapter 3. What's more, as I contend in Chapter 4, postcolonial anglophone writers are using their aesthetic innovations to propose novel means of reforming our present to establish justice for historical wrongs: by bestowing ghosts with legal personhood and enabling the 150 enslaved victims of the late eighteenth-century *Zong* massacre to pursue either a civil lawsuit for wrongful death or a criminal charge for murder against English slave traders, the Gregson syndicate and its heirs. Despite its many failings, the institution of law remains vital for building just futures.[48] Indeed, as this book shows, across Africa, Asia, and the Americas, colonial Britain's property laws are in the process of being transformed.

Distribution and Force: An Anti-Colonial Theory of Aesthetics

Like the law, aesthetics has been treated somewhat warily in postcolonial studies, and for good reason: in their colonial emergence, legal regimes and aesthetic philosophy coarticulated racially and culturally supremacist formulations of taste, judgment, and value.[49] Yet, if the law might be salvaged as a means of achieving anti-colonial justice in postcolonial jurisdictions, so, too, might the aesthetic.[50] Or, phrased more strongly: both law and aesthetics are vital for achieving anti-colonial world orders.[51] As this book demonstrates across four jurisdictions and four types of property law, literature frequently participates in transforming existing social formations. It does so not necessarily because of overt acts—like the toppling of Colston's statue, which can itself be read as an artistic intervention or form of protest art—but because aesthetic compositions frequently register and produce new structures of thought. Much as Hew Locke's *Colston* contributed to the emergence of a commitment to racial justice in contemporary Bristol, so too do literary works in their aesthetic configurations operate to slowly transform widely distributed ideas about how our worlds should be organized. These sensed and emerging ideas are not confined to works of art but are instead constitutively social, shaping institutions including, but not limited to, the law. Indeed, this book began as much when I identified logics of impropriety in postcolonial property laws as when I noticed those same improper logics in literary texts. It was only by aesthetically analyzing changes to property law as registered in legal instruments, like South Africa's Indigenous Knowledge Act (2019), that I was able to identify a substantive trend toward an emerging anti-colonial property law across the postcolonial anglophone world. As this book demonstrates, legal logics can be read aesthetically if aesthetic analysis means analyzing compositional structures or the relationship between component parts.

My theory of the aesthetic as a creative and analytic category that is constitutively forceful is built upon three propositions: first, aesthetics refers to those compositional arrangements that make up any given work of art; second, aesthetic engagement involves embodied perception that entails sensory rearrangement; and third, aesthetically configured ideas circulate diffusively and discursively. In establishing the aesthetic as a central component of a book that also examines the more expressly political fields of postcolonial studies and the law, I am participating in literary studies' resurgent interest in what is often, in one strain of scholarship, described as formalist analysis[52] and, in another, as aesthetic theory.[53] This attentiveness to literature's artistic or creative elements is much needed: after all, literary scholarship examines texts that are sculpted, shaped, and enjoyed. What's more, as this return to form and aesthetics suggests, understanding the world necessitates analyzing cultural, social, political, and legal relationships that are embedded in, or accessed through, artistic works of any medium. My own understanding of literature's aesthetic shaping of legal instruments is itself profoundly influenced by Joseph Slaughter's argument that postcolonial narrative form both responds to and discursively reworks human rights norms.[54] More broadly, my theorizing of the aesthetic as compositional, sensed, and diffuse emerges out of this rich body of scholarship that has variously theorized literary form in its political dimensions and aesthetic experience in its sensory capacities. While my primary analytic commitment is to aesthetics rather than form, for reasons that I will elucidate below, both frameworks have shaped this book's analytic claims.

In designating the aesthetic as fundamentally compositional, I make both a descriptive and an analytic claim: with respect to the former, a work's aesthetics are identifiable through the relationship between constituent parts; regarding the latter, these relationships produce both sensed aesthetic engagement and the dispersed circulation of emerging structures of thought. In the literary context, aesthetics' closest synonym is style (a disappointingly undertheorized category) followed closely by form, especially when the latter means that which is examined during the literary analytic practice of close reading. In a descriptive sense, in other words, aesthetics involves the assemblage of literary elements like genre, plot, narrative, voice, figuration, lineation, rhetoric, language, and syntax. Recent formalist literary scholarship usefully examines these features that I have identified as aesthetic to make a case for the constitutively enabling relationship between literature and politics. Revitalizing the field of literary formalism, Caroline Levine's 2015 book *Forms: Whole, Rhythm, Hierarchy, Network* conceptualizes form expansively, extending it from its typical sense as a singular and defined spatial structure to encompass all patterned, cohesive relationships in literary works or social institutions. Levine contends that forms "impos[e] order on heterogeneous materials";[55] that coherent forms can "collide with . . . an array of other forms in social situations";[56] and that "these formal collisions can produce strange and aleatory possibilities."[57] In an attempt to at once recognize heterogeneity and control it, Levine almost always describes forms as plural entities, including many relational patterns that would not ordinarily be defined as formal, such as rhythm, which moves across time. For Levine, form is a diagnostic tool that allows the literary or cultural critic to identify patterns and recognize how literary texts "set forms against one another in disruptive and aleatory as well as rigidly containing ways."[58]

Building on Levine's contention that the literary critic's role is to put forms "to strategic ends,"[59] Anna Kornbluh's *The Order of Forms: Realism, Formalism, and Social Space* argues that "formalism not only comprises the central proficiency of literary critics, but also funds their unique worldly purchase: ideas about making, about making relations, about making spaces and orders deliberately and justly."[60] Like Levine, Kornbluh aims "to undo the habitual political equation of freedom with formlessness"[61] but she does so by developing a more precise, more constrained conception of form. For Kornbluh, form refers to engineered entities, whether an architectural plan, a nineteenth-century realist novel, or a method in psychoanalytic theory. What's more, form is never static — never a means to contain or reflect — but always dynamic; form is the production of spatialized relationships and, as such, a projection of possible futures. Bringing together the Marxist conception of mediation with nineteenth-century mathematical theory, Kornbluh theorizes "aesthetic form's capacity to mediate [the] structuration of sociality,"[62] arguing that "the form of the novel works to actuate a projection of the social space in its world, a projection perceptible, after the time of reading, as a blueprint or model."[63] In Kornbluh's account, form is a powerful category because it provides prototypes for the astute reader of how structures, systems, or institutions might alternatively be organized.

Kornbluh's meticulous theorizing of form most usefully articulates the force that lies latent in how she conceptualizes the formal process of producing space, even as this generative potential is somewhat constrained by a fairly strict deployment of mediation and an accompanying emphasis, shared with Levine, on the literary critic's role in actualizing a work's transformative capacities. Without meaning to diminish the value of literary scholarship, whose role in understanding our existing social formations and producing new ways of being should not be underestimated, this book argues that the aesthetic bears greater dynamism than is typically recognized. The process by which aesthetic configurations actualize space, to use Kornbluh's framing, produces the generative force that begins to shift structures of thought. Like Raymond Williams, upon whom Kornbluh and Levine also draw, I am, then, recognizing that literary works are always evidence of "forming and formative processes."[64] In his influential concept "structures of feeling," Williams contends that a work's compositional features, or what he terms literary style, register changing values and institutions not after they have been formalized or concretized but during their process of emergence. These structures of feeling should be recognized as both evidence of changing social structures and a contributing factor to emergent means of organizing and making sense of our social contexts. The term "structures of feeling" thus serves to indicate not only the "specific internal relations" (structure) between constituent parts, whether stylistic or political, but also their processual, affective capacities (their feeling): they can "exert palpable pleasures and set effective limits on experience."[65] My own use of the phrase "structures of thought" consciously echoes Williams's concept, retaining its affective implications while also signaling the logics, proprietary or improper, that are evidenced in the literary works and legal instruments that are examined throughout this book.

Structure forms a bridge between formalist and aesthetic approaches to literary analysis because it articulates their shared interest in a work's composition. In this sense, structure conforms to my first proposition: that the aesthetic is always a reference to compositional arrangements. But structure also elucidates my second proposition: that aesthetic engagement involves embodied sensed perception and sensory rearrangement. While materialist formalism usefully theorizes compositional space as dynamic, aesthetic theory clarifies how engagement with literary or other art works is also always sensory. As David Lloyd brilliantly explicates in *Under Representation: The Racial Regime of Aesthetics*, aesthetic philosophy in the idealist tradition is built upon a colonialist, white supremacist understanding of aesthetic appreciation and political subjectivity. In the work of Immanuel Kant, Friedrich Schiller, and Georg Hegel, aesthetic taste and analytic judgment require the capacity to move from sensuous perception of an object to a disembodied understanding of its abstract principles.[66] This progression from sensory specificity to philosophical abstraction models and activates late eighteenth- and early nineteenth-century Europe's taxonomic racism that charted humans on a racial trajectory, proceeding from corporeal animal to rational human, from deepest complexion to palest skin tone. Significantly, idealist aesthetic philosophy's racial hierarchies bear political implications as well as social and cultural consequences. Explaining that representation is a central concept for the idealist tradition, Lloyd observes that the "movement from particular to general, common to universal . . . is intrinsic to the logic of representation."[67] Parsing representation's simultaneously aesthetic and political valences, Lloyd explains that "to assume the disposition to representation is also to assume the disposition to be represented by others. This slippage is crucial to the emergence of political representation as the self-evident form of modern liberal societies."[68] For Enlightenment idealist philosophy, in other words, the capacity for aesthetic analysis produces full subjectivity and its corresponding political rights: a capacity that is constitutively accessible only to white subjects.

Understanding aesthetic theory's racially discriminatory predicates is helpful both for recognizing the exclusions that are built into theories of aesthetic discernment and the affordances of affective aesthetic engagement. Much like the move from proprietariness to impropriety that this book charts, aesthetic philosophy can be approached improperly, from an anti-colonial perspective, by jettisoning its racially exclusionary assessments of sovereign subjectivity and acknowledging "the importance of artworks of every kind to both the imaginative survival of the racialized and the critical resistance to racism."[69] In *The Difference Aesthetics Makes: On the Humanities "After Man,"* Kandice Chuh makes the compelling argument that aesthetic experience and pedagogies of the aesthetic are a locus "for the realization of a radically different world."[70] Chuh builds a theory of aesthetics that actively works toward an anti-colonial world order by adopting and reworking the Aristotelian concept of the *sensus communis* from the idealist tradition and grounding it in an affective account of sensory experience by way of Black, feminist, queer, and anti-colonial theory. Whereas *sensus communis* in the Kantian tradition means something akin to "common sense," for Aristotle, the concept is expressly corporeal and refers to the process of perceiving all five senses together. Translated from the Greek *koine aisthesis* (literally, shared perception), *sensus communis* means both the cooperative work of the senses and the awareness of distinct senses in their shared operations. Chuh explains, "specific senses (sight, hearing, touch, taste, and smell) . . . coordinate syncretically what each distinctively perceives. This corporeal common sense leaves the specificity of each sense intact and understands each as equally but incommensurably contributing to the ability of the body to apprehend the world it traverses."[71] Sensory interactions physiologically and cognitively produce new ways of understanding the world.

In reclaiming sense and affect as fundamental to aesthetic theory, Chuh offers an enabling account of aesthetics for emancipatory humanistic inquiry. Recognizing that aesthetic encounters are always sensory, she explains that they involve "a combination of intellectual activity and embodied knowledge, from sense making through critique and sensory encounter."[72] Mobilizing the concept of sensibility, and especially its "double valence . . . as a reference to both what is held to be reasonable and what is viscerally experienced,"[73] Chuh argues that the humanities can "shif[t] the distribution of sensibility"[74] away from colonial racial capitalism's hierarchical and exclusionary forms of knowledge toward radically inclusionary modes of social organization. For Chuh, the co-occurrence of affective and cognitive perception can significantly alter a person's understanding of the world.[75] While the means by which this process actualizes is left somewhat implicit, it can be teased out through Chuh's proliferating aesthetic language, including repeated terms like "orientation," "sensibility," "arrangement," and "disposition." Reading Chuh's argument aesthetically — for its distribution of concepts and the disposition they imply — suggests that the relationships between a work's component parts register particular orientations toward the world that forcefully produce new orientations in turn.

If Chuh helps to explain my second proposition — that aesthetic engagement involves embodied perception that can then produce sensory rearrangement — it is another theorist of both Kant and the literary production of worlds who helps to advance my third proposition: that aesthetically configured ideas circulate diffusely and discursively. In *What is a World?: On Postcolonial Literature as World Literature*, Pheng Cheah develops a phenomenological account of the world that at once makes a case for literature's generative capacities and registers the enduring significance of the postcolonial as an analytic category that is required for understanding globalized inequality in the twenty-first century. Cheah rejects conventional accounts of the world as a spatialized container in favor of phenomenological analyses of the world as always in the process of coming-into-being. "In its fundamental ontological meaning," Cheah contends, "a world is a temporal process that brings all beings into relation or holds them together as a whole."[76] In place of analyses of form, which "presuppose a human subject who actualizes them as an objective world,"[77] Cheah offers an account of what he simply terms "literature": of how the literary operates temporally, particularly through the workings of narrative, to "performatively enact a world."[78] It is through the constitutively temporal relationship between its component parts that literature, like the world, can be understood as forceful. Literature's generative capacities neither replicate nor map materially existing formations; instead, "its formal structures enact the opening of a world by the incalculable gift of time."[79] Much like Williams's insistence on "structures of feeling" that are always in process, Cheah theorizes worlding as "a force that subtends and exceeds all human calculations that reduce the world as a temporal structure to the sum of objects in space."[80] By turning to what he terms phenomenological and postphenomenological accounts of the world, primarily by way of Martin Heidegger, Hannah Arendt, and Jacques Derrida, Cheah argues that literature necessarily participates in producing new social orders. Compositional relationships that are held together in productive tension, Cheah contends, generate new norms that themselves exert force upon the world.

Cheah's temporal analysis of literature's normative force usefully complements Jacques Rancière's distributive account of how works of art, through their aesthetic configuring, can bear material effects.[81] Using Aristotle's formulation of *koine aesthesis*, Rancière argues that both aesthetics and politics involve the "distribution of the sensible," meaning the process whereby sense perception "simultaneously discloses the existence of something in common and the delimitations that define the respective parts and positions with it."[82] The distribution of the sensible applies equally to works of art and political orders: to that which, perceived sensorily, is always at once a coherent whole and a set of constituent elements that can, in their dispersal, be subject to redistribution. In Rancière's thinking, "aesthetics" is neither art as such, nor an artistic medium or style, but the arrangement of elements that are perceptible to sense. Similarly, "politics" refers not to an organized political system but to the more general category of people's existence to one another as at once collective and individual. Politics and aesthetics share many significant features, including their generative capacities, because they both entail sensory distribution and redistribution: "Artistic practices," Rancière explains, "are 'ways of doing and making' that intervene in the general distribution of ways of doing and making as well as in the relationships they maintain to modes of being and forms of visibility."[83] Significantly, intervention comes not from the critic or artist but from the work itself, which always "steal[s] away to wander aimlessly without knowing who to speak to or who not to speak to."[84] While aesthetic forms are sometimes understood to evidence a particular political system, such as the assumed identity between closed literary forms and totalitarian regimes that Levine decries, Rancière's theory of aesthetics confirms that any "correspondence between the sayable and the visible" is neither innate nor incontrovertible.[85] Differently than new formalism's critique of critical theory that establishes a one-to-one relationship between political and conceptual forms, Rancière's theorizing of aesthetics clarifies that literary patterns both register emergent ideas (per Williams) and produce new modes of sensibility (per Chuh); what's more, they do so without any predetermined outcome because artistic forms "are susceptible to being assigned to contradictory political paradigms."[86] Works of art that are nonrepresentational, like the aesthetically experimental literary texts in this book, produce a formal discontinuity between the world of the text and the world beyond it; their interventions, or force, come from their own distributions of sensibility and their "sensible effectivity."[87]

Aesthetic force thus derives from the relationship between a work's constituent parts and the ways that particular configurations, in their sensory apperception, bear the potential to impact readers' understandings of epistemological distributions, reconfiguring the arrangement of component parts and producing new norms. This process of sensory and normative redistribution is significant for studying the law, especially law and the humanities, because forcefulness is the law's originary compulsion. In Jacques Derrida's influential assessment of legal violence in his essay "Force of Law," the law is *a priori* forceful; its enforceability is what makes justice possible.[88] For Derrida, force is either applied, in the sense of the police enforcing formalized laws, or abstract, in the sense of offering a mandate to act rightly or justly. Yet, the preceding theorizing of literature's aesthetic force indicates a more dispersed circulation of normative transformations that exist outside the law as an institution even as they engage with its presuppositions. A theory of diffuse force enables us to recognize anti-colonial legal reforms as they emerge organically but far from in isolation across dispersed but connected regions, just as it helps to mobilize anti-colonial sentiment that can itself produce additional reforms.

As this book shows by carefully assessing the aesthetics of late twentieth-century and early twenty-first-century postcolonial anglophone literature of multiple genres, works of art can gradually shift sensibilities because their constitutive elements, which they distribute and hold in relation, similarly bear the capacity for redistribution. The symbiotic relationships that Chapter 1 explores in work by Ben Okri and Chigozie Obioma do more than lament the catastrophic environmental and human harms inflicted on the Niger Delta;

they also indirectly articulate the kind of ecologically sustainable relationships that are being theorized in environmental philosophy and the remedies that are being sought in English courts for multinational petroleum corporations' distributed harms. Similarly, *The God of Small Things*'s laterally figured impropriety, discussed in Chapter 2, produces an alternative moral economy to that which is codified in Indian divorce law, anticipating significant political debates about feminist legal reform in the subsequent twenty years. Chapter 3's comprehensive analysis of Zoë Wicomb's experimental novel *David's Story* demonstrates that its aesthetically produced argument for anti-colonial intellectual property law preceded South Africa's markedly similar Indigenous Knowledge Act by nearly two decades. And my analysis, in Chapter 4, of M. NourbeSe Philip's *Zong!* identifies a radical new approach to pursuing legal remedies for historical wrongs: an approach that is made thinkable through *Zong!*'s powerful aesthetic dispersal of historical English legal doctrine. As *Aesthetic Impropriety* argues over the course of these four chapters, literature's indirect aesthetic distributions produce new structures of value that circulate discursively and shape the law.

Aesthetic Impropriety

The concept of aesthetic impropriety brings together an assessment of proprietary, English-derived property law with an anti-colonial theory of aesthetics, elucidating their sustained interaction during late twentieth- and early twenty-first-century global anglophone contexts. As this book's organizing conceit and central concept, aesthetic impropriety condenses two contradictory logics that appear together in postcolonial reforms to anglophone property law as well as in experimental contemporary literature across those same jurisdictions: on the one hand, the proper or proprietary logic that structures English-derived property law; on the other, the improper, nonproprietary logic of anti-colonial ideas about property. By using the term "proprietary" to refer to the development under colonial racial capitalism of property laws that facilitate appropriation, extraction, and dispossession, this book at once describes British colonialism's primary organizing drive and develops an analytically generative framework for reconfiguring postcolonial property laws and the forms of sociopolitical relation that they themselves produce. Unlike other widely used ways of characterizing Anglo-American approaches to property ownership, most notably possession and the possessive, the framework of the proprietary at once retains the core insight that possession entails exclusion and privation and also offers a way out of possession's closed analytic loop, in which the fact of dispossession is countered by making claims to ownership within the same dispossessive system. Proprietariness, by contrast, has no clear opposite and instead opens up to its cognate, propriety, and the latter's opposite, impropriety. Whereas possession is linked to lack, the proprietary is marked by its capacity for disruption: for improperly reworking the model of property ownership that emerged through British colonial domination.

In ordinary usage, impropriety is typically understood to mean indecorous behavior: a proclivity toward rejecting norms, whether out of stubbornness, ignorance, or a willful desire to stir trouble. In this sense, impropriety rejects that which is carefully contained and socially ordained. And yet, impropriety as I theorize it in this book is not a contrarian impulse. Instead, it operates specifically to counteract English-derived property law's proprietary logic. Impropriety derives from the Latin *improprius*, being a negative inflection of the Latin *proprius*, meaning already of oneself. As such, the term etymologically indexes that which is outside the borders of one's own being. In the first sense of impropriety that is given in the *Oxford English Dictionary*, this word describes the state of "[n]ot truly or strictly belonging to the thing under consideration; not in accordance with truth, fact, reason, or rule; abnormal, irregular; incorrect, inaccurate, erroneous, wrong." As the entry goes on to explain, this sense of impropriety was "[f]ormerly sometimes without implication of blame or censure, e.g., said of a meaning given to a word which is not the 'proper' or literal one, but metaphorical." Inasmuch as impropriety might refer not strictly to the thing under consideration but to a related entity, and inasmuch as it is not contained by the literal or concrete terms of how things are, it is definitionally constructed upon a propulsive movement. Impropriety recognizes the present structure of thought upon which it is built and moves toward something else: something related but radically distinct; something that is already in the process of becoming concrete.

As well as revealing a broad impetus toward anti-colonial critique and liberatory imagining, aesthetic impropriety names four ways of understanding the relationship between postcolonial property law and aesthetics, at once designating a distinct literary style, an entrenched system of property law, an emerging model of propertied relation, and a theory of aesthetic force. Whereas the first two categories address existing characteristics (a particular postcolonial literary style; a dominant model of property law), the third and fourth register an orientation toward the future (property as it should be; literature's capacity to generate new legal modalities). All four categories correspond to globalized forms of property law under colonial racial capitalism in both its aftermath and ongoing duration and all four categories are identifiable through a process of reading aesthetically: by looking for conceptual patterns in legal as well as literary contexts.

As a literary style, aesthetic impropriety names a loosely related set of aesthetic features that appear in postcolonial anglophone literature across a range of genres, nation-states, and cultural inheritances. Characteristically improper aesthetics are produced through all manner of literary devices, including recursive narrative plotting, distributed focalization, figures of connection and amplification, linguistic patterns, multiform narratives, and visual and aural dispersal. Each novel, short story, or poetry collection examined in this book is paradigmatically aesthetically improper, yet each also bears significant differences in legal, cultural, and political context, not to mention style. In epitomizing this new category of aesthetic impropriety while remaining culturally distinct, the literary works examined in *Aesthetic Impropriety* register impropriety's many possible literary and legal forms. In their simultaneous affinities and distinctions, this book's curation of work by Ben Okri, Chigozie Obioma, Arundhati Roy, Zoë Wicomb, and M. NourbeSe Philip demonstrates aesthetic impropriety's usefully capacious reach.

Over the course of four chapters, this book charts a journey through four different variations of aesthetic impropriety: from symbiosis, to reciprocity, to accretion, to dispersal. When combined with critiques of property law, improper aesthetics should be seen to register radically inclusionary modes of relation that are likewise established in emancipatory legal proposals for protecting ecologies, economic security, Indigenous knowledge, and legal personhood. Each version of aesthetic impropriety rejects proprietary property law's hierarchical, exclusionary, and privative logics in favor of egalitarian, liberatory, sustainable forms of association. At the same time, each aesthetically improper variation accords with its specific context: the symbiotic relation that is theorized in Nigerian writing about petroleum production suggests ecological interdependence in place of regional resource extraction; the reciprocal aesthetic modality of Chapter 2 responds to patriarchal Indian law by producing a feminist socialist configuration of equitable Indian society that is affirmed in India's Constitution; the accretive style examined in Chapter 3 operates according to Indigenous principles of creative production that have been newly introduced as a protected mode in South Africa's intellectual property regime; and the dispersive process identified in Chapter 4 pushes apart English admiralty law's racially hierarchical structure to grant full legal personhood to ghosts. By categorizing each chapter's literary and legal work as forming a distinct mode of producing equitable legal relation, *Aesthetic Impropriety* at once recognizes difference across context and location while identifying a common challenge to proprietary property law: a pairing whose global scope provides reason for hope.

In their sequencing, these four variants of aesthetic impropriety register the concept's own propulsive movement and intrinsic momentum. By opening with symbiosis and reciprocity, *Aesthetic Impropriety* begins with the two aesthetic modalities that most clearly demonstrate property law's internal logics and the emergent, contradistinctively anti-colonial reformulations of land law and inheritance law. As my argument gains cumulative force, I turn to a chapter that theorizes the similarly accretional process whereby literary aesthetics bear normative impact through their dispersed articulation over time. The book's primary chapters close with dispersal, an aesthetic modality that names my argument's similar analytic trajectory, dispersing privative colonial law in order to open into a viable and radical future. Mobilizing aesthetic impropriety's propulsive possibilities, these four body chapters proceed from potential success to significant legal reform: from an in-process action in Chapter 1, "Symbiosis"; to an example of some successes and some losses in the second chapter, "Reciprocity"; to a recent and substantial legal reform in Chapter 3, "Accretion." Similarly registering impropriety's dynamism, this book moves from examining cases that involve a known legal remedy (compensatory damages, in the opening chapter) to a possible precedent-setting case that adapts existing doctrine (granting legal personhood to nonhuman beings or objects, in the final chapter). In their propulsive sequencing, this book's four chapters register the necessary optimism for social change that anti-colonial efforts to reform property law require. In its theoretical premises, *Aesthetic Impropriety* maintains its movement toward future promise, exemplified in a short concluding chapter that recognizes impropriety as necessarily hopeful.

Much like this book's analytic momentum, aesthetic impropriety operates according to hope's trajectories: it engages directly with the limits of society's current organizing structures in order to participate in the process of generating more just social formations. Aesthetic impropriety is at once a way to name an aesthetic response to the vast and connected forms of privation that are produced by the seemingly intractable Anglo-American property regime and a means to participate in building more equitable, sustainable, and fulfilling ways of living in common. Yet, despite its hopefulness, impropriety is never quite utopian, even as it might bear utopian sympathies; instead, it remains adamantly committed to justice that can be concretely achieved. Unlike theories of justice which articulate a messianic future that has not yet come into being and which must remain fulfillable only within an ethical framework, and unlike a significant body of postcolonialist scholarship that reasonably remains deeply skeptical of legal systems as offering any kind of justice because of the law's role in colonial violence and dispossession, *Aesthetic Impropriety* affirms law's usefulness.

Aesthetic Impropriety returns us to a politically engaged theory of aesthetics by recognizing that this concept operates to at once register a given literary work's distinctive style and the relationship between multiple aesthetic works; to signal art's power not only to move us emotionally but also to slowly shift our structures of thought; and to index literature's materially forceful capacities, its generative potential, in the sense not of instrumental impact but of forcefully producing new modes of sociality. Just as important, *Aesthetic Impropriety* recognizes that significant, even radical legal and political transformations can accrue from engaging with the law as a viable entity.

Chapter Summaries

Aesthetic Impropriety builds its argument through four chapters and a conclusion that separately offer contextually precise legal and literary analysis and together build a successive argument for a forcefully improper postcolonial aesthetic. Chapter 1 examines twentieth-century Nigerian legal history and contemporary literary engagements with petroleum extraction to argue that Nigerian writers are retheorizing ecological relationships and contributing to significant legal change. "Symbiosis: Oil Extraction in the Racial Capitalocene" shows how proprietary land law took hold during English colonial rule and intensified during postcolonial governance, especially through The Mineral Oils Ordinance (1914) and the Land Use Act (1978), both of which facilitated intense oil extraction with devastating ecological and human consequences in the Niger Delta. Analyzing Ben Okri's "What the Tapster Saw" and Chigozie Obioma's *The Fishermen*, I argue that these authors aesthetically configure a symbiotic model of ecological relation that closely corresponds to models that are being developed in Indigenous ecological philosophy, Indigenous legal theory, West African animist theory, and progressive environmental law. Moreover, these aesthetically produced formulations of symbiosis accord with contemporary environmental legal actions, including the ongoing tort suit *Okpabi v. Shell* and proposed legal reforms to the Land Use Act. In these shared philosophical commitments to symbiotic relation, writers and legal theorists refuse to identify the Delta as merely a locus of negation and death but instead recognize that a hopeful, sustainable, and abundant future requires developing radically different forms of ecological relation. In affirming mutual interdependence as the only viable, sustainable mode of human-land relation, these writers, activists, and legal actors are theorizing the kind of relationship that this book identifies as necessarily improper: as im-properly refusing proprietary ownership.

Building on the opening chapter's analysis of proprietary English property law as it was developed in colonial Nigeria, my second chapter turns to examine gendered propriety in India's divorce and inheritance laws. "Reciprocity: Female Dispossession in Inheritance and Divorce" contends that feminist challenges to patriarchal Indian inheritance and divorce laws, among jurists, activists, and writers, articulate a model of reciprocal legal relation that refuses women's legislated economic dispossession and proposes viable, urgent reforms. I argue that while the plot of Roy's novel offers a necessary critique of India's patriarchal property laws, its aesthetics offer something more generative: they participate in rewriting ownership's formal logic. Drawing on scholarship by feminist legal theorists and historians, I argue that *The God of Small Things* balances two conceptual structures: the first is a proprietary model of ownership that largely restricts property ownership to men and upholds India's patriarchal juridical economy; the second conceptual structure is improper, egalitarian, and reciprocal, and it registers Roy's vision of a feminist socialist legal system that is equitable and just. *The God of Small Things* at once responds to a landmark Supreme Court case addressing female inheritance, *Mary Roy v. Kerala* (1986), and precedes proposed amendments to Indian property law that would protect women's property rights upon marriage and divorce (the unsuccessful Marriage Laws Amendment Bill 2013). By aesthetically restructuring property law's formal logic, *The God of Small Things* participates in a broader shift in public discourse toward granting women equal property protections under the law.

Chapter 3 moves from examining legislative and literary accounts of property law's core elements, moveable and immoveable property, to addressing an area that in legal practice is distinct yet shares the same proprietary logics. "Accretion: Decolonizing Intellectual Property Law" argues that Zoë Wicomb's novel *David's Story* offers an early example of retheorizing South Africa's intellectual property laws according to Indigenous principles of collective, inherited, and ephemeral creative production. I identify these three tenets of anti-colonial intellectual property law as accretive, contending that, as a version of aesthetic impropriety, accretion engages with capitalist-colonial property laws in general and intellectual property laws in particular. *David's Story* is typically analyzed in relation to apartheid, but it also confronts globalized intellectual property law's neocolonial enabling of intellectual resource extraction. Indeed, the ending of apartheid coincided with an Indigenous-led movement across the world for substantive intellectual property protections against Global North profiteering, while *David's Story* precedes substantive intellectual property law reforms in South Africa by two decades. By interpreting Wicomb's account of the systemic silencing of Black and multiracial women as engaging with intellectual property's significant limitations, I not only offer a new reading of this novel, but I also provide a clear example of how a literary work's aesthetic engagement with complex legal ideas has preempted significant reform. Wicomb's early theorizing of what would become a concerted effort by South African politicians, legal theorists, and activists to expand intellectual property's purview, culminating in the Indigenous Knowledge Act (2019), extends the argument that *Aesthetic Impropriety*'s first two chapters have been developing: that new legal ideas circulate discursively, and often through aesthetic means, well before they are signed into law.

Chapter 4 builds on this book's cumulative theorizing of aesthetic force to show how contemporary literature about historical injustice might transform contemporary legal doctrine. In "Dispersal: Admiralty Law and Raising the Dead," I argue that M. NourbeSe Philip's epic poem *Zong!* undertakes an aesthetic act of legal figuration by breathing poetic life into the dead and granting legal personality to ghosts. Philip's collection responds to the 1781 killing of 150 Africans on the slave ship *Zong* by aesthetically dispersing the logic of racial propertization that was enshrined in English admiralty law and which made the massacre thinkable and legal. This chapter combines readings of seventeenth-century admiralty law, especially the Navigation Acts (1650s) and *Butts v. Penny* (1677), with theories of legal personality that recognize the law's figurative processes, arguing that figuration makes literary works similarly capable of creating new legal conditions. Philip uses the poetic space created by dispersing eighteenth-century law's racist predicates to breathe life into the ghostly spirits of the *Zong* victims, granting them spectral personhood through an extended act of incantation. Philip's process of aesthetic resurrection is not entirely without precedent: the Anglo-American legal system has long made space for ghosts, as both English and US case law reveals, so bestowing personhood on spectral beings should be understood as more than an act of imagination. In opening up visual and aural space not only to mourn the dead but also demand redress, *Zong!* prefigures the forms of justice that might yet be established in an English court.

The conclusion to *Aesthetic Impropriety* synthesizes my argument for postcolonial aesthetic impropriety in particular and aesthetic force in general, and in doing so it proposes possibilities for emancipatory literary analysis. In the context of renewed attention to racial violence, global inequities, and gender injustice, and after prolonged attacks on humanistic methods, emancipatory modes of inquiry offer a vital mode for building a more just world. As the preceding chapters will have shown, my model of aesthetic impropriety brings together materialist formalist analysis with recent theories of aesthetics to show how literature engages forcefully with the world. Just as legislative change occurs by formally encoding new ideas and enshrining them in law, so too do literary texts aesthetically encode new ideas: as such, they participate in the process of discursively producing change. *Aesthetic Impropriety* ends with a call for a renewed faith in the forceful capacities of both creative production and critical analysis as a way of addressing the raced and gendered violence built through colonial modernity that remains entrenched in our globalized present.

1
Symbiosis
Oil Extraction in the Racial Capitalocene

The extreme ecological degradation inflicted on the Niger Delta through unchecked petroleum production is by now widely known, thanks largely to the combined efforts of activists, journalists, filmmakers, and artists. In the sustained engagement of Ken Saro-Wiwa and the Ogoni Nine; in the journalism and nonprofit work of more recent activists like Nnimmo Bassey; in the petroaesthetics of writers including Ben Okri, Buchi Emecheta, Isidore Okpewho, and Helon Habila; in the militarism of the Movement for the Emancipation of the Niger Delta (MEND); in the coordinated actions of Platform London, Liberate Tate, and the Art Not Oil Coalition; and in the activist scholarship of thinkers like Rob Nixon, Jennifer Wenzel, and Cajetan Iheka, the catastrophic ecological and human harms caused by this particularly merciless form of oil extraction have been advertised widely not only in Nigeria but around the world. Multinational petroleum companies and their local subsidiaries have destroyed what was once one of the world's most biologically diverse regions[1] through disproportionately large and frequent oil spills, grossly inadequate clean-up operations, and near-constant gas flaring.[2] Successive Nigerian governments are likewise to blame, having ignored their own environmental regulations that would limit ecological harms to the Niger Delta and instead permitted petroleum companies to operate with minimal oversight. Under both military and civilian regimes, the Nigerian state has passed laws that facilitate depletive extraction in order to maximize its own profits.[3] In the meantime, an uncountable number of people have died or suffered serious illnesses ranging from birth defects to cancer;[4] traditional occupations like fishing and farming have been rendered largely impossible;[5] and the sovereignty of the region's ethnically minoritized populations has been persistently undermined.[6]

Behind the Niger Delta's well-documented experience of extreme ecological dispossession is a property regime imposed by colonial Britain and intensified by postcolonial Nigerian governments. Central to English-derived land law's predication on individual ownership and capital accumulation is an assumed right to extract value from real or immoveable property. Anglophone land law's proprietary predicates are acutely apparent in petroleum production, which uses up nonrenewable energy sources, fuels Global North comforts, and exploits racially minoritized peoples. While the oil industry is recognizably global in that it extracts oil and gas in one region and transports it to another, it also remains deeply colonialist. Most obviously, multinational conglomerates such as Royal Dutch Shell or British Petroleum employ far stricter health and environmental protocols in wealthier countries than in poorer regions: for instance, cleanup operations in the United States after spills like Deepwater Horizon are significantly faster and more comprehensive than similar disasters in Nigeria, which endure what Rob Nixon has influentially termed the "slow violence" of ecological destruction over extended periods.[7] Similarly, large petroleum companies commonly employ colonialist financial structures and business practices, typically operating through local subsidiaries that allow for the greatest profit extraction with the least possible oversight. Constructed upon complex networks of ownership, parent companies like BP and Shell can effectively transfer responsibility to their subsidiaries in order to largely evade consequences for ecological damage and harms to human health. Much like the trading companies that operated from the sixteenth through to the twentieth centuries, the multinational petroleum industry siphons raw materials from the Global South to pursue wealth that accrues most substantially in the Global North.

The petroleum industry's colonialist business operations and ongoing ties to European legal frameworks have been at the center of recent litigation that has challenged centuries of extraction by the Global North from the Global South. On January 29, 2021, the Hague Court of Appeal made a decision in the case of *Four Nigerian Farmers v. Shell*, finding Royal Dutch Shell (RDS) liable for oil spills in the Niger Delta villages of Oruma and Goi.[8] The court determined that RDS has a duty of care to the litigants, even though it does not itself operate in Nigeria, because it is the parent company of Shell Petroleum Development Company (SPDC), whose business operations in the Niger Delta have involved extensive spills and limited clean-up.[9] As Lucas Roorda observes, *Four Nigerian Farmers v. Shell* "is the first time a court of the home state of a transnational corporation has found a subsidiary located outside of its jurisdiction liable on the basis of harmful acts."[10] The Dutch decision's global impact could be felt only a month later when the UK Supreme Court ruled that a similar case, *Okpabi v. Shell*, could proceed with a different claim against RDS and SPDC for Niger Delta oil spills caused by negligence. The Supreme Court's decision rested on whether the appellants had an arguable case that RDC owed them a common law duty of care given that it "exercised significant control over material aspects of SPDCs operations and/or assumed responsibility for SPDC's operations."[11] Lord Hamblen and his fellow Supreme Court judges found that the High Court had erred in 2018 by conducting a mini-trial instead of assessing whether enough evidentiary material had been supplied to "satisf[y] the summary judgment test of real prospect of success."[12] [13] While the lower court's ruling was overturned due to procedural error, the Supreme Court inferred from *Four Nigerian Farmers v. Shell* a reasonable likelihood that extensive evidentiary materials will be produced during disclosure, meaning that Shell will likely be found similarly liable under UK law.[14]

These recent judgments reveal less about Shell's particular business practices than they register changing juridical opinion regarding resource extraction, racial capitalism, and distributed corporate responsibility.[15] Both 2021 rulings were made possible by a 2019 case in the United Kingdom Supreme Court, *Lungowe v. Vedanta*, in which nearly 2,000 residents of the Zambian city of Chingola successfully pursued damages from Vedanta, a UK-domiciled copper mining parent company, and its local subsidiary, Konkola Copper Mines (KCM), after mining runoff had polluted waterways that supplied drinking water and farmland irrigation.[16] Like the 2021 judgments against Shell in both the Netherlands and the United Kingdom, the judges in *Lungowe v. Vedanta* found a multinational corporation, registered in Europe yet benefiting from resource extraction in Africa, responsible for the ecological and human consequences of its industrial practices. In a significant departure from precedent, these recent court cases effectively assess whether extractive companies based in the Global North will face legal and financial repercussions for their activities in the Global South.[17] Further, they implicitly recognize what certain scholars of environmental justice have long identified: that the distribution of ecological harms is substantially racialized.[18] Whether within communities in the Global North or between locations in the North and South, extractive practices disproportionately harm communities of color and disproportionately benefit white populations. In the putatively postcolonial present, systemic environmental harms accrue from Global Northern extractive practices that are at once anthropocentric and racialized, sustaining capitalist-colonialist violence through the structuring of multinational corporations that have long allowed wealthy, predominately white beneficiaries to evade justice.

As these recent cases against petroleum and copper companies demonstrate, the legal arena is finally catching up with the cultural sphere. Works of literature, art, journalism, and activism have made clear for decades if not centuries that northern companies are profiting from the ecological violence that they inflict upon racialized others and distant landscapes. If litigants are successful in achieving some degree of redress for the extractive harms inflicted by copper mining in Zambia or petroleum production in the Niger Delta, it will be as a result of not only legal processes but also literary actions and activist pursuits whose discursive impacts accrue only slowly and over many years. Certainly, the aforementioned court cases, which all provide redress for victims of transnational resource extraction, represent notable shifts in legal thinking, but these changing ideas about globally distributed responsibility for ecological and human harms are established not only within the legal sphere but also beyond it. The broad creative arena that includes fiction, poetry, sculpture, visual art, and anti-oil activism is as notable as legal decisions in confronting corporate approaches to resource extraction because, much like activist protest or environmentally attuned litigation, aesthetic works bear discursive effects. Differently than the more common ecocritical response to the urgency borne of climate crisis, I am not arguing that aesthetic inquiry can help to redress ecological devastation through the expository mode of making oil visible, revealing the scale of a crisis that had gone largely unrepresented so that action might follow.[19] Nor am I heedless to warnings that the perceived need to identify solutions to practical problems is often part of the "market friendly sustainability discourse" that sustains the neoliberal university.[20] Instead, I am arguing that aesthetic processes bear dispersed material consequences. By engaging aesthetically with significant ideas and legal contexts, works of literature and other arts necessarily participate in the discursive process by which structures of thought gradually change over time, just as recent environmentally attuned litigation redefines globally distributed responsibility for extractive harms.

While the abovementioned cases against Shell and Vedanta are tort suits in which litigants sue for harms, their conditions of possibility stem as much from English land law and its proprietary formulation of property ownership as they do from the branch of law redressing injury. Even though tort law regulates some of the most egregious consequences of resource extraction, it is property law that explains, legislates, and provides the rationale for depleting nonrenewable resources in ways that have profoundly racialized consequences. In

Nigeria, as in most former British colonies, the legal system draws significantly from English common law, as Lord Hamblen explains in the *Okpabi* judgment: "It is agreed that the issue of governing law should be approached on the basis that the laws of England and Wales and the law of Nigeria are materially the same."[21] Quite apart from the jurisdictional issues raised in cases like *Lungowe v. Vedanta* and *Okpabi v. Shell*, which newly establish that harms caused abroad can be tried in English courts if the parent company is based in the United Kingdom,[22] Lord Hamblen recognizes that Nigerian law remains substantially structured upon the British legal system that colonial legislators forcibly imposed. Like all forms of colonial law, statutes regulating oil derive substantially from British formulations of proprietary land ownership that have historically benefited Britain economically, dispossessed colonized regions, and fueled climate change. From 1903, British companies were granted licenses to search for oil in the Niger Delta;[23] from 1907, the Southern Nigerian Mining Regulation (Oil) Ordinance "made the search for oil in Nigeria a British monopoly";[24] and from 1914, the Mineral Oils Ordinance and its subsequent versions maintained the provision that crude oil exploration was reserved only for British subjects while also vesting mineral rights in the Crown. Since independence, Nigerian petroleum laws have maintained and even intensified this extractive approach to mineral ownership.

Inasmuch as these tort suits reveal an emergent legal understanding of globally dispersed responsibility for ecological and human harms, they enact ideas that are being most forcefully developed in a substantial body of contemporary Nigerian fiction and poetry. This chapter traces twentieth-century Nigerian legal history and analyzes contemporary Nigerian literary aesthetics to argue that Nigerian writers are retheorizing ecological relationships in ways that are contributing to significant legal change. A history of Nigeria's land and mineral laws reveals that the country's petroleum industry is built upon colonial statutes that facilitated resource extraction and wealth generation by radically changing Nigerians' legislated relationship to land. In turn, postcolonial land laws from the 1960s and 1970s deepened the potential for unmitigated extraction, building prosperity for the nation and its elite at the expense of Niger Delta ecologies and the region's primarily ethnically minoritized populations. In the face of petroleum production's devastating ecological and human consequences, contemporary artists of all genres, including the fiction writers examined in this chapter, are effectively participating in the slow process of reformulating land law. I take Ben Okri's "What the Tapster Saw" and Chigozie Obioma's *The Fishermen* as representative of a significant body of work that also includes Buchi Emecheta's *Destination Biafra*, Kaine Agary's *Yellow-Yellow*,

Isidore Okpewho's *Tides*, Ogaga Ifowodo's *The Oil Lamp*, and Helon Habila's *Oil on Water*, not to mention visual art including Victor Ehikhamenor's installation *Wealth of Nations*, ceramicist Ngozi-Omeje Ezema's sculpture *Man of Fishes*, or Ayò Akínwándé's video installation "Ogoni Cleanup." In their stylistically distinct but aesthetically similar works, Okri and Obioma at once critique extractive relationships to natural resources and aesthetically theorize a symbiotic relationship between all living beings (and past and future lives) within the Niger Delta. While Okri's style is often inadequately identified as magic-realist and Obioma's dialogue and plotting take a more substantially realist form, both writers theorize ecological symbiosis through metonymically and figuratively rendering the consciousness of beings, human and nonhuman, in their past and present lives.

Like Okri and Obioma, a small but not insignificant group of legal theorists and environmental philosophers have begun to reframe the human-land relationship by casting it in terms not of ownership but care. Working primarily in Indigenous ecological philosophy, Indigenous legal theory, West African animist theory, and progressive environmental law, these thinkers are putting pressure on existing legal frameworks and contributing to a broader epistemological shift that is also evidenced among Nigerian writers and artists. Interpreting this broad assessment of ecologies as symbiotic, in contrast to English-derived land law's proprietary predicates, this chapter argues that legal actions and literary texts similarly undertake the slow process of changing structures of thought. Sometimes these legal or literary works are explicit about their intentions and other times less so, and sometimes they act in concrete ways and other times their ideas are rendered aesthetically, but all are crucial for establishing a more just ecological landscape that is sustainable for all forms of life. In these shared philosophical commitments to symbiotic relation, writers and legal theorists refuse to identify the Delta as merely a locus of negation and death but instead recognize that a hopeful, sustainable, and abundant future requires developing radically different forms of ecological relation than those that exist in current Nigerian land and mineral laws. In affirming mutual interdependence as the only viable, sustainable mode of human-land relation, these writers, activists, and legal actors are theorizing the kind of relationship—one that includes but does not revere humans—that this book identifies as necessarily improper: as im-properly refusing proprietary ownership. This chapter concludes that symbiosis offers more than a way of conceptualizing ecological relation that necessarily challenges proprietary forms of land and mineral law; it also registers the redistributive work that activists, writers, and theorists undertake when they aesthetically participate in reconfiguring existing structures of thought.

Nigerian Land Law's Colonial History

Long before the British government signed a contract with the Royal Niger Company to take control of what is now Nigeria, the region had been a noted source of potential wealth for acquisitive Europeans. By the time Britain took sovereign possession in January 1900, its emissaries had been engaged in extensive property speculation throughout western Africa for nearly three hundred years.[25] During the seventeenth and eighteenth centuries, British merchants traded in enslaved peoples from the Delta region;[26] throughout the nineteenth century, Britain began asserting sovereignty in West Africa, annexing Lagos in 1861 and creating the Oil Rivers Protectorate in 1884, in the process facilitating its merchants' robust hold over the Delta's palm oil industry;[27] from 1900 to 1960, Britain consolidated its colonial domination by acquiring sovereign rights to well over 350,000 square miles of the region it named Northern and Southern Nigeria, which was home to countless ethnic groups, as well as the Benin, Oyo, and Hausa Empires; and even after independence, British corporations have maintained neocolonial property interests in the form of business deals that allow direct or indirect profit from oil. To a greater or lesser extent, British formulations of property ownership, whether of people, goods, or land, have been extracting value from Nigeria and dispossessing the region and its people since the seventeenth century.

In the strictly legal sense, English property law was only implemented in Nigeria once the whole country was forced under colonial rule in 1900, but the British system of land alienation that justified resource extraction took root during the century and a half spanning 1807 to 1960, with significant consequences for the postcolonial Niger Delta. During this longer period of coercive imperial power that preceded explicit colonial domination, Britain imposed its administrative, political, and juridical control under the guise of benevolent care. Legal historian Inge van Hulle explains that Britain's touted involvement in 1807's abolition of the slave trade was equally "a vector for introducing Western legal techniques in West Africa, and for the employment of a discourse shrouded in international law."[28] Justifying its regional presence through the humanitarian framework of abolition, Britain signed treaties "in which strategically located regions were ceded to Britain and which might, at a later point, be used to justify forcible intervention against African communities."[29] One such agreement was the Lagos Treaty of Cession (1861), leading to the Registration of Deeds in Lagos in 1883, which R. K. Udo identifies as Nigeria's first colonial land law.[30] Along with its goal of future political sovereignty, Britain enjoyed immediate monetary gains. No longer able to exploit enslaved people's forced labor to fuel its own economic growth, Britain used its increasing jurisdictional authority to tap into the Niger Delta's existing trade in palm oil and engage in a new form of colonial extraction. Recognizing that palm oil had brought significant wealth to the Oil Rivers region, British traders signed business agreements that favored their own interests and shipped this commodity back to Europe to power their nation's factories. Significantly, as legal theorists Rhuks T. Ako and Patrick Okonmah explain, "[f]oreign traders . . . exclude[d] the indigenous population from the trade by dealing directly with the producers in the hinterland. Their intention at the time was to ensure the steady and cheap supply of palm-oil, which was strategic to maintain the industrial revolution in the West."[31] Not only was the nineteenth-century British trade in palm oil ecologically and economically extractive, in other words, but it was also racialized, proving lucrative largely by displacing the ethnically minoritized communities that had been central to its initial production.

If Nigeria's transition to petroleum was continuous with earlier forms of colonial extraction, being at once racially dominative and ecologically depletive, it was made possible by a complete overhaul of Nigerian land law. By the early twentieth century, with speculators seeing the promise of oil in the Niger Delta's swamps and wetlands, the newly empowered colonial administration began to restructure the country's land laws in ways that would consolidate Britain's power, ensure its economic growth, and allow for unlimited petroleum production. Fifty years before oil was found, colonial officials granted search permits only to British companies and their affiliates, excising the Niger Delta's Indigenous populations from the potential wealth that petroleum would eventually yield. Political theorist Cyril Obi identifies a sequence of legislative measures throughout British rule that sought to control petroleum access, explaining that "the oil industry in Nigeria is rooted in the country's colonial history."[32] As Obi enumerates, the industry "was formalized by the passing of the Mineral Oils Ordinance of 1914, which was subsequently amended in 1916, 1925, 1945, and 1959. The Mineral Ordinance . . . favored British oil companies in the exploration and extraction of oil destined for the world market."[33] Left only implicit in Obi's analysis is that petroleum's particularly depletive consequences were enabled by the colonial state's fundamentally rewriting Nigerians' legal relationship to land. Prior to colonial domination, land tenure systems across what is now Nigeria shared significant similarities, despite variations between ethnic groups. As Udo explains in his exhaustive report on 1978's Land Use Act and its precursors, "broadly, land belonged to the entire community, to the living, the dead and generations unborn."[34] In marked distinction to the British tradition, land was inalienable, even as a specific person might hold tenure for a time, and it was meant to be maintained for the collective good.

While customary law still operates under certain strict limitations within Nigeria's plural legal system, colonial administrators overrode its doctrine of shared land rights when, in the early twentieth century, they established English common law as the basis for legal statutes[35] and imposed on the region their proprietary formulation of property ownership. In 1910, as part of the process of bolstering sovereign power in Northern Nigeria, High Commissioner Percy Girouard signed the Land and Natives Rights Ordinance No. 9, which implemented Frederick Lugard's 1902 misreading of land law in Fulani territories and vested all land in the state.[36] Udo identifies Girouard's ordinance as "the mother of all basic land policy legislation in Nigeria" because, for the first time, it codified all jurisdictional land as state property and set precedent that would determine postcolonial land law.[37] Similarly consequential for shaping Nigeria's petroleum industry and its ecological and human costs was 1914's Mineral Oils Ordinance, which "vested all oil control in mainland Nigeria in the British colonial government."[38] In subsequent updates to this ordinance, like 1945's Minerals Act, the state intensified its ownership claims, stipulating that "The entire property and control of all minerals and mineral oil in, under or upon any land in Nigeria, and of all rivers, streams and water courses throughout Nigeria is and shall be vested in the crown."[39] In Ekanade Olumide's analysis, "this colonial ordinance . . . set the standard for the economic injustice" that would persist long after independence.[40] Owning not just the land but all minerals found within it, colonial Nigeria newly followed an ecologically and economically extractive system of property ownership that rewarded not just the use but also the using up of natural resources. If the very act of imposing colonial law is a form of property assignation, in that "treaties . . . transfe[r] sovereignty and property rights,"[41] English land law's central tenets and material forms at once provided British colonialism's conditions of possibility and facilitated its continued harms.

Postcolonial Nigerian land law retains British property law's formulation of property as defined by alienable ownership, along with the extractive predicates and depletive consequences that Britain saved for its colonies, while also adding new delimitations that make its oil-producing regions particularly vulnerable to extraction, exploitation, and depletion. Following independence in 1960, and after a three-year civil war fought partly over oil rights, the Petroleum Act of 1969 confirmed that the federal government owned all Nigerian oil.[42] In this first major petroleum law since oil's discovery in 1956 and the country's independence in 1960, postcolonial Nigeria disregarded customary approaches to land use and instead followed the strictures laid out in the colonial-era Mineral Oil Ordinance. Under Nigerian customary law, land comprises only the soil and includes neither structures built upon it nor minerals found beneath it.[43] By contrast, the Petroleum Act provides that "[t]he entire ownership and control of all petroleum in, under or upon any lands to which this section applies shall be vested in the State."[44] In 1978, the Land Use Act consolidated the state's property rights by allowing for land to be appropriated if doing so were deemed in the "overriding public interes[t]."[45] This controversial law disproportionately benefits the state and its affiliates not only by extending the nationalization of natural resources from oil to land but also by providing for the sale of private immoveable property with insufficient mechanisms to ensure appropriate compensation.[46] In its introductory paragraph, the Land Use Act expressly "vest[s] all Land comprised in the territory of each State (except land vested in the Federal government or its agencies) solely in the Governor of the State, who would hold such Land in trust." The Land Use Act remains controversial: proponents argue that it "ensure[s] that there is sound land and environmental development and that the ecological and aesthetic values of the nation are preserved and enhanced,"[47] while critics charge that "it is a confiscatory piece of legislation which expropriates land in favour of the rich and their multinational business partners against the poor."[48] The Constitution of the Federal Republic of Nigeria 1999 further strengthened the Land Use Act's violent privations when it similarly vested "the entire property in control of all minerals, mineral oils and natural gas in, under or upon any land in Nigeria or in, under or upon the territorial waters and the Exclusive Economic Zone of Nigeria . . . in the Government of the Federation."[49] Building on British administrators' almost wholesale reshaping of the region's property laws, postcolonial legislators have entrenched in Nigeria a model of land ownership that licenses depletive resource extraction and facilitated large-scale, proprietorial ownership of Niger Delta minerals.

Impropriety as Critique: Proprietary Land Law's Persecutory Consequences

In the extensive collection of Nigerian literary production that has been variously described as "petrofiction,"[50] "petroleum aesthetics,"[51] and "petro-magic-realism,"[52] writers have engaged with changing legal ideas about land ownership and use, often understood in terms of the petroleum industry's ecological harms and political violence. The aforementioned aesthetic categories have been helpful in understanding the breadth of literary engagement with Niger Delta oil extraction, albeit not without cost. With the exception of Wenzel's *petro-magic-realism*, these categories only address genre in the broadest sense (*petrofiction* refers only to novels or short stories) or aesthetics in the loosest sense (*petroleum aesthetics* describes works of art generally rather than specific aesthetic styles, techniques, or practices). Even *petro-magic-realism*'s satisfying complexity somewhat reduces the concept's scope to the specific genre of magic realism, excluding many works — including *The Fishermen* — from consideration. Even the "petro" prefix somewhat diminishes the aesthetic complexities and intellectual breadth of these works, characterizing and categorizing them primarily through their engagement with oil. More significantly, these categories tend to encourage literary scholarship that blames postcolonial political corruption for the environmental and political violence inflicted on the Niger Delta and its predominately Indigenous peoples, even as Nigeria's writers and artists pay significant attention to the juridical principles that facilitate ecological degradation.

In the first of this chapter's literary analyses, Ben Okri's "What the Tapster Saw" astutely alludes to Nigeria's proprietary model of land ownership in a dystopian vision of the multinational petroleum industry that identifies land law as the main culprit of the Niger Delta's near total destruction. Published in 1986 and offering one of the earliest examples of a large corpus of Nigerian literature that addresses petroleum extraction's human and ecological costs, "What the Tapster Saw" narrates the near-death experience of a palm wine tapster after he unwittingly trespasses on land that has been newly purchased by the fictional Delta Oil Company. The story is bookended by a conversation between the tapster and his friend the herbalist, both of whom practice professions that are economically and culturally important to the region, while the bulk of the plot concerns the tapster's hallucinatory experience after falling from a palm tree for the first time in his thirty-year career and being knocked unconscious. The first indication that something awful is about to happen is a signboard that warns: "DELTA OIL COMPANY: THIS AREA IS BEING DRILLED. TRESPASSERS IN DANGER."[53] Okri registers the strangeness of this legal notice — and the property regime by which it is legitimated — in the way the tapster "stare[s] at the signboard without comprehension," seemingly unable to understand that a once-familiar environment is now owned by a petroleum company and that he is barred from entry. The tapster's shock at this new epistemological and legal landscape is likewise registered in the sudden representational shift from the frame narrative's substantive realism to Okri's characteristically fantastic mode. Immediately after passing the signboard, the tapster "notice[s] a strange cluster of palm-trees" and rides his bicycle through "thick cobwebs" to reach them, only to find that their red-green bark releases a smell that "intoxicate[s] him."[54] Poisoned by the fumes that these uncanny palm trees emit, the tapster climbs a tree to tap for wine, but "[t]he morning sun, striking him with an oblique glare, blinded him. As the golden lights exploded in his eyes the branches of the palm-tree receded from him. It was the first time he had fallen in thirty years."[55] Overwhelmed by a newly potent cognitive and physical environment, one that has been ushered in by the oil company's proprietorial notice, the tapster falls to the ground and is knocked unconscious.

Inasmuch as the concept of *trespass* unlocks the horrors inflicted on the tapster and introduces this story's fantastical, embedded episode, it functions narratologically to mark the structural connection between Nigerian land law's proprietary impulses and the region's experience of catastrophic ecological and human loss. In this first of several references to private property and the associated crime of trespass, Okri recognizes that Nigerian land law inflicts suffering upon Niger Delta peoples and ecologies even as it is presented by the state as beneficial to the nation. The tapster's initially delighted reaction to unconsciousness reflects the government's insistence that oil and land appropriation is in the country's best interests: feeling "unbelievably light and airy," he at first believes that "the fall had done him some good."[56] Like "the spectacle of opulence" that Andrew Apter identifies as characterizing Nigeria's public persona during the 1970s when oil wealth was abundant, the tapster's preliminary response to his changed ecological and juridical environment is positively coded, even as he fails to recognize its imminent and present dangers. Apter uses the metaphor of magic to describe the ideological and economic hollowness of Nigeria's boom years and to convey the simultaneity of exorbitant wealth and profound poverty that have together resulted from the postcolonial nation's extractive practices. Whereas Apter addresses petroleum in materialist economic terms, identifying the "mysterious value" of the country's oil revenues and lamenting "what was a symbolic mode of production all along,"[57] Okri explores economic and sovereign dispossession in relation to land's legal dimensions.

"What the Tapster Saw" rhetorically identifies land law as causing human and ecological harms when the tapster encounters a second noticeboard that reads: "DELTA OIL COMPANY: TRESPASSERS WILL BE PERSECUTED."[58] Announcing the petroleum industry's legislated violence with the rhetorical modulation from "prosecution" to "persecution," and simultaneously recalling the widely publicized oppression of Indigenous and ethnically minoritized peoples in the Delta by oil companies relying on paramilitary support, this signboard is explicit about the exclusionary intentions and violent consequences that are only implicitly encoded in land law statutes. Shifting focalization quickly from the persecutorial notice to the landscape, Okri shows the tapster realizing that "around him were earth-mounds, grave-stones, a single palm-tree, and flickering mangrove roots. He made a mark on the tree-trunk. Suddenly it became a fully festered wound."[59] The speed with which the tapster's "mark on the tree-trunk" becomes a suppurating injury invokes the rapidity, in the scale of deep time, of catastrophic levels of destruction in the Niger Delta. Moreover, Okri's characteristically sudden transition between the measured, realist description of his frame narrative to that which is extravagantly hyperabundant renders the known world strange, refusing the norms of properly precise observation in favor of an improper account of extractive violence wherein affective immersion produces a more accurate sense than detached observation of the scale of ecological devastation.

Invocations of the strange or weird function as markers of critical impropriety in this story, revealing the violence that Nigeria's land laws conceal. As soon as the tapster enters the Delta Oil Company's territory, he sees the curiously immobile water, which is "viscous and didn't seem to move," much like the waterways of the Niger Delta, where tens of thousands of gallons of oil are spilled each year.[60] The tapster watches a peculiar explosion "of green smoke" that alludes to the common practice of planting dynamite to rapidly clear forests and drill for oil: "When the smoke cleared the tapster watched a weird spewing up of oil and animal limbs from the ground. The site was eventually abandoned. Agapanthus grew there like blood on a battlefield."[61] The "green smoke" caused by this explosion is matched in its unnatural color and destructive extent by the earth's "weird spewing up" of oil and body parts. Invoking strangeness more obliquely, too, the tapster is surrounded by an all-encompassing silence: "When his eyes stopped itching the tapster wandered beneath the copper bursts of the sky. He noticed that there were no birds around."[62] Okri ties the region's strange avian lack to the practice of gas flaring, itself indexed metonymically in the sky's "copper bursts." Natural gas is a byproduct of oil extraction and setting it alight is the cheapest and most dangerous method of disposal; the process releases a substantial proportion of carcinogens into the atmosphere while the intense light pollution it emits disrupts sleep patterns and damages mental health.[63] Multinational oil companies like Shell have historically tended to reserve this cheaper form of gas disposal for activities far from their Global North headquarters,[64] a mark of not only their desire to cut costs where legislation allows but also their disregard for majority Black and brown regions, especially in the Global South.

Okri registers the damage caused by proprietary land laws through descriptions that are at once extremely violent and, according to the definition provided in this book's Introduction, aesthetically improper. The tapster experiences an array of ailments that commonly result from petroleum extraction and whose oblique rendering and diffuse characteristics refuse the proprietary logic of enclosure that Nigerian land law attempts to uphold. The tapster suffers chest pain, recalling the oil-related respiratory problems plaguing inhabitants of the Niger Delta; his "eyes itch," invoking the copious dermatological conditions that are experienced throughout the region;[65] and he notices "an acid in the feel of things," signifying the acid rain that results from gas flaring.[66] This acidity is figured improperly, or outside the proper's demarcated bounds, because it is not presented as a quality or attribute of the rain itself but as a dispersed, diffuse, affectively registered form of knowledge. The effects of flaring are also alluded to in this strange world's unremitting light: "the sun did not set, nor did it rise. . . . In the evenings the sun was like a large crystal. In the mornings it was incandescent. The tapster was never allowed to shut his eyes."[67] Afflicted by environmentally induced insomnia, the tapster is subjected to gas flaring's incessant light emissions, described by Nixon as "the blazing false sun of interminable flares."[68] Okri's hauntingly beautiful prose — his careful rhetorical constructions and his rendering of human-produced horrors in expressly aesthetic terms — make the extensive reach and gratuitous quality of these ecological devastations stark.

In allusively itemizing the variety of ill-effects inflicted by the petroleum industry on all forms of life in the Niger Delta, and in connecting petroleum extraction to Nigerian land and mineral law's proprietary predicates, "What the Tapster Saw" acknowledges that Nigeria's land and mineral laws bear extreme ecological consequences. Since first discovering oil in 1956 on the cusp of independence,[69] Nigeria has passed a slew of legislation which ostensibly protects national and environmental interests by regulating the oil and gas industry, but which has instead restricted land and resource ownership in order to maximize oil extraction and control access to profits. A partial list of these legal instruments includes the Oil Pipelines Act of 1956; the Oil in Navigable Waters Act of 1968; the Petroleum Act of 1969; the Offshore Oil Revenue Decree of 1971; the Land Use Act of 1978; the Associated Gas Re-Injection Act of 1979; the Environmental Impact Assessment Decree of 1992; and the Constitution of the Federal Republic of Nigeria of 1999. Some of this legislation is categorized as environmental law and several of the aforementioned statutes explicitly address pollution, especially the Oil in Navigable Waters Act and the Environmental Impact Assessment Decree (EIA). Implemented after an illegal dump of toxic waste was discovered in 1988, the EIA was followed by government commitments to sustainable development,[70] including a constitutional provision to "protect and improve the environment and safeguard the water, air and land, forest and wild life of Nigeria."[71] Yet these laws remain largely ineffectual because Nigeria's state agencies are notoriously lax in enforcing preventative or recuperative measures against an overwhelmingly powerful oil industry.[72] The lack of effective industry regulation primarily stems from high-level conflicts between legal rulings affirming human and ecological wellbeing and illicit practices ensuring elite wealth generation. As Toyin Falola and Matthew Heaton explain, the combination of oil riches and a rent-seeking economy has created in Nigeria "a comprador class of politicians and bureaucrats, who work in conjunction with foreign companies to siphon off surplus wealth for personal benefit."[73] While profits for a select few have been immense, especially during the nation's oil-rich years from the 1970s to the early 2000s,[74] petroleum's ecological costs have also been notoriously high. Effectively, environmental law and land law have been co-conspirators in protecting Nigeria's petroleum industry and its economically, ecologically, and culturally extractive practices.

While the Land Use Act seemingly instantiates a form of property ownership that in fact bears a longer colonial history, the mechanisms it introduces for land alienation, including and especially across the nation's oil-rich regions, have led to both economic and sovereign dispossession as well as extensive ecological harms. According to Ako, the Land Use Act has turned the Niger Delta into "a land speculator's paradise," making the region's inhabitants "tenants-at-will" of the powerful multinational oil industry.[75] Like Okri's figuration of trespass in "What the Tapster Saw," Ako explicitly links Nigeria's Land Use Act to proprietary models of ownership that make Niger Delta residents subject to the oil industry's desires. Identifying the Land Use Act as "a fundamental cause of the high incidence of violent conflicts in [the Niger Delta] due to the environmental injustice it instigates,"[76] Ako connects the legal and economic processes of land speculation to the consequences of colonially imposed and postcolonially consolidated land law.[77] Less expressly but still significantly, Jennifer Wenzel also indicts Nigeria's land and environmental laws for the ecological and sovereign violence they enable and sanction. Employing the conceit of disposability, Wenzel establishes an expansively materialist analysis of petroleum extraction that attends to its political, ecological, and affective dimensions. In *The Disposition of Nature*, Wenzel argues that "The 1969 Petroleum Act and the 1978 Land Use Act claimed mineral rights for the federal government and privileged oil-related uses of land over all others. Here the right to dispose of natural resources as an aspect of postcolonial sovereignty entails a temperamental disposition toward oil extraction as a mode of consolidating state power" (109–10). In at once ideological and affective terms, Wenzel links the "disposal" of extracting natural resources to the "disposition" of a newly postcolonial nation's political aims. While *The Disposition of Nature* remains primarily focused on state power and political machinery, its integration of Nigeria's land laws into its assessment of petro-violence, political corruption, and civil unrest marks a vital development in analyses of the petroleum industry's environmental harms in the Niger Delta. Even as Nigeria's political elite have facilitated the accrual of inordinate wealth by a small number of multinational corporate executives and Nigerian politicians, the country's land and environmental laws are as significant a shaping condition for depleting the Niger Delta as the more commonly identified perpetrator, political corruption.

Blood and Oil: Metonymizing Proprietary Land and Environmental Laws

Inasmuch as Okri's improper aesthetics respond to English property law's proprietary tenets, as well as to British colonial property law's additionally racialized presumptions, they help to clarify the deep connections between land laws and political unrest in Nigeria. Okri is far from alone in his analysis of political upheaval's association with land and mineral laws that have polluted the Niger Delta and effectively restricted land access for local communities. To take just one of many possible examples, Chigozie Obioma's 2015 novel *The Fishermen* similarly registers petroleum's consequences by charting the relationship between oil extraction, state power, and land use in the Niger Delta. Stylistically and thematically establishing itself as an heir to Chinua Achebe's *Things Fall Apart*, *The Fishermen* is an expressly political novel, narrating a story of curtailed youth, aborted political promise, and ecological degradation in 1990s Nigeria. Much like *Things Fall Apart*, Obioma's novel uses a tragic family plot as a prism through which to assess the country's political deficiencies. At the same time, in revolving around a metaphorically polluted river, *The Fishermen* also offers a sustained examination of petroleum extraction's extensive ecological and human harms. Focalized through its titular fishermen, this novel improperly retheorizes the relationship between humans and their environment in ways that confront Nigeria's proprietary land laws and the dispossession they enable. Whereas *Things Fall Apart* prefigures postcolonial Nigeria's troubled birth, telling the story of colonial subjugation through the hubris and deadly violence of its adult protagonist Okonkwo, *The Fishermen* addresses the disappointments of independence through the doubly twinned stories of the four Agwu boys: older brothers Ikenna and Boju, who are driven to fratricide and suicide after believing a madman's prophecy; and their younger siblings, Obembe and Benjamin, who seek vengeance for their brothers' deaths and face imprisonment and exile as a consequence. The cause of their downfall is the river at which they have secretly pretended to be fishermen, and which is a locus of fear for the town's residents. In its overt references, *The Fishermen* engages expressly with social pressures and electoral politics during the fragile democracy of the mid-1990s, but in its symbolic resonances, Obioma's novel is inexorably tied to environmental concerns.

The Fishermen obliquely anchors itself in the particular human and ecological harms afflicting the Niger Delta by making the fictional Omi-Ala river the primary site of this novel's successive acts of violence. Variously described as "dreadful," "dangerous," and "deadly," the river's name translates to Ala's Water, where Ala is the Igbo goddess of the earth and "omi" means *water* in Igbo.[78] In its name, Omi-Ala registers the persistence of autochthonous religious beliefs that are grounded in local contexts and which grant power and respect to ecological systems. In its present-day function, however, this river serves as a site of pollution and fear, which the retrospective child narrator, Benjamin, links to external influence: "when the colonialists came from Europe, and introduced the Bible . . . the people, now largely Christians, began to see [the river] as an evil place."[79] Contemporary residents maintain these colonial beliefs: Christian villagers fear the animist congregation from the nearby Celestial Church, sharing reports of fetish rituals, which they associate with evil, washing up on the riverbank. Omi-Ala's malevolent reputation is cemented when, in 1995, one year prior to the novel's setting, "the mutilated body of a woman was found in the river, her vital body parts dismembered."[80] The river's ecological life-system foretells these tragedies: *esan* grass grows prolifically along its banks and throughout the area, its "strange botanical name" meaning "retribution or vengeance" in Yoruba.[81] In the "strangeness" of this grass's name, Obioma reveals his shared interest, with Okri, in the at once figurative and affective potential of the weird and esoteric. As Kate Harlin's animist materialist reading of the scene explains, "the Yoruba name for esan suggests an ontology that views the grass as alive and animate. That the grass's animate nature continues into death reveals the path to the Omi-Ala to be a 'spectral space', populated by the spectres of no-longer-living nettles."[82] It certainly seems to Benjamin that the river is seeking reprisal for some unnamed act, as "schools of prickly dead nettles . . . flogged our bare legs and left white welts on our skin."[83] Like the workings of colonial British land law in postcolonial Nigeria, Omi-Ala's history freights its present.

Registering the human harms that accrue from polluted waterways, the Omi-Ala river is both the site and vehicle of this novel's central conflict, prompted by a prophecy so frightful that it causes a fatal argument between the four Agwu boys. Breaking their mother's interdiction to stay away from the Omi-Ala and their father's command to spend all of their free time studying, Ikenna, Boja, Obembe, and Benjamin style themselves as fishermen and go to the river daily to catch tadpoles and tilapias, only stopping when their neighbor, Mama Iyabo, sees them and informs their mother. Framed through a temporally improper narrative structure, Mama Iyabo's actions and Mother's outrage narratively precede but chronologically follow the more serious event that occurs at Omi-Ala, which triggers its own cascade of consequences. One afternoon as the boys are leaving the riverbank, a local madman, Abulu, prophesies that Ikenna will die in a "river of red" and "by the hands of a fisherman."[84] A few months later, just as Abulu had forewarned, Ikenna dies in a river of sorts, stabbed in his own kitchen and found lying in a pool of blood. The precision of Abulu's prophecy extends to his predicting not only the murderer but also the assailant. Several weeks before Ikenna is killed, after Mama Iyabo had informed Mother of the boys' forbidden trips, Boja had stabbed a cock and left its corpse in their neighbor's yard. Much as Boja punishes their informant with a bird's lifeless body, so Abulu had prophesied that Ikenna would "die like a cock dies."[85] Omi-Ala's perilousness recurs a symbolic third time when, in an act of poetic justice, Obembe and Benjamin use fishing hooks to murder Abulu in retribution for Ikenna's death and Boja's suicide. Obembe is forced into exile in Benin, while his younger brother (and this novel's narrator) is imprisoned for over five years.

Charting the material connection between proprietary land and mineral laws and their human and ecological consequences, the red river of Abulu's prophecy symbolically registers the oil spills that plague the Niger Delta as much as it denotes the blood of a traumatized child who has been afflicted with the promise of certain death. The figurative association between spilled oil and spilled blood has a long literary history in contemporary Nigerian oil literature and petroactivism: in his poem, "We thought it was oil . . . but it was blood," for instance, poet and environmental activist Nnimmo Bassey denounces the security forces' common practice of killing ethnically minoritized groups who protest oil extraction. Alongside its titular refrain, this poem asks: "First it was the Ogonis/Today it is Ijaws/Who will be slain this next day?"[86] Elsewhere, Bassey explains that "[t]he colour of oil in much of the world runs red—and nowhere more so than in Nigeria, where fossil-fuels extraction is deeply linked to militarisation and repression."[87] Much like Bassey, Obioma leverages the trope of spilled oil as spilled blood in Ikenna's death, which confirms Abulu's prophecy. When Obembe, Benjamin, and Mr. Bode find Ikenna in the kitchen of the Agwu home, they notice "[a] pool of reddish palm oil mapped across the top of the board beside the sink. . . . A fork lay like a dead fish, still, in the pool of red oil."[88] This brutal scene of domestic violence is also deeply political: the "ma[p]" of "reddish palm oil" that spills across the cutting board metonymically invokes nineteenth-century Britain's trade in Niger Delta palm oil; meanwhile, the fork that "lay like a dead fish" figuratively registers twentieth-century petroleum extraction and its consequences for the region's aquatic life. Echoing the bloody river in which Ikenna has died, the kitchen's domestic objects and their use for violent ends marks the similarly bloody transition from a nineteenth century form of capitalist-colonial oil extraction to a postcolonial version that maintains similarly racialized consequences.

It would be easy to read Nigerian petrofiction in the tragic mode, and *The Fishermen* certainly recognizes the tragedy of late twentieth-century Nigeria's political turbulence and the resource wars that bear partial responsibility for the postcolonial nation's cycles of violence. Like Achebe's landmark postcolonial novel, *The Fishermen* seems to be stuck in tragedy's recursive time, with Obioma reproducing Achebe's own echo of W. B. Yeats's refrain about unrest in his own colonized nation: "things fall apart; the center cannot hold."[89] Recalling the very first line of Yeats's "The Second Coming" and its invocation of spiraling unrest, Ikenna gets into a fight with another boy early in *The Fishermen*, during which "their feet drew an imperfect gyre" in the sandy ground.[90] Consecutive chapters near this novel's center reference critical motifs in Yeats's poem and Achebe's novel: Chapter 7, "The Falconer," recalls Yeats's line "the falcon cannot hear the falconer," metaphorically describing a master who is no longer in control of its subject, like Britain over its colonies or Abulu over his infamous prophecies, while Chapter 8, "The Locusts," marks a narrative turning point, much as the swarming insects in *Things Fall Apart* not only prefigure but metonymically embody the arrival of white British missionaries and their tragically disruptive legal system. Even Abulu's prophecy that Ikenna "will swim in a river of red but shall never rise from it again" echoes both "The Second Coming" and its Nigerian counterpart;[91] as Yeat's poem describes, "the blood-dimmed tide is loosed, and everywhere / The ceremony of innocence is drowned."[92] Indeed, as Achebe and Obioma recognize, and as I discuss in Chapter 4, prophecy is a constitutive feature of legal reasoning.

Yet Nigerian petroliterature is less beholden to tragedy's recursive time than such plottings of story and symbolism might suggest. While Nigerian petroaesthetics are typically understood within a political framework, thanks largely to what was, as Jennifer Wenzel explains, the nation's "simultaneous entry into global print and petro-capitalisms on the eve of independence,"[93] the petroleum industry must be understood in relation to land laws as much as national and global economic processes. Okri and Obioma both substantially address the ecological and human consequences of extant juridical formulations of land ownership even as they recognize that political corruption and paramilitary violence are also significant factors in petroleum extraction's many harms. In their aesthetically improper engagement with petroleum production, "What the Tapster Saw" and *The Fishermen* reject Nigeria's proprietary land and mineral laws and the extractive practices that they both enable and sanction. As the rest of this chapter demonstrates, Okri and Obioma pair their critique with proposed solutions that align remarkably closely with emergent legal practice and environmental philosophy. In their aesthetic impropriety, Obioma and Okri separately figure an ecologically sustaining relationship between humans and the places they call home. Aesthetically, in other words, they theorize a symbiotic relation between people and their environments that at once aligns with, and extends, a significant emergent trend within progressive areas of legal scholarship.

Theorizing Ecological Land Law

Across the world, in regions that largely follow British models of proprietary ownership, a small but not insignificant number of legal theorists is seeking to recalibrate property law for more life-sustaining ends. Countering the primary strain of at least four centuries of British-derived property law, these scholars reject the anglophone model that identifies human relationships to territory in terms of ownership, instead theorizing ways of protecting natural resources, managing land claims, and providing for housing that would preserve rather than deplete the necessary resources for sustaining both present and future life. Many of these theorists, who typically work from either an Indigenous or Global South perspective, promote a stewardship model that reframes the human-ecological relationship by casting it in terms not of ownership but care. Under the concept of stewardship, land is neither something to be owned nor an entity over which one might exercise exclusive control but is instead part of a mutually sustaining relationship between human and nonhuman actors. In moving away from capitalist colonialism's proprietary model of ownership, the stewardship model seeks to protect peoples and environments that have been most threatened by a globalized property regime that is predicated on territorial acquisition and land alienation. Given that the beneficiaries of the property-as-ownership paradigm are based primarily in the Global North, it is hardly surprising that stewardship's most vocal proponents have worked from a Global South or Indigenous perspective. It should be equally unsurprising that white, settler-colonial academics in the environmental humanities have arguably co-opted Indigenous philosophies of stewardship and kinship, extracting practices and systems of thought from which they benefit professionally.[94]

When legal scholars employ the concept of stewardship, they are typically engaging an Indigenous formulation that specifically theorizes relationships between people and land, sometimes (but not always) in a legal context, and sometimes (but not always) in relation to property. In an especially clear formulation, Anishinaabe philosopher Kyle Whyte argues that colonialism destroys Indigenous relationships with the environment, a term that he employs expansively "to reference many different relationships connecting human and nonhuman living beings (plants, animals, persons, insects), nonliving beings and entities (spirits, elements), and collectives (e.g., forests, watersheds)."[95] By granting equal significance to all forms of biotic and abiotic life, Whyte shows how ecological interdependence is crucial for both environmental justice and Indigenous sovereignty. He brings together ecosystems and stewardship under the concept of "ecologies" to explain how, differently than the anthropocentric principles that characterize settler-colonial law, stewardship extends from any and all components in an ecosystem: for instance, not just from humans toward animals but also from soil toward insects. Citing Deborah McGregor's collaborative work with Josephine Mandamin and Anishinaabe women's water movements, Whyte explains how "water supports 'plants/medicines, animals, people, birds, etc.' and — reciprocally — there is 'the life that supports water (e.g., the earth, the rain, the fish).'"[96] When Whyte argues that "settler colonialism, as an ecological form of domination, is environmental violence," it is not just because colonialism perpetuates extractive modes of resource use and proprietary systems of land ownership but also because it imposes these systems on Indigenous peoples, thereby "undermining the qualities of relationships that are constitutive of any society's social resilience or collective continuance."[97] In other words, proprietary colonial land laws are environmentally destructive as much because of the human, animal, biotic, and abiotic relationships they damage as the specific forms of degradation they inflict. By substantively and comprehensively eroding human and environmental interdependence, the European colonial enterprise has been one of the primary causes of anthropogenic climate change as well as genocidal harms to Indigenous peoples.

While Whyte focuses broadly on North American contexts, particularly Anishinaabe philosophies, his analysis of colonial resource extraction's depletive consequences both resonates with and is extended by Nigerian petrocritical thought. In literary theory, Cajetan Iheka shows how African literature often formally encodes human and nonhuman lives as interdependent. Unlike postcolonial studies, which has "retained the anthropocentric leaning of the Western epistemology it critiqued," Iheka combines Africanist literary scholarship with work from the environmental humanities to "orien[t] readers to a critical practice attentive to interspecies relations."[98] In his reading of Okri's *The Famished Road*, Iheka points out that "the intermingling of different realms serves an ecological function," while Isidore Okpewho's *Tides*, an epistolary novel set in the Niger Delta, similarly formalizes "an interconnection that is central to ecological thought."[99] For Iheka, Okpewho's novel and other Niger Delta works establish the "shared vulnerability" of "humans and other life forms" in the face of merciless petroleum extraction, while Okri's "Yoruba cosmological vision" reveals the incompatibility of anthropocentric humanism with African literary traditions, thereby signaling the limits of postcolonial studies as traditionally conceived.[100]

In these examples and others, Iheka recognizes that European colonial epistemologies — including Anglo-American property law — both conflict with and undermine African systems of thought. If oil extraction is part of what Iheka terms "the prevailing exploitative thrust of human relations with the nonhuman world,"[101] it has put what Whyte names the "collective continuance" of Niger Delta peoples at grave risk.[102] While the question of whether the peoples who live in the Niger Delta can be considered Indigenous is the subject of some debate,[103] it remains true that the colonial logic of extraction and depletion underpinning Nigeria's petroleum industry, as well as the proprietary land laws on which it was built, has disrupted the region's cultural and environmental equilibrium and disproportionately harmed the region's minoritized peoples. Whereas European colonialism's approach to land ownership and use was premised, like contemporary anglophone legal systems, on the perceived right to individual possession, African cosmologies and Indigenous philosophies alike acknowledge ecological connectedness in a way that has only just begun to be identified in the Global North.

Recognizing anglophone property law's individualist and acquisitive precepts and its at once ecological and neocolonial consequences, a growing number of legal scholars are using the concept of stewardship to develop more sustainable and equitable models of codifying human and nonhuman relationships. In her extensive scholarship on cultural property, Kristen Carpenter draws upon Indigenous formulations of stewardship to suggest necessary revisions to the English-derived property law that operates in a North American context. In an essay with Sonia Katyal and Angela Riley, "In Defense of Property," Carpenter and her collaborators connect contemporary United States' property law to a broader anglophone formulation of appropriative and individualist ownership:

> The classic view of property law, including its ownership model, is intimately tied to a paradigm of liberal individualism. Current theories of property acquisition grounded in this tradition . . . fail to take into account the prospect of group-oriented claims of custody and control that are so critical to the protection of indigenous cultural property.[104]

In their assessment of new legal methods to protect ideas and materials that have frequently been stolen by non-Indigenous entities, particularly by settler-colonial museums, Carpenter et al. push back against the liberal tradition of understanding property in terms of individualist rights to accumulation, instead explaining why property rights must also be formulated in collective, intergenerational, and custodial terms. Carpenter et al. build their case by drawing together two strains of North American jurisprudence: on the one hand, the well-established account of property as a bundle of relative rights that emerged in the twentieth century; on the other, the Indigenous stewardship principle of assuming responsibility to care for land independent of title.[105] Working with Indigenous, corporate, and environmental theory, Carpenter et al. construct a model of responsive relationship to land as place, asserting that "a stewardship model disaggregates title, possession, and exclusion."[106]

The argument that Carpenter and her various co-theorists establish as part of a broader attempt to protect Indigenous cultural property shares significant similarities with comparative environmentalist analyses of land law. Lin Heng Lye's assessment of Singaporean property law's ecological consequences, for instance, leads her to argue that "land ownership should be recognized as a species of 'stewardship.'"[107] As in Nigeria, Singapore's legal system derives from English common law, which Britain imposed by Letters Patent in 1826.[108] Today, Singapore's property regime largely retains common law's amenity to individualist ownership and capital accumulation, resulting in "ecological impoverishment, as land is cleared for economic benefits and put to 'productive use.'"[109] As Singapore has no environmental protection requirements accompanying its property laws, it continues to prioritize land's economic benefits rather than its ecological function. Lye advocates introducing stewardship to Singapore's land law through the principle of public trust, which has been successfully implemented in India, Australia, and the United States to protect against ecologically harmful development projects.[110] In proposing a robust juridical conceptualizing of stewardship that follows the public trust principle, Lye implements lessons from environmental law that understand land as ecologically valuable, and therefore needing to be collectively experienced and intergenerationally dispersed, rather than primarily identifying land as valuable because it can produce large profits that accrue to an individual land owner.

Environmental law's proposals for establishing more sustainable relationships to land offer a necessary corrective to the depletive consequences of English-derived property law. Indigenous theories of stewardship broadly recognize reciprocal relations between all ecological elements, while African animist theories of ecological interdependence similarly maintain a philosophy of reciprocal relation within a collective whole. Refusing to ascribe greater value to humans than any other ecological component, Indigenous and animist ecological philosophies operate outside the logic of proprietary ownership upon which anglophone property law is predicated. While they do not conform to property's current logic, property does bear the capacity for expansion into something other than the proprietary model that was established in colonially imposed, English-derived law.

Symbiosis: Theorizing Ecological Relation through Aesthetic Impropriety

Inasmuch as Indigenous formulations of stewardship and African animist philosophies presuppose a relationship of symbiotic, mutually sustaining care between all components of an ecological system, they function similarly to Okri's and Obioma's renditions of collective life. Both Okri and Obioma theorize ecologies as symbiotic through recurrent motifs, and in both, spiders appear repeatedly, as with the cobwebs that improperly weave together the fantastical landscape of the tapster's dream. Entering this strange world after cycling through "thick cobwebs," the tapster's briefly enamored response to his new environment is rendered in his initially noticing their "glittering" form.[111] Almost immediately, however, the tapster is disabused of his metaphorically sparkling optimism: a "foul-smelling creature" uses cobwebs to "stuff his eyes,"[112] causing an itching sensation that both references gas flaring's ophthalmological consequences and augurs the tapster's awakened consciousness to the Nigerian petroleum industry's particular harms. On the cusp of waking from his coma, the tapster is subjected once more to the cobwebs' anaesthetizing work: "a creature came and stuffed his eyes with cobwebs. His eyes itched again and he saw that the wars were not yet over."[113] In his final moment of unconsciousness, he notices that "[s]treamers of cobweb membranes weaved over the wounded palm tree."[114] Fluttering in the breeze like flags to honor the dead, these cobwebs call attention to the unnerving absence of creaturely life, including not only the birds who would typically rest on the area's trees but also the spiders that presumably produced these webs yet whose existence is never noted. Spreading across atmospheric space, these filaments register the distributed ecological injuries inflicted by petroleum extraction upon the Niger Delta. At the same time, the membranes' woven structure binds Okri's story together, functioning tropologically to register and construct a symbiotically organized world. In their symbiotic rendering, the spiders' webs aesthetically produce an improper alternative to the proprietary tenets of Nigerian land and mineral laws.

Much as in Okri, Obioma likewise employs the trope of cobwebs as a method of symbiotic cohesion and to register the falling apart of a known world. As Obioma's occasionally omniscient narrator recognizes, "spiders were beasts of grief: Creatures whom the Igbo believe nest in the houses of the aggrieved, spinning more webs and weaving noiselessly, achingly, until their yarns bulged and covered vast spaces."[115] In presenting the spiders' obsessive and tireless weaving as a form of "achin[g]" care, their webs "bulg[ing]" across "vast spaces," Obioma casts them as part of a compassionate ecosystem in which they weave webs not for their own benefit but, with deep pain, on behalf of the bereaved. Spiders serve metaphorically to signify Mother's successive mental breakdowns after the deaths of Ikenna and Boja, followed by Obembe's absence and presumed death. Mother attempts to undo the reality of her losses by eliminating the webs that publicize her grief: "by the end of her second week at the institution, every speck of spider web had been removed from the vicinity and every spider smashed to bits."[116] These episodes describing Mother's "psychic wound"[117] theorize in psychological terms that which, in Okri, is cast as cosmological: "There had been a cataclysmic explosion of her mind, and her perception of the known world had been blasted into smithereens. Her senses became imbued with extraordinary sensitivity."[118] As either a result or symptom of her painfully excessive sensory perception, Mother suffers nyctophobia, in which "[b]ig things shrunk to incredible smallness while small things bulged, bloated, and turned monstrous."[119] In these processes of shrinking and bloating, bulging and expanding, Obioma represents Mother's capacity to perceive and interpret — her skills in aesthetic analysis — as improperly operative, horrifyingly exceeding ordinary bounds and expectations. Bringing together the living and the dead, Mother is haunted by the ghosts of the Biafran war, especially of her father, "who was blasted to bits by artillery fire" and who "c[omes] frequently to dance in the centre of the hospital room."[120] Both Okri and Obioma render the spectral as ordinary and ever-present, just as they both use animist structures of thought to aesthetically configure a fundamentally symbiotic relationship between all parts of an ecological system.

By aesthetically rendering symbiosis as a constitutive feature of both natural and political life, "What the Tapster Saw" and *The Fishermen* participate in broader discursive attempts to formulate different ecological relationships than those that are codified in Nigerian property law. Much as Wenzel insists that the Niger Delta be understood "as a site both of resource extraction and world-imagining,"[121] the framework of symbiotic aesthetics reveals how fiction writers and legal theorists alike refuse to see the Delta as merely a locus of negation and extraction and instead engage in the process of producing alternate forms of land relation. Wenzel cautions that world-building can remain extractive: as she points out, "oil has fueled the imagining of national community and the production of the Nigerian state, underwriting its international visibility and viability."[122] Wenzel's model of "eco/materiality" identifies oil "as a material substrate of national imagining and unimagining,"[123] effectively pairing the material conditions of petroleum extraction with the social and political forms it engenders: namely, ethnonationalism and statist resource sovereignty. But multiple imaginative models can coexist, and the symbiotic world that is being built by many Nigerian writers, thinkers, activists, artists, and legal theorists through their impropriety, aesthetic or otherwise, is increasingly taking hold and bearing identifiable material consequences. In contrast to colonial and postcolonial proprietary formulations of minerals and natural resources ownership, anti-petroleum aesthetics instead formally theorize and enact a philosophy of symbiotic relation.

Okri and Obioma's ecologically minded fiction aesthetically establishes the interdependence of human and nonhuman forms of life, including rivers, grasses, trees, fish, birds, insects, spiders, mammals, snakes, fungi, and spirits. In *The Fishermen*, Obioma configures an expansive, symbiotic lifeworld, as signaled in the naming of this novel's eighteen chapters, each of which refers to specific biotic and abiotic figures, including "The River," "The Tadpole," and "The Roosters." The only exception to Obioma's ecological naming convention is his opening chapter, whose simple "Fishermen" at once echoes the novel of which it is a part and, in removing the expected definite article, figures the collective protagonists as archetypes rather than singular individuals. Similarly, in "What the Tapster Saw," Okri establishes a symbiotic relationship between human characters and his story's other ecological constituents: some characters appear as two things at once, such as the turtle bearing the face of the herbalist, Tabasco; some beings seem to share properties with other elements, like the snake who slides from a borehole into the river and back again; and on other occasions, characters expand beyond their own embodied consciousness, as when the tapster finds that "he had multiplied. He was not sure whether it was his mind or his body which flowed in and out of him."[124] This kind of metamorphosis is a common stylistic conceit in Nigerian writing, often traced to animist cosmologies and oral traditions, and is identified in work ranging from Okri to his well-known predecessor Amos Tutuola.[125] Just as important, Okri's metamorphic aesthetics register an ecological understanding of the juridical land relation rather than one that conforms to Nigeria's extractive current model. Through the tapster's corporeal and spiritual amplification, Okri constructs an expansive and symbiotic ecosystem that rebuts the property regime that at once underpins and facilitates Nigeria's unsustainable extractive practices.

For Obioma, too, metamorphosis operates as a device that is simultaneously literary, biological, and philosophical. Engaging the concept of metamorphosis in both figurative and material terms, Obioma uses it to at once register the biochemical processes by which an organic substance goes through several life stages and signal Ikenna's changed personality after hearing Abulu's prophecy. Whereas Ikenna had been known in his life as a python — as strong and powerful — his tragic death turns him into "a sparrow": "a curious traveler that journeys out of his own body."[126] Boja is similarly understood through the framework of metamorphosis and, after his own death by suicide, is considered to have transformed into a microorganism. In a passage that slips from objective description to metonymy, Benjamin reports that his older brother's "body was filled with fungi. His heart pumped blood filled with fungi. His tongue was infected with fungi. . . . Just as a fungus hides in the body of an ignorant host, Boja lived on unseen in our compound for four days after Ikenna's death."[127] In a sequence of metonymic slippages, Boja is first taken over by a fungus that gains new life in its unwitting host; he is then so fully consumed by the parasitic microorganism that he himself becomes fungal; and finally, he infects a new host in turn. Boja's microbial metamorphosis represents both the Agwu brothers' consumption by fear after Abulu's prophecy and the psychological as well as juridicopolitical consequences of colonization. What's more, Obioma renders the process of Boja's metamorphosis as biological as well as figurative. Boja is ecologically hosted by his living family members: in the time that he is submerged in the well from which they have been drawing water to make tea, microorganisms cause his body to gradually decompose, merge with the liquid in which it has settled, and be consumed by his family in turn. Even though Boja has not "lived on" in any ordinary sense, as he remains unseen from the moment he kills Ikenna until he is found four days later when his decomposed body belatedly floats to the well's surface, his autolytic corpse plays host to millions of bacteria that generate chemical changes, releasing gases and causing the bloating that is habitual in drowning. In a literal sense, Boja metamorphosizes, living on ecologically after his death.

In contrast to Nigerian property law, which, over the course of the twentieth century, has significantly weakened the legal bonds between Nigerians and the land, especially Niger Delta peoples and their homelands, Obioma's figuration of Boja's death aesthetically reestablishes customary law's motivating logics and effects a challenge to the tenets of contemporary Nigerian property law. Under customary law, which operated throughout almost all of Nigeria's southern states until the Land Use Act came into effect in 1978, land belonged to all members of a community, including both ancestral and future generations, and it was entrusted temporarily to a patrilineage.[128] Differently than in the British system of fee simple, or absolute ownership, a customary landholder "[bore] a possessory title which he enjoy[ed] in perpetuity, and which g[ave] him powers of use and disposition scarcely distinguishable from those of an absolute freeholder."[129] While customary law bears some similarities to freeholding, a proprietor under customary law "cannot alienate his holding so as to divest himself and his family of the right to ultimate title."[130] In disallowing land alienation, customary law codifies perpetual connection between people and the place in which they live, juridically sustaining a multigenerational relationship. Under customary law, as was found in a significant early colonial legal decision, *Amodu Tijani v. Secretary of Southern Nigeria* (1921), "land is conceived as belonging to a vast family of which many are dead, few are living and countless members yet unborn."[131] Thus, when Boja is described as "living on unseen" in the Agwu family's compound,[132] Obioma is doing more than employing figurative language to signal the psychological impact of Boja's death and Ikenna's murder. Given *The Fishermen*'s critique of Niger Delta petropolitics and its associated land legislation, Boja's organic and spectral endurance encodes customary land law's multigenerational presumptions. What's more, in siting Boja's death and ecological afterlife in the Agwu's well, Obioma extends his challenge to colonially imposed land law, which redefined what counted as land and vested this newly expansive definition of land in the state. Unlike the Minerals Act of 1946, which declared that "the entire property in and control of all mineral oils on, under or upon any lands in Nigeria, and all rivers, streams and watercourses throughout Nigeria, is and shall be vested in the crown,"[133] Obioma symbolically reconnects vitally sustaining water to land owned by Nigerian individuals and families. In contradistinction to the existing property regime and its many privations, Boja's death reveals the symbiotic ecological underpinnings of Nigerian customary law.

Both "What the Tapster Saw" and *The Fishermen* identify symbiosis as an aesthetically and philosophically improper mode that is crucial to overcoming Nigerian land law's extractive and depletive formulation of property ownership. Okri's uncanny rendering of the tapster's extraordinary reality as both commonplace and shared by all living beings in the Delta Oil Company's terrain theorizes symbiosis as necessarily localized. When the tapster is brought out of his coma, seven days after he has been knocked unconscious, it is largely through the herbalist's capacity to reintegrate his patient within his ecological environment. In the traditional West African procedure marking the beginning of a ceremony, Tabasco breaks a kola nut and then lights a pipe, but "[i]nstead of tobacco, he use[s] alligator pepper seeds."[134] Rejecting a substance that represents colonial trade and instead using seeds that are local to the Niger Delta and West African wetlands, Tabasco symbolically and phenomenologically reconnects the tapster to his material environment, thereby saving him from the nightmare of phantasmagoric oil and the transitional existence of unconsciousness. The "black ticklish smoke" of the locally grown alligator seeds gradually brings the tapster out of his coma, "making [him] float into a familiar world."[135] Rescued from the nightmare experience of ruinous methods of petroleum extraction, the tapster is reconnected to his body in the present moment through local ecological and cultural practice. Once he has fully reawakened, all of the markers of his nightmare, including the oil-spill snake and the signboard warning against trespass, are blown away by "green liquids" that "spe[w]" like vomit from the borehole.[136] In framing his dystopian tale of environmental ruin with a utopian story of local triumph, Okri acknowledges the two principal formulations of land relation that currently operate in Nigeria: on the one hand, the model of proprietary land ownership that colonial Britain imposed and which the postcolonial Nigerian state has maintained; on the other, the improper, symbiotic system that activists, legal theorists, and creative writers alike uphold. Aesthetically, in other words, "What the Tapster Saw" renders in fantastical terms two approaches to land law: one that has had catastrophic ecological and human effects and one that might restore regional ecologies.

Similarly, *The Fishermen* positively renders customary law's spectral and symbiotic temporality through its own seemingly recursive structure. The opening lines of Obioma's analeptically narrated novel are nearly, but not quite, its final words; in this way, Obioma rejects tragedy's cyclical form even as he uses it to aesthetically theorize symbiotic modalities of land relation. In *The Fishermen*'s final chapter, Benjamin recounts the time when, over five years earlier, he had begun testifying while on trial for killing Abulu. Just like *The Fishermen*'s opening sentences, Benjamin begins his testimony with the proclamation: "'We were fishermen. My brothers and I became —'"[137] Yet, unlike the novel's opening, these sentences, when they appear in the final chapter, narrate not only Benjamin's testimony but also his mother's notable interruption in the form of "a loud piercing cry."[138] After Father has calmed Mother, and Benjamin has calmed himself, and the judge has "knocked his staff on the table three times and bellowed: 'You may now proceed,'" Benjamin continues.[139] More than momentarily delaying Benjamin's defense, Mother's wail effects a substantive change in these near-closing lines. In the temporality of his trial, Benjamin repeats his opening words, but in the framing of his retrospective narration, he describes rather than reiterates them: "I opened my eyes, cleared my throat, and started all over again."[140] In these analeptically recounted and contextually variant final words, Obioma at once gestures toward repetition while also deferring it, leaving what had been said as only a spectral presence. Not only does *The Fishermen* thereby register the affective and material reality of ordinary Nigerians' confinement in an oppressively repetitive political present but it also invokes the kind of variant repetition that in customary law allows for continuity of ownership across generations.

Together, Okri and Obioma recognize the workings of ecological interdependence through the improper, symbiotic aesthetic mode that establishes mutual connectivity across all kinds of ecologies, in this world and in others. When Okri invokes the multiple worlds of Yoruba cosmology to present the tapster as bearing counterparts in other worlds, he is establishing, like Obioma, two temporal moments in the space of one narrative episode and figuring, like customary law, continuity of land rights between the worlds of the living and the dead. In the passage detailing the tapster's new awareness of the petroleum industry's ecological impact, Okri uses the traditional oral storytelling device of anaphora to chart his story's compressed narrative trajectory beyond the perceptible realm:

> That night he fled. Everything fled with him. Then, after a while, he stopped. . . . Then, as the eggs tormented him with the grating noises within them, . . . he learned patience. He learned to watch the sky. . . . He learned to listen to the birth groaning within the eggs. He also learned that when he kept still everything else around him reflected his stillness.
> And then, on another day, the voice came to him and said:
> "Everything in your world has endless counterparts in other worlds."[141]

Okri's anaphoric repetition of both "then" and "he learned" rhetorically marks both temporality and consequence. In a passage that lauds "patience," "stillness," and psychological serenity, this story's third-person narrator invokes the chronological movement of time and the teleological structure of narrative through the cumulative logic of knowledge acquisition. During this final period of the tapster's unconsciousness, Okri's use of anaphora build connections through time and space, echoing the apparent pairing of all living things with "endless counterparts in other worlds." Aesthetically, Okri and Obioma establish symbiotic relation on a vast scale: as fundamentally structuring not just this world but other worlds, too.

Discursive Redistribution

The framework of symbiosis as a variant of aesthetic impropriety reveals how creative writers and legal theorists alike refuse to see the Delta as merely a locus of negation and extraction but instead engage in the process of producing alternate forms of land relation. While the process of undoing English-derived land laws will necessarily take time, the shared philosophical commitments that can be seen across progressive approaches to land law, Indigenous ecological theory, West African environmental philosophy, and literary work suggest that significant changes are already underway. These commitments to symbiosis and stewardship are evidenced in increased resistance among legal scholars and practitioners to Nigeria's Land Use Act; they are at least partially identifiable in the successes of *Okpabi v. Shell*, *Four Nigerian Farmers v. Shell*, and *Lungowe v. Vedanta*, all of which recognize limitless extraction's globally distributed agents and benefactors as well as its depletive and localized consequences; and they are apparent, too, in petroleum companies' decreased cultural capital.

Multinational oil corporations have been particularly supportive patrons of the visual arts, one of the most generous being Nigeria's largest and most active oil company, Royal Dutch Shell. In the United Kingdom, which has been Okri's home since 1978, Shell's sponsorships have long included the National Gallery, the British Film Institute, the National Theatre, the Natural History Museum, and the Southbank Centre. Thanks to sustained activist pressure, particularly from visual arts groups like the Art Not Oil Coalition, Platform London, and Liberate Tate, many of these sponsorships have ended, while others, such as the British Museum's sponsorship by BP, are under increasing pressure to similarly cut oil funding.[142] While these philanthropic relationships' extended duration testifies to the Global North's history of consuming in art and leisure that which is produced through violent modes of extraction in the Global South, their recent or imminent suspension affirms a significant turn against petroleum production.

If "What the Tapster Saw" and *The Fishermen* pose a challenge to the traditionally exploitative relationship between art and oil, it is because their symbiotically improper aesthetics engage in the slow, redistributive process of reformulating possible legislated relations to land. It is not just that these works of fiction offer an alternative to the proprietary property relation that is upheld in Nigeria's English-derived land law, and not just that their improper aesthetics reveal the commitments they share with progressive theories of property jurisprudence from an Indigenous and Global South perspective, but also that they engage aesthetically in a broader process of redistribution that is also occurring in more obviously impactful venues, such as in law courts, at approximately the same time. Whereas current property law pretends that goods and harms are neither distributed nor shared, legal theorists and creative writers working within Indigenous stewardship or African animist traditions are recognizing the fullness of ecological relation. These acts of theorizing are not merely utopian but are part of the slow process of legal transformation that is more expressly registered in British and Dutch courts recognizing the harms inflicted in the Global South by companies headquartered in the Global North. As Christopher Riley and Oludara Akanmidu argue in their analysis of the Okpabi case, courts can be a forum for publicity, and not just for compensation: "[T]he fear of reputational harm," Riley and Akanmidu observe, "can also provide a strong incentive to improve one's behaviour and . . . this may be more effective when aimed at the parent and when achieved through publicity-attracting proceedings in the courts of the parent's domicile."[143] In other words, it is not just literary works and political activism that provide necessary public attention to proprietary land laws and their consequent harms; litigation, too, is materially consequential because it functions to slowly change behavior and legislation through visible legal actions that are important partly because they might establish new case law and partly because of the embarrassment they might cause. The law operates on a similar timescale to the literary, in that it almost always only incrementally shifts our understanding of what is possible.

While the process whereby legal actors or literary works participate in cultural change typically occurs only slowly, especially within the context of modifying legislation, its gradual pace should not be mistaken for impotence. As Iheka's theorizing of ecological agency within an animist framework clarifies, dispersed forms of agency are forceful despite their lack of purposeful intention or coherent and cohesive action. When Iheka articulates the interconnectedness of all living components within an ecological system in order to offer a more accurate understanding of the world we live in, especially as understood by African writers, he "rethinks the dominant notion of agency based on intentionality."[144] Like the new materialist theories on which he partially builds his framework, Iheka is invested in reorienting humans to ecological consciousness, or "ways of conceiving distributed agency or varieties of agency functioning between human beings and other environmental actors."[145] Ultimately more animist than new materialist, Iheka's conception of agentive impact as ecologically dispersed recognizes that a system's component parts symbiotically affect one another. In a similar fashion, as my analysis of Nigerian land law and symbiotic aesthetics has suggested, the process of establishing more ecologically attentive land laws is necessarily diffuse. Operating discursively across many different fields, including in law, activism, and literature, emergent ideas about reorganizing legislated approaches to land are occurring in concert. Even without purposeful intent, this process of discursively engaging changing structures of thought bears a slow but forceful impact.

Inasmuch as symbiosis functions as a form of redistribution, it offers a model for the intellectually redistributive work that is not only ecologically vital in our current moment but also useful for theorizing generative scholarship. The diffusively forceful model of symbiotic ecologies and aesthetics that I have identified as operating in Nigerian literary work and progressive legal actions offers a way of conceptualizing ecological relation that challenges petroleum laws' extractive predicates; what's more, it suggests that humanities scholarship and the creative arts bear the capacity to engage in material redistribution. Just as creative texts and legal actions similarly participate in analyzing pressing social concerns, so too does critical scholarship engage in the slow process of shifting cultural norms. The kinds of symbiotic, mutually sustaining relationships that progressive legal theorists as much as Nigerian writers have theorized as vital to challenging ecological devastation in the Niger Delta are at once diffuse and forceful, much like the processes of discursive change. It is not just that symbiosis offers a way of conceptualizing ecological relation that challenges petroleum laws' premising on rapacious resource extraction and participates in establishing a more just and sustainable ecological landscape. Just as important, in its very logical structure, symbiosis stages the need for activists, thinkers, and writers to engage in intellectually redistributive work: to redistribute structures of thought away from depletion and toward justice.

2

Reciprocity

Female Dispossession in Inheritance and Divorce

At the heart of India's gendered inequities lies a complex system of patriarchal inheritance and divorce laws, whose codification under British colonial rule entrenched local patriarchies, diminished many existing economic protections, and systemized legal dispossession. Since the late nineteenth century, and with increased intensity from the 1930s, Indian feminists from across the political spectrum have sought legislative changes that would protect women's property rights upon marriage or divorce and establish the same inheritance rights for women as exist for men.[1] As feminist activists and progressive jurists have recognized, female vulnerability to exploitation derives from a system of sharply unequal access to property of all types, both moveable and immoveable, and especially of land ownership, which provides the benefit not only of financial accrual in a capitalist political economy but also of secure accommodation in a patriarchal society. The right to a home, as India's feminists have long recognized, enables women to leave misogynistic, violent, or otherwise undesirable family arrangements; a home of one's own enables women, like men, to meet their daily needs. While analyses of gender injustice and women's rights are often most publicly framed in the immediate and highly visible terms of bodily vulnerabilities, including sexual violence or reproduction,[2] the very grounds for achieving gender equity are established through a much less spectacular area of struggle that remains quietly fundamental: equal and unobstructed access to a home.

This chapter reveals the importance of assessing property law through a feminist lens by addressing significant developments in Indian inheritance and divorce law in relation to Arundhati Roy's debut novel *The God of Small Things*. Despite some retrenchment during the Modi years, India has seen a general trend toward improving women's property access, particularly since the 1980s, an achievement that not only corresponds to the liberalizing of India's economy[3] but also results from tireless work by progressive activists, jurists, and public thinkers. As Supreme Court Justice Katikithala Ramaswamy declared in his 1996 opinion in a pivotal case assessing tribal women's property rights, *Madhu Kishwar v. State of Bihar,* "Law is an instrument of social change as well as the defender of social change."[4] In this landmark case, Madhu Kishwar and her co-complainants leveraged the Indian Constitution to successfully argue that the unequal inheritance laws of the Chota Nagpur Tenancy Act 1908 violated the constitutional provision of gender equality. In its decision, the high court explained that "customary law operating in the Bihar State and other parts of the country excluding tribal women from inheritance of land or property . . . being founded solely on sex is discriminatory."[5] Kishwar and her co-petitioners' action built upon a similar suit a decade earlier that Mary Roy and two co-petitioners had won after being denied equal inheritance to their respective intestate fathers' estates. Under the Travancore Christian Succession Act, 1062 KE (1916 CE), a Syrian Christian widow of an intestate man received only a life interest in the estate, while a daughter received one quarter of the son's share, or 5,000 rupees, whichever was less.[6] As Roy and her co-complainants identified, this statute violated their rights to gender equality under articles 14 and 15 of the Constitution. *Mary Roy v. State of Kerala* 1986 found in favor of the complainants, albeit not because the Supreme Court agreed that their rights to equality were compromised but because the Travancore Christian Succession Act should have been repealed after independence. Under the Part-B States (Laws) Act 1951, the former princely states of Travancore and Cochin had been incorporated into the newly constituted nation-state of India and were subject to its laws. According to the relevant Indian statute, the Indian Succession Act 1925, men and women inherited equally from intestate parents, so "it becomes unnecessary," the judges argued, "to consider whether sections [of the TCSA] . . . are unconstitutional and void."[7] While the court's decision answered a jurisdictional question that resulted from the process of inaugurating a new nation instead of addressing a more wide-ranging constitutional question about gender equality, it did give these claimants in particular, and Syrian Christian women in general, equal succession rights as men.

The Mary Roy case is one significant example of broader attempts across India to reckon with the female economic vulnerabilities that result from a system of male property ownership. Evidence for a gradual shift in public and legal opinion lies in subsequent cases, including not only *Madhu Kishwar* but also *Bahadur v. Bratiya* 2015;[8] in the earlier suits that paved the way for Mary

Roy's claim, like the successful action *Solomon v. Muthiah* 1974[9] and the suit that overturned it, *D. Chelliah v. G. Lalita Bai* 1978;[10] in attempted legislative reform like the Christian Succession Acts (Repeal) Bill that had been introduced in 1958 by Kerala's law minister, Justice V. R. Krishna Iyer;[11] in statutory amendments like the Indian Succession (Amendment) Act 2002 and the Hindu Succession (Amendment) Act 2005, both of which entitle women under their jurisdiction to equal inheritance rights as men;[12] and even in failed attempts at legislative overhaul, like the Marriage Laws (Amendment) Bill 2010, which would have provided Hindu women with an equal share in all marital property upon divorce or separation, including property that had been acquired by the man alone during marriage.[13] While the Marriage Laws (Amendment) Bill 2010 stalled in the Lok Sabha, India's lower house of parliament, it passed in the Rajya Sabha, the upper house, and a partial success during this period of right-wing ethnonationalism, with its patriarchal as well as racialized and heterosexist motivating logics, is not to be underestimated.

The temptation to rail against the law for its conservative capacities abounds in literary scholarship, including postcolonial studies, yet law is often a means of establishing gender equity as well as other forms of social justice. Even though the process of legal reform is slow, involving significant time and effort by a range of actors across legal as well as social venues, and even though the improvements that are introduced through new laws can be stymied by delays in implementation, gender-just bills remain vital for guaranteeing women's security and potential.[14] In India, Ratna Kapur confirms, "feminists across the political spectrum have frequently sought recourse to law as one means of securing women's freedoms and emancipation."[15] For Kapur, recognizing law's transformative potential is a way of refusing to reduce feminists to "the status of permanent hecklers to power."[16] Certainly, many Indian feminists have remained cautious about the law's emancipatory capacities, as Rajeswari Sunder Rajan acknowledges, in part because of a common "hostility to the state, to legal reform, and to the promises and premises of liberalism."[17] In our current moment of rampant ethnonationalism, in India as across much of the world, valid anxieties over state repression need to be carefully differentiated from liberalism's failures, including its political quietism and its preference for gradual, moderate change. Given the Hindu far-right's increasingly successful attempts at demanding a homogenous national identity that violently dispossesses Indians who belong to minoritized religions or ethnicities, liberalism's limitations are less compelling a reason for rejecting the law's potential than they were at the turn of the twenty-first century when Rajan's authoritative *The Scandal of the State* was published. Instead, as Rajan anticipated, the rise of Hindu chauvinism has intensified a process of recognizing extensive variety in forms of gendered experience that feminist organizing worldwide has likewise been forced to address.

Over the past two decades, Indian feminist debate has marked its distinction from right-wing ethnonationalism by recognizing many types of female experience that are themselves shaped by forces including caste, religion, labor, regional location, sexuality, and gender identity.[18] In acknowledging variance, Indian feminists have more significantly revised their understanding of how best to achieve gender justice than at any point since the emergence of a consolidated feminist movement in the early twentieth century. Feminists once roundly advocated for a Uniform Civil Code (UCC) that would standardize India's complex system of personal and secular laws, observing that "the personal laws of all communities are discriminatory toward women."[19] Governing marriage and divorce, inheritance and maintenance, and adoption and custody, personal laws relegate family life to a separate domain than the professedly neutral laws that administer areas of legal life including torts, contracts, and constitutional protections. Personal laws were codified under colonial rule to at once establish bureaucratic efficiencies and maintain the pretense of deferring to Indian preference,[20] and they broadly correspond to the customary practices of four main religions: majority Hindu; and minority Muslim; Christian; and Parsi; other religious groups, meanwhile, fall under Hindu law. Standardizing these laws into a common code that abolished religiously influenced personal law was long seen as the best way to comprehensively address gender discrimination. Yet, after the regressive Muslim Women (Protection on Divorce) Act 1986 that effectively overturned a controversial 1985 case, *Mohd. Ahmed Khan v. Shah Bano Begum*, in which a Muslim female defendant had been granted maintenance from her ex-husband, feminists began to recognize how women's religious, ethnic, and other alignments competed and intersected.[21] Sensing political opportunity in the *Shah Bano* suit, not least because of the extensive interethnic patriarchal outrage it elicited, Hindu nationalists co-opted the cause of the UCC, understanding that standardization would allow majority Hindu politicians to establish a supposedly universal law according to their own beliefs. A universal secular law would, for instance, allow Hindu nationalists to codify monogamy against the "image of a polygamous Muslim," assuaging far-right fears of decreasing Hindu influence in the face of a growing Muslim population.[22] Responding to rising patriarchal communalism, Indian feminists have recognized that legal reform needs to be carefully individuated, now broadly advocating for establishing gender-just laws within each religion's codes, among other constellated actions.[23]

Taken together, *Mary Roy* and *Shah Bano* reveal how feminist demands for equitable property protections have been met with ethnonationalist patriarchal retrenchment. Both lawsuits sought to improve or achieve economic protections for women, one through establishing equal succession law and one through pursuing maintenance upon divorce, and both cases reveal the importance of assessing property law through a feminist lens. As an object of analysis, property is fairly fraught, especially in the context of socially just legal reform. Beyond the Marxist observation that private property ownership is not only inherently inequitable but leads to uneven development, property is associated in late twentieth-century India with communalist politics. As Nivedita Menon explains, "the state's gradual granting of property rights to women under Hindu law . . . [is] more than a simple triumph of feminist demands. It also represents the establishment of a bourgeois regime of property for the Hindu community."[24] Paradoxically, gender-just reforms to property law in the twenty-first century have broadly functioned to support the Hindu state's nation-building project by turning ancestral land into individual property and thereby enabling large-scale acquisition of land that was previously community-owned. Yet, even as property rights are entangled with a right-wing, ethnonationalist model of nation-building, and even as private property ownership is typically inaccessible for women from impoverished families, property remains a significant site of dispossession for millions of Indian women, including for low-wage families who own small parcels of land, as well as for Adivasi women. As Archana Mishra argues in her assessment of several decades of case law that responds to the Mary Roy case, "[d]eprivation of property rights is the root cause of the secondary status of women in India."[25] In its 2018 consultation paper "Reform of Family Law," the Law Commission of India similarly identifies "discriminatory provisions under all personal laws," arguing that "regardless of whether the wife 'financially' or 'monetarily' contributes to the family income, her contribution to a household in terms of household labour, home management, and child bearing and care should entitle her to an equal share in a marriage."[26] Employing a Marxist feminist perspective, the Law Commission recognizes that women's unpaid reproductive labor remains extremely valuable to the Indian economy. In recommending equal access to property and economic protections upon divorce, the Law Commission has seemingly learned from Indian feminists' concerted efforts to address not just spectacular forms of misogyny that garner public outrage but, more particularly, gendered economic inequities, especially in terms of labor law,[27] sex work,[28] and the category of woman as worker.[29]

As the slow process of improving Indian women's delimited property rights suggests, changing the law involves significant imaginative labor, work that not only conceptualizes new forms of legal being but brings them into effect. By identifying the relationship between feminist legal activism and *The God of Small Things*, this chapter charts the interrelated imaginative mechanisms of both literary texts and legal processes, thereby revealing the imagination's generative juridical capacities and making the case for literature's legally impactful discursive operations. *The God of Small Things* at once exposes the consequences of Indian property law's gendered exclusions and aesthetically participates in the legal process of producing new modes of propertied relation. To the extent that Roy's 1997 novel offers a fictionalized account of her mother Mary Roy's dispossession under the Travancore Christian Succession Act, it might be seen as a mere response to *Mary Roy v. the State of Kerala*. Yet, *The God of Small Things* also anticipates and enters into broader public discussions about the urgency of feminist legal reform, including not only women's inheritance rights, which are currently unevenly distributed across personal laws, but also equal property rights upon divorce, which stalled in the Lok Sabha for Hindu women in 2014 and which remain unequally allocated for Indian women of all other religions, too. Much as Rohit De argues of the Indian Constitution, which "came so alive in the popular imagination that ordinary people attributed meaning to its existence,"[30] *The God of Small Things* recognizes the law's imaginative liveliness, activating vivid public debates about property law's appropriate delimitations. For De, India's Constitution represents both radical possibility and conservative continuity: on the one hand, it insists that fundamental human equality can be achieved only by addressing material inequalities, to which end, it establishes affordable mechanisms for citizens to pursue legal remedy against the state;[31] on the other, it maintains repressive colonial laws and the British colonial model of centralized juridicopolitical control. More than recognizing that independent India's founding document dwells in contradiction, De most significantly finds that "the Constitution did not descend upon the people; it was produced and reproduced in everyday encounters."[32] In showing how the Constitution provides both the model and mechanisms for Indians to remake the law, De recognizes, like Roy, that the legal system is a product of human imagination and constant discursive renegotiation.

Engaging in the process of reimagining the very contours of legal thought, *The God of Small Things* enacts the kinds of necessary reimagining that spur public action and prompt jurists to start the process of legal reform. By establishing very different arguments at the levels of plot and style, Roy's novel demonstrates how literary texts productively participate in changing legal norms. In its plot, *The God of Small Things* rails against India's gendered property laws for making women physically, psychologically, and economically vulnerable; thus, one of its central characters, Ammu, dies as a direct result of her delimited economic rights under Indian succession and divorce laws. Yet Roy's style goes beyond strident critique, instead establishing the principle that needs to underpin all Indian laws: the equal worth and equal rights of all citizens. In other words, *The God of Small Things* models the distinction between Indians' constitutional rights to equality and their much more curtailed rights under personal laws, which operate in accordance with discriminatory social norms. In the outcomes traced by its plot and in its differently egalitarian style, *The God of Small Things* balances two conceptual structures: the first is a proprietary model of ownership that largely restricts property ownership to men and upholds India's patriarchal juridical economy; the second conceptual structure is improper, egalitarian, and reciprocal, and it registers Roy's vision of a feminist-socialist legal system that is equitable and just. By aesthetically restructuring property law's formal logic, *The God of Small Things* participates in a broader shift in public discourse toward granting women equal property protections under the law.

The Costs of Patriarchal Inheritance Laws

In its plot, *The God of Small Things* largely takes the form of a tragedy, detailing the events that befall the wealthy Syrian Christian Ipe family — a family that somewhat resembles Arundhati Roy's own.[33] Set in Ayemenem, a small town in the southern Indian state of Kerala, this novel's twin temporalities mirror the timeline of Syrian Christian succession law: the main events unfold in the late 1960s, when the Travancore Christian Succession Act was still in effect, and their traumatic aftereffects are explored in the mid-1990s, when Mary Roy's lawsuit had effectively established gender-equal inheritance rights for Syrian Christian women. A series of cascading events prompts this novel's tragic climax: a climax that is partially revealed in the opening pages, when Chacko's daughter, Sophie Mol, lies in a coffin after drowning in the Meenachal River during a short visit from her home in England. Chacko blames Ammu for his daughter's death: his sister, he reasons, had married a Hindu man without her family's consent; she had subsequently divorced her alcoholic, abusive husband and returned to Ayemenem with her twins, Estha and Rahel; she had established a short but impassioned relationship with a Dalit man named Velutha, whose status as a so-called Untouchable made him even more damaging to the family's social status; she had been furious after Mammachi, their mother, and Baby Kochamma, their aunt, had locked her in her room after learning of the affair; and her twins had run away with his daughter in response to the turbulence at home. Yet it is not Ammu who is to blame, Roy suggests, for the violence and tragedy that occur that night, but caste-based discrimination and the perceived demands of social propriety that the Ipe family upholds. After Mammachi and Baby Kochamma falsely accuse Velutha of sexually assaulting Ammu and kidnapping her children, Velutha also escapes across the river, where he is brutally beaten to the point of certain death by a group of police officers who face no consequences for what is seen as a reasonable response to a social infraction. In the aftermath of that night, Estha is sent back to his father in Bengal and separated from his beloved sister and mother, while Ammu is forced to leave the family home, dying alone and destitute only four years later.

Among its many forms of social commentary, including the horrors of caste prejudice and the enduring impact of British colonial rule, *The God of Small Things* uses Ammu's untimely death to expose the consequences of women's curtailed access to property. Ammu dies young, when Estha and Rahel are only eleven years old, because her brother, in his grief and fury, exiles her from the natal family home. Chacko is able to evict his sister not just because of "His bigness. His bullying power"[34] but because, under the Travancore Christian Succession Act, he had inherited the family's estate in full when their father died. By contrast, Ammu is entitled to only 5,000 rupees[35] — approximately 23,900 rupees in today's terms, or 300 US dollars — which she anyway does not receive.[36] Even Mammachi is beholden to her son, holding a lifetime interest in her home but no financial stake in the property. Under the system of male inheritance that was codified and calcified in the Travancore Christian Succession Act, extended families would share a home and men would be morally compelled to economically support female family members. As Amali Philips explains, Syrian Christian women "are socialized into . . . forfeit[ing] property claims in return for security, support and protection by men."[37] Whereas Baby Kochamma and Mammachi support the patriarchal distribution of power that is enforced first by Pappachi and then by Chacko, and as such benefit from "the traditional compensatory mechanisms justifying women's exclusion from equal family inheritance,"[38] Ammu rejects misogynistic social norms, so she is excluded from the kinship support that would somewhat compensate for lacking property rights.

When Chacko furiously banishes Ammu from the natal family home, blaming her for his daughter's death, *The God of Small Things* dramatizes women's vulnerability to patriarchal caprice under gender-inequitable inheritance laws. Ammu takes a sequence of poorly paid jobs that leave her unable to afford adequate housing, pay her medical bills after developing chronic asthma, or financially support Estha and Rahel. In a kind of perverse justice, in which her fate is tied directly within the novel's symbolic economy to that of Sophie Mol, Ammu's death from an asthma attack four years later replicates her niece's death by drowning. While Sophie Mol dies in a tragic accident in the tumultuous Meenachal River, the result of an ill-fated nighttime voyage orchestrated by her twin cousins, Ammu's nighttime drowning is in the tides of her own phlegm, in circumstances prompted by familial revenge and underwritten by the patriarchal legal system that authorizes her economic dispossession.

While *The God of Small Things* establishes a clear line of causation between Ammu's death from asthma and the eviction that leaves her homeless and without access to medical care, Roy's assessment of Indian women's legislated economic dispossession has garnered scant scholarship.[39] Critical aversion to this novel's explicit condemnation of property law corresponds to the phenomenon that Srila Roy has identified as popular attentiveness to spectacular forms of misogyny, including sexual violence against women, rather than to more quotidian varieties of patriarchal subordination.[40] Disregard for this novel's explicit engagement with property law might also be attributed to *The God of Small Things*'s more obvious attack on global capitalism[41] or its more spectacular invective against caste,[42] both of which appeal to Roy's global readership; if globalization is part of an international audience's everyday knowledge, caste's exclusions have long been denounced in orientalist and anthropological accounts of culturally specific forms of oppression. Critics who offer sustained and insightful analyses of Roy's feminist interventions typically employ the tools of cultural criticism, addressing Ammu's significant social ostracism rather than exploring her similarly precarious legal status.[43] Yet, Ammu dies not because she "wast[es] herself away into an unnecessary death," as Aijaz Ahmad declares, but because India's gendered succession and divorce laws leave her homeless, forcing her to live in squalor and without required medical treatment.[44] Her precarity must be understood within the specific context of limited female property rights, not just within what Ammu glibly refers to as "our wonderful male chauvinist society."[45] As *The God of Small Things* makes clear, the law structures our daily lives in complex ideological and material ways, so analyzing the legal embeddedness of literary texts is as crucial as addressing social, political, or cultural factors.

Inasmuch as Ammu's legislated economic dependence upon her brother is a significant factor in not only her death but also the twins' loss of their mother, Roy recognizes that inequitable inheritance laws bear significant social repercussions. In an otherwise minor disagreement while driving to fetch Sophie Mol and her mother from Cochin airport, Chacko angrily informs Ammu that she and the twins are "millstones around his neck."[46] As a film-loving seven year old, Rahel realizes the dangers that inhere in dependency: "In *Mutiny on the Bounty*, when people died at sea, they were wrapped in white sheets and thrown overboard with millstones around their necks so that the corpses wouldn't float."[47] Much like *The God of Small Things*, the fictional scene that helps Rahel to make sense of Chacko's anger at his effective moral and legal financial responsibility for his sister and her children derives from historical events. The 1962 film to which Rahel refers dramatizes a 1789 mutiny in the South Pacific, when sailors on HMS *Bounty*, which had been collecting Tahitian breadfruit trees to take to the West Indies as a cheap food source for enslaved people, rebelled against their captain's violence and caprice. This Hollywood scene that at once communicates Rahel's unusual emotional maturity and registers this novel's critique of British colonial dispossession is later replayed in both the mode of Ammu's death (being a drowning of sorts) and the treatment of her corpse. Like those who die at sea, Ammu is wrapped only in "a dirty bedsheet" before her body's disposal, while she similarly lacks a final resting place, having been refused a church burial in Ayemenem and cremated in a furnace whose "eternal fire" explicitly invokes Hell.[48] Thrown metaphorically overboard by her church as well as her family, she is deprived, in her lack of a burial, of spiritual salvation. While Chacko uses a metaphor of forced drowning to describe his undesired financial support for his sister and her children, his legally sanctioned decision to banish Ammu from the natal family home in fact prompts her own fatal submerging.

Attentive to the broad social consequences of gender-inequitable inheritance laws, *The God of Small Things* further registers their intergenerational impact through Chacko's inheriting the family pickle factory. Mammachi had run the pickle factory to great local acclaim as a "small but profitable enterprise" that operated successfully in the informal economy.[49] Her personal stake in the business is identified in the products' informal appellation by way of her first name, "Soshamma": "Until Chacko arrived in Ayemenem, Mammachi's factory had no name. Everybody just referred to her pickles and jams as Sosha's Tender Mango, or Sosha's Banana Jam."[50] Upon Chacko's return from England, where he had been studying at Oxford as a Rhodes scholar, he seizes control of Mammachi's venture. Disregarding Mammachi's personal investment in her enterprise, as signaled in the pickles' naming, Chacko claims ownership of the business, "had it registered as a partnership[,] and informed Mammachi that she was the Sleeping Partner."[51] In failing to first consult with Mammachi, and in designating her a "sleeping" or silent partner, Chacko effectively excludes his mother from operational decisions while ensuring her continued productive labor. His executive failures lead to huge financial losses, so he "mortgag[es] the family rice fields" — again without consultation — in an attempt to buoy the sinking business.[52] As the mortgaged rice fields symbolize, Chacko's aggressive business decisions threaten not only Mammachi's commercial enterprise but also her ability to feed herself. In the male heir's unilateral power to mortgage fields that produce food, *The God of*

Small Things insists that the Travancore Christian Succession Act and similar Indian succession laws put women's livelihoods, and even their lives, at risk.

Beyond the material consequences of gender-exclusionary inheritance laws, Roy recognizes that patriarchal systems of ownership uphold male dominance in all forms of cultural and political life: that property ownership corresponds to political power and social status and that systems of legislated dispossession enforce social hierarchies. Chacko gains cultural capital by advertising his proprietary position to state-sponsored business regulators, diminishing the value and significance of Ammu's labor: "Though Ammu did as much work in the factory as Chacko, whenever he was dealing with food inspectors or sanitary engineers, he always referred to it as *my* Factory, *my* pineapples, *my* pickles. Legally this was the case, because Ammu, as a daughter, had no claim to the property."[53] Much like my discussion, in Chapter 1 of *Aesthetic Impropriety*, of "What the Tapster Saw," where the tapster has no right to tap sap from palm trees on land that is newly owned by the Niger Delta Company and is punished when he proceeds, the proprietary tenor of Chacko's "*my, my, my*" triptych signals not only his arrogance but also the exclusionary logic of India's male-oriented property law. Chacko's comparatively large property portfolio — he owns the factory, the pineapples, and the pickles — obtains from the substantial exclusion of women from inheriting immoveable property, marked in his easy appropriation of Mammachi's business and Ammu's inability to stake any such claim for the family inheritance. Unlike her nonfictional forebear Mary Roy, Ammu is unable to see that she could challenge either the constitutionality or jurisdiction of her legislated dispossession; she is diminished legally, economically, and socially by the power that Chacko gloatingly wields.

By drawing attention to the dire consequences of inequitable inheritance laws, Roy recognizes, along with feminist economists, that property access is one way of ensuring female economic security. As Bina Agarwal argues, "[t]he links between gender subordination and property need to be sought in not only the distribution of property between households but also in its distribution between men and women, in not only who owns the property but also who controls it."[54] Roy is attentive to the uneven distribution of property and wealth between families, navigating material inequalities most particularly through various characters' relationship to communism. Comrade Pillai, who runs Ayemenem's printing press and leads the local Communist Party, "[holds] his poverty like a gun to Chacko's head."[55] Other characters are far poorer than Comrade Pillai, like the protesters who subscribe to a more radical form of communism and whom the Ipe family encounter in Cochin: these protestors, among them Velutha, demand that wages are raised, that rice-paddy workers receive a lunch break during their twelve-hour days, and Untouchables are not marked by their caste names. Yet, alongside her assessment of Kerala's sharply unequal distribution of wealth, Roy is also alert to the gendered components of economic dispossession. To that end, Ammu is scathing about Chacko's professed communism given that he routinely exploits his status to sexually harass female laborers. Recognizing the material and ideological continuities between colonial and postcolonial Indian elites as well as the economic and physical components of patriarchal domination, Ammu accuses her brother of "playing *Comrade! Comrade!*": of being "[a]n Oxford avatar of the old zamindar mentality—a landlord forcing his attentions on women who depended on him for their livelihood."[56] Roy recognizes, as Agarwal goes on to argue, that even comparatively well-off women "can be rendered economically vulnerable in the absence of independent economic resources in case of divorce, desertion, separation, or widowhood."[57] Despite Ammu's relative security compared to the female factory workers, she dies in poverty because she has no legal right to the family's property.

The legal underpinnings of Ammu's destitution are signaled in one of the twins' many neologisms; as Chacko seemingly gloats to Estha and Rahel, Ammu has no "Locusts Stand I."[58] In the legal Latinate misheard by the twins, Ammu, as a Syrian Christian woman in 1960s Kerala, has no *locus standi* or "place to stand." She has no right to the family property: no legal standing to object to her gender-based exclusion from the protections that access to a home affords. The incomprehensibility of such gender discrimination from a social justice perspective is conveyed through the twins' unsurprising failure to understand the term *locus standi* in its Latin guise. Just as *locus standi* is an idiom from a foreign and long-dead language, so too is it an alien concept for Ammu's young children, who translate it into a more familiar lexicon. Equally important, the twins' neologism diminishes the likelihood of a reader identifying the original term, not least because *locus standi* has a specific application to Indian property law that will be unknown to many readers, especially Roy's global audience. While Mary Roy's challenge to the Travancore Christian Succession Act is well-known throughout India, especially in Kerala, and while the senior Roy is as controversial an activist as her daughter, international readers will be unfamiliar with either the well-known personalities involved in this case or the complexities of Indian personal law.

"Die-vorce": Economic Destitution and Divorce Law Reform

As *The God of Small Things* recognizes, female economic dispossession is tied as much to diminished property rights upon marriage as it is to exclusionary inheritance practices, meaning that, from a feminist perspective, succession and divorce laws cannot readily be teased apart. When Comrade Pillai aptly coins the neologism "die-vorc[e]" in a conversation with the grown Rahel,[59] newly returned from the United States and divorced like her mother, he unwittingly points to Indian women's doubled economic dispossession under both inheritance and divorce laws. Comrade Pillai serves as a cipher for Keralan social mores, conveying divorce's gendered stigma throughout the period of this novel's setting, both when Ammu's divorce was processed in the 1960s and thirty years later when Rahel returns, sharing both her mother's age and marital status. Moreover, given the sequence of events that lead to Ammu's death, Comrade Pillai's neologism registers divorce's economic consequences as well as their social impact. To be a divorced woman in India is to be economically vulnerable because Indian courts tend to devalue female contributions to marriage when awarding maintenance and dividing assets. As Kirti Singh identifies in a thorough and much needed study of divorced and separated women's economic entitlements, "the reality is that there is a sharp plunge in [a divorced woman's] status and standard of living. She is then forced to live with or depend on her relatives/natal family. . . . A lot of women, therefore, do not leave even violent marriages. They know it will be impossible to survive outside."[60] Ammu's economic destitution and subsequent death indexes the significant material hardship that divorce currently inflicts upon many Indian women and their children.

Indeed, divorce compounds the dispossession that is authorized by gendered succession law precisely because inheritance is understood to be granted upon marriage through dowry. Historically, and under laws that operated well into the post-independence period, Indian women received their inheritance in the form of jewelry and other gifts upon marriage that were both significantly less valuable than male inheritance entitlements and were vulnerable to expropriation. While different personal laws allowed for different degrees of security, Muslim women retained the most substantial protections of property and decision-making upon marriage. Under the Islamic legal code of *mehr*, a prospective husband was required to give an agreed sum of moveable or immoveable property to his prospective wife as part of the marriage contract. If the husband failed to provide the agreed amount, the woman could refuse cohabitation, a "stipulation [that] was meant to balance the husband's power of arbitrary oral divorce."[61] Hindu law provided a delimited form of female property ownership named *stridhan*, which granted a married woman absolute ownership over select categories of property: these generally included gifts received at marriage; gifts after marriage from her father, mother, brother, husband, or in-laws; and a marriage fee upon any subsequent marriage of her husband.[62] As *stridhan* reverted not to a woman's heirs upon her death but to the heirs of the last male property holder, female ownership was only ever temporary and limited.[63] Syrian Christian law largely followed Hindu code, granting a small portion of family property to daughters upon marriage as dowry or *stridhan*, at most totaling one quarter of a son's share.[64] When inheritance practices were codified in 1916's Travancore Christian Succession Act, they were shaped by "the rising economic profile of an influential if small section of the community" that sought to consolidate wealth and power through succession laws that kept property within a family.[65] In other words, the 1916 act did not simply codify an ancient practice into law but implemented a modern system that was shaped by contemporary economic forces. For some, the act remained too lenient: a dissenting statement to the 1916 committee declares, "If daughters are given share along with their brothers and the widow is allowed to have any claim whatever, except maintenance in the property of their husband, it would destroy the domestic tranquility, throw open the flood-gates of litigation, bringing all sorts of calamities and eventually ruin the community."[66] By formally limiting female property acquisition and by allowing a measure of economic security only through marriage, succession laws are inextricably connected to legislation governing the distribution of female property upon marriage and divorce.

Roy registers women's compounded vulnerability under both inheritance and marriage law in the theft of Ammu's dowry. Like many Indian women, Ammu receives her own, very small portion of the family inheritance as dowry at the time of her marriage, yet she no longer has access to that property because it was stolen by her father-in-law on her wedding day. In the time and manner of this theft, Roy symbolically positions gendered succession law as a double-cross: instead of inheriting property, a woman is given an inferior sum upon marriage; that sum is frequently understood by her marital family as belonging to them; consequently, a woman receives no inheritance at all. Not only is Ammu's inheritance stolen by her father-in-law, much as many Syrian Christian women find their dowries taken from them by their marital families, but as the practice of dowry was already illegal, she could not claim recompense even if she tried. With the passage of the Dowry Prohibition Act in 1961, immediately prior to Ammu's marriage, dowry payments were prohibited, yet they remain an ongoing cultural practice among Syrian Christian families, as they do in communities across India. In banning dowry (or *stridhan*) for all women except Muslims—the more protective measure of *mehr* remained legal—legislators attempted to modernize Indian marriage practices and make them more gender-just. Yet, feminist legal scholars have observed that the Dowry Prohibition Act has also caused harm: "By making dowry transactions illegal," Philips explains, "the Dowry Prohibition Act has unintentionally removed the traditional safeguards that were available to women."[67] Pointing to "the overwhelming evidence that the enactment of legal rights does not necessarily change social practice," Rachel Sturman concludes, in her analysis of colonial Indian law and the intersecting patriarchal interests that diminished women's de facto and de jure legal protections, "[p]rogressive laws do not directly transform existing values or common sense."[68] Legislative reform can serve to undermine protections for women both because legal change can be gender-regressive and because legal regimes do not map neatly onto social practice.

The economic, psychological, and physical harms that Ammu and her children experience can be substantially attributed to divorce laws that neglect women's economic needs and force them to depend on natal family members. During the mid-twentieth century, when *The God of Small Things* is primarily set, and under statutes that persist into the present, divorced women are entitled only to maintenance payments upon divorce and not to an equal division of marital property.[69] As such, divorced women retain their status as the economic dependents of male relatives, despite recent attempts at legal reform, including the Married Women's Amendment Act (2010), the Irretrievable Breakdown of Marriage Bill (2013), and the Personal Laws (Amendment) Bill (2018).[70] *The God of Small Things* registers divorced women's legally inscribed vulnerability through Ammu's economic responsibility for raising the twins alone. Upon her return to Ayemenem, she severs all relation with her abusive ex-husband, who had tried to conscript her into sex work with his manager in return for keeping his own job, so she receives no maintenance payments to help her raise their children. Indeed, most divorced Indian women face such significant barriers to receiving maintenance, as Kirti Singh explains, that they instead raise their children without financial support from their former husbands. For a variety of reasons, including the cost of trying to access legal services, the limited amount awarded by gender-biased judges, and "tiers of litigation that may last anywhere between 3 and 20 years," divorced Indian women frequently avoid pursuing maintenance altogether.[71]

The God of Small Things demonstrates that divorce bears a disproportionately negative impact on women and children compared to men through Ammu and Chacko's respective experiences of marriage dissolution. Chacko's comparative freedom over his business affairs and sexual liaisons function as a foil to Ammu's distinctly female experience of economic insecurity and social ostracism. Chacko is feted on his return to Ayemenem as a divorcé and, unlike Ammu, he is welcomed back into the family home. In his many sexual liaisons with women from the pickle factory, Chacko both gratifies his own desires at the expense of women who cannot afford to refuse his advances and exemplifies the gender relations that are formalized within India's inheritance and divorce laws which make women financially dependent upon men. Mammachi tacitly but actively endorses these liaisons on the basis that Chacko has "Men's Needs,"[72] building a separate entrance to his room so that he can fulfill his sexual desires without permitting laborers to walk through the family home. By contrast to her encouragement of Chacko's sexual activities, Mammachi is disgusted by Ammu's sexual relationship with Velutha, her revulsion motivated both by caste prejudice and the conviction that respectable women do not engage in extramarital sex. Just as the family property is modified to provide an extra door for Chacko, encouraging sexual profligacy, so too is it made the site of Ammu's expulsion when she develops a meaningful and loving sexual relationship with a Dalit man. Architecturally, the Ayemenem home becomes a site of patriarchal endorsement of male ownership and male sexual freedoms even as it also becomes the location of female property exclusion and caste-based discrimination.

Configuring Reciprocity: Roy's Aesthetically Improper Challenges to Indian Law

I have been arguing that *The God of Small Things* explores the injurious effects of legally sanctioned dispossession and makes a convincing case against misogynistic property laws that systematically exclude women from ownership, make them dependent on male family members, and precipitate significant emotional and physical harms. Yet, Roy's political critique is more generative than straightforward opposition, despite the weight that has been given to this novel's contestatory stance by critics and reviewers.[73] Beyond exposing the structural violence that was built into India's patriarchal system of property ownership, established over hundreds of years and compounded under British rule,[74] *The God of Small Things* aesthetically builds an argument for how the Indian legal system needs to change. Contending that all Indians must be treated equally under the law, Roy's novel shares ethical commitments with the Indian Constitution, which not only identifies fundamental rights to equality under articles 14 to 18 but also specifies welfare protections in article 39, including "the right to an adequate means of livelihood" and the requirement "that the ownership and control of the material resources of the community are so distributed as best to subserve the common good." If this novel's plot demonstrates the consequences of excluding certain groups from material resources and the rights that attach to others, its aesthetics differently — improperly — insist on the fundamental interconnectedness and intrinsic equality of all living beings. Through figures of equitable relation that are established narratively, rhetorically, and tropologically, *The God of Small Things* aesthetically affirms the Constitution's egalitarian ideals, configuring a model of feminist, socialist community that differs significantly from 1960s Ayemenem. Crucially, therefore, in both its critique and its assertion of alternative legal rights and protections, *The God of Small Things* corresponds to arguments made by feminist activists in the fifty years prior to its writing as well as in the twenty-five years following publication. In the continuity between Roy's analysis and that of progressive thinkers and jurists who have been pressing for feminist changes to India's property laws, *The God of Small Things* demonstrates how literary texts engage discursively in the process of rethinking the law.

Stylistically, *The God of Small Things* counters the legal regime that its plot exposes, a system under which women are subjected to misogynistic violence and patriarchal domination and under which Dalit people are routinely persecuted and exploited because of their caste status. To an extent, *The God of Small Things* stylistically acknowledges the patriarchal, socioeconomic, and caste domination that its plot interrogates: this novel repeatedly employs tropes of enclosure, from the Ipe family's confinement within their car during the communist rally in Cochin, fearful of attack given their landowning status, to the opening scene of Sophie Mol lying trapped in her coffin; from Kerala's Foreign Returnees being "trapped outside the History House" of India by their newfound shame of their country of birth,[75] to the Orangedrink Lemondrink Man cornering Estha at the Abhilash Talkies, first sexually abusing him and then warning "I know where your factory is" to confine him in the fear of further abuse.[76] In their cumulative capacity, tropes of enclosure such as these establish a sense of claustrophobia and domination: of characters having little agency over their narrative trajectories and of being subjected to an organizing system that is beyond their control. The repeated references to "History," its capitalization serving to index its totalizing facility, explain the affective claustrophobia that is established through these tropes of confinement. In a Foucauldian vein, the assessment seems to be that institutional formations inexorably structure our daily realities, an analysis that is seemingly also upheld in the deaths of both Ammu and Velutha after they contravene the so-called Love Laws prohibiting intercaste sexual liaison.[77]

Alongside these tropes of enclosure, *The God of Small Things* aesthetically configures a commitment to egalitarian relation that consistently undermines the structures of domination that seem to constrain the lives of this novel's characters. Examples include linguistic refrains (like the references to Pappachi's moth) that echo throughout the text, subtly connecting seemingly disparate scenes that are instead shown to bear crucial bonds; the narrative's recursive structure, which challenges the sequence of events that trap Ammu and the other characters in tragic time; and the imagery of excess that patterns this novel's environmental descriptions, where objects consistently burst their bounds. Before the monsoon, for example, "the countryside turns an immodest green. . . . Wild creepers burst through laterite banks and spill across the flooded roads. Boats ply in the bazaars. And small fish appear in the puddles that fill the PWD potholes in the highways."[78] Much as in the tapster's corporeal and spiritual amplification in Okri's "What the Tapster Saw," or in Boja's microbial metamorphosis in Obioma's *The Fishermen*, *The God of Small Things* repeatedly identifies living beings and inanimate objects as exceeding their own structural limitations, the confines of their own objecthood, and mixing with other elements from their surrounding environment. Thus, the creepers in Ayemenem "burst" and "spill" from their original locations, draping themselves over "flooded roads" that, similarly "immodest," overstep the bounds of expectation by carrying boats to market and playing host to marine life. This scene's metaphysics contradict the logic of containment that inheres in a system of limited, male-oriented property ownership and strict social hierarchies, undermining gendered legal exclusions through a contrasting modality of reciprocal relation.

In its self-professed aesthetic immodesty—its aesthetic impropriety, in this book's terms—*The God of Small Things* elaborates an alternative set of legal principles to those that underpin mid-twentieth-century Indian succession and divorce laws. Whereas India's gendered property laws and the social mores that they both reflect and sustain are hierarchical and exclusionary, *The God of Small Things* aesthetically operates according to socialist-feminist principles that are much more akin to those that are found in India's Constitution. My analysis of Roy's aesthetic style and its consequences presupposes a clear conceptual relationship between property, possession, and propriety, concepts which together serve as organizing tropes in *The God of Small Things*, each configured upon lines of exclusion and enclosure. Scholars of property law have long acknowledged the close association between property and exclusion, especially in relation to private property: as Morris R. Cohen and Felix S. Cohen explain, "the essence of private property is always the right to exclude others."[79] So too do legal scholars recognize the close conceptual relationship between property and propriety; according to Gregory Alexander, property law's primary concern is "maintaining the proper social order."[80] In *The God of Small Things*, Roy similarly connects property ownership, legislated exclusion, and bourgeois propriety, excoriating the rigid moral codes that sustain and facilitate women's legal and economic dispossession.

From a stylistic perspective, *The God of Small Things* associates propriety with enclosure and impropriety with openness, a distinction that is perhaps most obvious in Mammachi's and Ammu's radically different attitudes to social decorum. Whereas Mammachi "fit[s] properly into the conventional scheme of things," accepting her subservience to male family members, Ammu repeatedly and deliberately contravenes social norms.[81] Mammachi's acquiescence includes submission to her physically abusive husband, Pappachi, whose "lurking manic violence . . . a sort of contained cruelty" is "contained" only insofar as it is effectively condoned by the prevailing social order; he releases it not infrequently on his wife.[82] By comparison, Ammu's rebellion against Indian property law's gendered exclusions and its corresponding social codes is registered in her consistently flouting rules and expectations: her liaison with Velutha, for example, demonstrates her rejection of "the smug, ordered world that she so raged against."[83] Roy encourages a direct comparison between the closed structure of propriety, evidenced in the way Mammachi "fit[s]" into the properly demarcated space of convention, and the open, equitable structure of impropriety, shown through Ammu's contempt for "order." *The God of Small Things* registers Ammu's impropriety not only through her refusal to conform to patriarchal sociopolitical hierarchies but also through her unpredictability, variously describing her as having a "reckless streak" and an "Unsafe Edge."[84] Whereas Mammachi's behavior is predictable and proper, Ammu's is unpredictable and improper; whereas Mammachi adheres to convention, Ammu rejects social respectability. If the *proper* is carefully delineated, contained within strict boundaries, the *improper* thwarts such easy demarcation and, in its recklessness, is less easily subject to control.

Roy builds a case for the political exigency of impropriety through Ammu's and the twins' persistent flouting of decorum and the logic of the proper. Ammu is notable for her "effrontery" and her refusal to abide by bourgeois codes of behavior, manifest not least in her status as a divorcée, unusual for the period as well as her caste.[85] In addition, she actively considers reverting to her maiden name, an act that would symbolically undermine—by concealing— her legally formalized dependence upon her ex-husband. She undercuts heteronormative family structures by insisting to her children that they need only her: that she can be their Ammu and their Baba.[86] And she establishes a nonmarital sexual relationship with a Dalit man, through which *The God of Small Things* not only challenges caste segregation but also, as Anuradha Needham argues, "transform[s] the ideological grounds of a hetero-normative family structure" in which the male partner bears greater power.[87] By identifying the reciprocity between Velutha and Ammu, as well as by determining the nonphallocentric tenor of their sexual congress and Velutha's "subversion of hetero-normative masculinity and sexuality," Needham suggests that *The God of Small Things*, and novels more generally, can transform political horizons by changing the grounds of analysis.[88] What's more, Ammu and Velutha's relationship offers one instance among many of how *The God of Small Things* theorizes egalitarian association. In this novel in which so many relationships are formed through domination, Roy identifies the love between Ammu and Velutha as tender and fulfilling: as an ethical good. Inasmuch as their relationship refutes caste-based discrimination as well as bourgeois ideals, both of which enforce hierarchical modes of association, it asserts its commitment to equality rather than domination.

Impropriety, then, registers far more than the breaking of convention; more significantly, it indicates a form of egalitarian reciprocity that *The God of Small Things* establishes as a necessary alternative to mid-century India's patriarchal and class-based social hierarchies. When Roy identifies normatively improper behavior that contravenes gendered expectations, she employs tropes of lateral movement and horizontal association. Much like their mother, Estha and Rahel disregard expected gender roles, causing widespread familial and societal consternation. Baby Kochamma cannot comprehend the pleasure that Estha derives from performing housework, a task that is firmly gendered female, and Rahel's teachers are mystified by her "waywardness":[89] to their perturbation, "[i]t was . . . *as though she didn't know how to be a girl.*"[90] Ironically, Rahel's teachers are concerned less with their pupil's minor but persistent acts of disruption, such as stealing and setting alight a teacher's false-hair bun, than her lack of interest in adhering to gender norms. Roy counters the teachers' narrow understanding of expected and accepted behavior through her associational schematic. Just as "waywardness" refers to Rahel's refusal to submit to social norms, metaphorically indicating her divergence from a designated path, so too does it imply lateral movement, indexing her demands that girls be treated equally to boys. If *The God of Small Things* signifies patriarchal domination through vertical hierarchies, it registers equality through horizontal relations and figures of lateral movement. In its laterally figured impropriety, Roy's novel rejects structures of domination that are codified in law, including in patriarchal succession and divorce laws.

In its recursive narrative, *The God of Small Things* establishes its commitment to egalitarian relationships and repudiates patriarchal property law's hierarchical structure. While the sequence of events that make up this novel's plot identifies discriminatory property law as instigating Ammu's death, the narrative is framed to counter domination with equality, hierarchy with reciprocity, exclusion with inclusion. Roy immediately undercuts expectations and rejects novelistic propriety by beginning with Sophie Mol's funeral, the event that, for Ammu and her children, is in many ways an end. From the start of the novel, the reader knows that Sophie Mol dies in a tragic accident; that Ammu dies at the "viable die-able age" of thirty-one; that Velutha dies in suspicious circumstances, "dark blood spilling from his skull like a secret"; and that Estha and Rahel are separated for twenty-three years, during which time Estha is "steeped in the smell of old roses, blooded on memories of a broken man."[91] The novel's recursive plot, shifting continually between the 1960s and 1990s, bears two significant implications: on the one hand, it traps the reader in the certain knowledge of encountering death, loss, and long-lasting suffering, and through this confinement replicates the stifling effects of exclusionary and dominative legal systems; on the other, it creates an associational formation that not only registers this novel's frustration with legislated hierarchies of domination and exclusion but also establishes its logic of operation as fundamentally improper, in the terms identified in the Introduction to *Aesthetic Impropriety*.

The God of Small Things at once facilitates its readers' navigation of its temporally complex plot and establishes a politically significant logic of equitable relation through its linguistic refrains and repeated imagery. Prominent examples of such repetition include references to Pappachi's moth and its "unusually dense dorsal tufts,"[92] the lucky silver thimble brought by Sophie Mol from London to Ayemenem, and the sickly sweet smell of roses on a breeze. These motifs all evoke traumatic memories: Pappachi's moth references his professional frustrations and his assertion of power through domestic violence, and as such its textual invocation is always an index of fear and misogyny; Sophie Mol's thimble is found clutched in her dead hand, not having provided her with the luck she knew she needed to safely cross the Meenachal River; and the sickly smell of roses is an olfactory reminder of the location of Velutha's murder and, therefore, of caste-based violence. As well as enabling Roy to address the workings of memory and psychological trauma,[93] these motifs aesthetically establish a schematic of egalitarian relation that bears political implications. Like Aarthi Vadde, whose critical assessment of *The God of Small Things* focuses on the "ecological collectivity" evinced in its pages, and like the symbiotic ecologies that I discussed in this book's first chapter, I am making a case for "the revolutionary potential of Roy's narratives of connection."[94] Whereas Vadde argues that Roy formally establishes a relational epistemology that draws on ecological forms of interrelation to counter caste- and gender-based hierarchies of domination, I am claiming that Roy's reciprocal aesthetics function to challenge exclusionary property laws, engaging in the imaginative labor that brings new forms of legal being into effect.

By requiring her reader to look for associational clues to understand *The*

God of Small Things's temporality and plot, Roy undermines the dominative and exclusionary logic that prompts Ammu's death. The novel's lateral structure effectively refuses what Leela Gandhi terms "the crisis of nonrelation upon which juridico-transcendental and universalizing forms of power... are predicated."[95] If power is organized hierarchically and vertically, as Gandhi argues, the repeated tropes and refrains in Roy's novel establish a lateral schematic that registers a radically different vision of feminist socialist equality than is identifiable in contemporary Indian legislation. According to Gandhi, colonial Britain deployed vertical structures of power to enact its political domination while fin-de-siècle radicals organized their actions horizontally. Late nineteenth-century anti-colonialists used their coalitional politics, their "solidarity with foreigners," and their eschewal of inherited communities of belonging to undermine "the embargo on relationality through which power, colonial or otherwise, orchestrates its divisions and exclusions."[96] What Gandhi terms "relationality" might be more precisely termed egalitarian or socialist relation because, with some exceptions, British colonial governments did not deny relation itself. To effect political domination, as Britain did in India and elsewhere, is not to reject relationality as such but to insist that it must operate hierarchically: for the relationship to be one of superiority and inferiority. Similarly, in *The God of Small Things* as well as under mid-twentieth-century succession and divorce laws, women's legislated position in relation to men is one of subordination and subjugation. Yet, Gandhi's analysis, broadly understood, is crucial for identifying the political implications of Roy's aesthetic style. The lateral relationality that is aesthetically produced in *The God of Small Things* is more than a metaphor for how power might be better distributed or how property law might be better organized. Roy's aesthetic schematic is neither incidental nor symbolic; instead, Roy recognizes, like Gandhi, that power is organized in aesthetic ways.

As an alternative to the exclusionary implications of prevailing legal and social systems, *The God of Small Things* develops a nonascendant, laterally relational, nondominative aesthetic economy, evidenced not only in Ammu and Velutha's relationship but also in Estha and Rahel's extreme closeness.[97] Before Sophie Mol's death and its traumatic aftereffects, the twins had felt themselves to be "physically separate, but with joint identities": they "thought of themselves together as Me, and separately, individually, as We or Us."[98] Rahel remembers, for example, "waking up one night giggling at Estha's funny dream," just as she remembers, even "though she hadn't been there," Estha's assault by the Orangedrink Lemondrink Man.[99] The splitting of the twins' shared identity occurs when Estha is "Returned" to his father in Bengal at the urging of Baby Kochamma, who fears he might reveal her role in Velutha's death. As Estha sits on the train at Cochin railway station, with Ammu and Rahel outside on the platform and Ammu holding his hand through the window, he is overcome by loss: "Estha's voice lifted into a wail. . . . He left his voice behind./On the station platform Rahel doubled over and screamed and screamed./The train pulled out. The light pulled in."[100] Estha and Rahel's closeness, and the psychological effects of their shared loss, are signaled in their shared scream. In the moment that "Estha's voice lift[s] into a wail" and promptly stops, Rahel "double[s] over" in pain, her own scream resuming the sound that her brother can no longer make. Estha's silence persists until he is reunited with Rahel fourteen years later; his vocal and psychological hibernation are a strategy by which he copes with his grief and guilt. (His name, "Esthappen" in full, hints at his long hibernation—his estivation—from the world.) Rahel's dormancy is emotional rather than verbal but like Estha's it begins with their separation. She finds herself emptied with his departure and the scream she emits on his behalf: as the train pulls away, carrying her shared self, "[t]he light," or emptiness, "pull[s] in."

In reconnecting the twins' jointness through the sexual intimacy they share after returning to Ayemenem as adults, *The God of Small Things* rejects the outcomes that Indian succession and divorce law require. Whereas this novel's plot results in death and trauma, a consequence of gender-inequitable inheritance and divorce laws, Roy's narrative shaping of that plot repudiates legislated economic exclusion. Within the logic of the novel, Estha and Rahel's single act of sexual union is psychologically restorative, enabling "Quietness and Emptiness" to "fi[t] together like stacked spoons" and rejoin what had been torn asunder.[101] Even though "what they shared that night was not happiness, but hideous grief," the sharing of their sorrow seems to facilitate a peacefulness that had long been affectively absent from *The God of Small Things*.[102] It is, therefore, significant that the twins' union occurs in this novel's penultimate chapter, just before the retrospective narration of Ammu and Velutha's similarly propitious sexual liaison. By concluding with Estha and Rahel's emotional reunification, as well as with Ammu and Velutha's relationship, *The God of Small Things* ends with the promise of future happiness, even as that promise is tempered by the "hideous grief" that accompanies the twins' sexual coupling and the knowledge of Ammu and Velutha's certain deaths.[103] While this novel's conclusion leads some critics to suggest that Roy envisions an end to caste prejudice through Ammu and Velutha's romance and others to argue that she prescribes personal and erotic fulfillment as the only viable response to institutional injustice,[104] such readings initiate a false choice between optimism and despair, between creative reimagining and feminist critique, in a novel that consistently balances both possibilities. Instead, *The*

God of Small Things at once condemns existing conditions and productively imagines them otherwise.

Much like challenges to unjust laws, *The God of Small Things* both identifies a specific problem and engages in the process of posing a credible alternative. Just as the Travancore Christian Succession Act was overturned through concerted legal challenges, culminating in the *Mary Roy* judgment, and just as the Indian Succession (Amendment) Act 2002 and the Hindu Succession (Amendment) Act 2005 provide women under their jurisdiction with equal inheritance rights to men's, *The God of Small Things* participates in the long, collective process of theorizing feminist legal protections by revising the logics of existing succession and divorce laws. In place of the proprietary system that saw property consolidated in male hands, especially under British colonial rule, Roy's novel aesthetically establishes an improper logic of equitable and reciprocal relation. Extending beyond female property protections, *The God of Small Things*'s reciprocal schematic insists on equality for all those who make up a community, without regard for discriminatory hierarchies based on caste, gender, or class, or even for distinctions between human and nonhuman lifeworlds. In direct contradistinction to Indian inheritance and divorce laws, *The God of Small Things* makes an impassioned case for the radical egalitarianism that is outlined in India's Constitution.

What We Expect from Literature and the Law

In arguing that Roy's relationally egalitarian aesthetics construct a more just model of Indian property law, one in which all women have the same rights and protections as men and in which material resources are equitably distributed, I am suggesting not simply that *The God of Small Things* presents both a critique of India's patriarchal property laws and an alternative formulation of legislated land rights but that their careful balancing registers the slow and messy process of legal change. *The God of Small Things*'s critical interventions depend on its offering neither solely a critique of embattled opposition against a system of domination nor a utopian narrative of merely imaginatively transcending injustice but an account that instead recognizes how both critique and the generating of alternatives necessarily and productively coexist during the process of transforming the law. As *The God of Small Things* itself suggests, and as the feminist legal context in which it is embedded demonstrates, the process of challenging unjust laws, not to mention changing the social structures that give rise to them and which they also endorse, is typically exceedingly slow, involving at once optimism and despair, possibility and limitation, small victories and countless losses. The history of recent feminist improvements to Indian succession laws, along with ongoing attempts to reform divorce laws, confirm what all political and legal activists know: that persisting to advocate for justice often successfully leads to reform, even if change is slow.

My analysis of *The God of Small Things*'s reciprocally relational aesthetics in contrast to its charting of mid-century India's system of gendered property law thus bears similarities with David Scott's argument, in *Conscripts of Modernity*, that the history of colonial resistance can be plotted simultaneously as oppositional critique and utopian overcoming: in his terms, as both tragedy and romance. Indeed, the very same incident can be narrated both ways, as Scott identifies through his analysis of the 1938 edition of C. L. R. James's *The Black Jacobins*, a monumental biography of Haitian revolutionary Toussaint L'Ouverture, and its slightly revised 1962 edition, released after independence's promise had already begun to wane. For Scott, tragedy is politically salient in the twenty-first-century postcolonial context because it simultaneously acknowledges the material limitations that inhibit transformation and opens up the necessary critical space to facilitate change. In his reading of *The Black Jacobins*, and drawing upon Hayden White's theory of tragic and romantic emplotment, Scott claims that tragedy is the "less determinative, more recursive" of the two genres, arguing that it challenges the "hubris" of total revolution and "reopens a path to formulating a criticism of the present."[105] Scott's argument that political change can be better conceived not as emancipatory overcoming but as opening up critical space corresponds closely to the narrative structure and aesthetic style of *The God of Small Things*, whose plotted resignation to its tragic events by no means negates its juridical interventions. This novel's recursive plot and tropes of confinement identify the hierarchical legal system in which the narrative unfolds while its reciprocally relational aesthetics theorize an alternate system of gender-equitable property protections. The pivotal connection between, on the one hand, the legislation that is critiqued in *The God of Small Things* and, on the other, the aesthetic strategies that function to reimagine India's property laws produces a novel that at once opposes oppressive legislation and participates in the broader public process of discussing and reformulating those laws. Like Scott's assessment of tragedy, my reading of Roy's novel through the framework of aesthetic impropriety refuses to choose resignation over utopia, critique over imagining: instead, it participates in a necessary project within both law and literary studies and postcolonial studies by making a case for the aesthetic's transformative potential.

The aesthetic's materially generative capacities and its involvement in establishing property law reform is staged most acutely in Roy's treatment of Kathakali, Kerala's traditional artform that combines narrative, drama, and dance. *The God of Small Things* draws its narrative structure from Kathakali, which "discovered long ago that the secret of the Great Stories is that they *have* no secrets. The Great Stories are the ones . . . you can enter anywhere and inhabit comfortably. . . . You know how they end, yet you listen as though you don't."[106] In claiming that epic stories narrate what is already known and yield pleasure in that telling, Roy at once recognizes tragedy's consolations and offers a belated piece of guidance on how to navigate a novel whose complex temporality includes partially revealing the characters' fates from the start.[107] Yet, if *The God of Small Things* satisfies on recurrent rereadings, it is only partly because its heart-wrenching account of the deaths of Sophie Mol, Ammu, and Velutha, as well as its rendering of Estha and Rahel's decimated lives, provides a safely managed experience of cathartic release. Just as important as its plot, *The God of Small Things* is captivating on multiple readings because of its attention to detail: to the reciprocally relational, aesthetic rendering of the world through which it offers its account of tenderness, love, and the equal value of all living beings. Even as *The God of Small Things* tells a tragic tale of misogyny and casteism that leads to violent deaths, thwarted love, and painful bereavement, it also aesthetically participates in the process of achieving legal reform.

The God of Small Things is both as tragic as the Kathakali plays watched by Estha and Rahel after their return to Ayemenem as adults and as committed to art's politically generative capacities as the twins' psychologically restorative experience of watching these performances. The opening play, *Karna Shabadam* ("Karna's Oath"), prefigures Ammu's tragic separation from her beloved children, telling the story of Kunti from the Hindu epic the *Mahabharata*. Separated from her first son, to whom she had given birth prior to marriage, Kunti now faces the loss of another child. Like Roy, Kunti "invoke[s] the Love Laws" when she tracks down her long-lost son, Karna, and begs him not to kill her five other sons during an impending battle.[108] Karna cannot comply because he has already vouched loyalty to Duryodhana, his benefactor and half-brothers' enemy, but he promises that Kunti will lose only one son: either he or his brother Arjuna will die, but not both. Inasmuch as "Karna's Oath" is a story of maternal and filial loss that is borne out of prohibitions against unmarried mothers, it echoes the chain of events in *The God of Small Things*, where gender-exclusionary succession and divorce laws cause needless deaths and familial bereavement. Likewise, the emotional pain suffered by Kunti and Karna as a result of their long separation recalls Estha's distress at being sent away as a child: "*Where were you*, he asked her, *when I needed you most? . . . .* In reply Kunti took the regal face in her hands. . . . *Did you know how much I missed you?*"[109] Kunti and Karna's reunification stages the deep love of mother for son, and grief at their forced separation, that Ammu could never prove to grown Estha because of her tragically early death.

While *Karna Shabadam* narrates the consequences of gendered social norms on the relationship between a mother and her children, the second play, *Duryodhana Vadham* ("the Death of Duryodhana and his brother Dushasana"), recalls Roy's critique of land ownership's historical predication upon female dependence. *Duryodhana Vadham* recounts how another major character in the *Mahabharata*, Draupadi, is won in a game of dice and is "strangely angry only with the men that won her, not the ones that staked her."[110] As the *Mahabharata* narrates, one of Draupadi's five husbands, Yudishthira, is convinced by his cousin Duryodhana to stake his kingdom in a game of dice. After progressively losing to Duryodhana each brother's freedom, and then his own, Yudishthira finally gambles away his wife. Angered, Draupadi questions the legality of his bet: in staking his own freedom prior to gambling hers, her husband had lost his legal personhood while she was still the Pandava queen. Without legal personality, Yudishthira had no standing to make any bet at all. Duryodhana's brother Dushasana tries to disrobe Draupadi in an attempt to humiliate and subjugate her, and in return, one of her five husbands, Bhima, avenges her honor by clubbing Dushasana to death.[111] In staging *Duryodhana Vadham* within *The God of Small Things*, Roy identifies a long regional history of gendered land ownership that includes the presumed right to claim land by putting a woman's legal personhood at stake.

Even as the Kathakali episode suggests that misogynistic property laws and corresponding theories of female subordination endure largely without change, *The God of Small Things* uses this scene to reject the foreclosures that are implied in tragedy's preordained conclusions. While the Kathakali performance's narrative, conceptual, and affective resonances cause Estha and Rahel to revisit the trauma of their youth, this recurrence bears promise as well as pain. Despite the gendered domination that is built into the Kathakali stories, and despite the misogyny of the performers, who displace their frustration at their artform's cultural depreciation by "[going] home to beat their wives,"[112] the performance facilitates the repair of Estha and Rahel's emotional intimacy. When Estha silently arrives to join Rahel at the temple, his twin senses his presence: "Something altered in the air. And Rahel knew that Estha had come./She didn't turn her head, but a glow spread inside her. *He's come.* She thought. *He's here. With me.*/Estha settled against a distant pillar and they sat through the performance like this, separated by the breadth of the kuthambalam, but joined by a story. And the memory of another mother."[113] If the twins' extended separation registers the enduring impact of mid-twentieth-century India's misogynistic legal system, their silent assembly at the kuthambalam, or temple theater, suggests art's productive capacities. Just as Kathakali brings the twins together, diegetically uniting them within this novel's own narrative logic, *The God of Small Things* bears a generative legal function, challenging India's gender-exclusionary property laws and their consequences while also conceptualizing new modes of legislated relation.

In refusing the tragedy that is inscribed in a patriarchal legal system that subjugates women as well as harming their children, and in aesthetically constructing an alternative moral economy that is built on openness and egalitarian relation, *The God of Small Things* enacts both a critique of Indian succession and divorce law and a generatively improper account of how these laws should be reformed. Taking the form of a tragedy in its plot and a romance in its style, *The God of Small Things* reckons with the constraints of historical conditions and the promise of their capacity to be changed. By combining both tragedy and romance, Roy's novel models the process of legal activism, which similarly involves both critiquing harmful laws and proposing valid alternatives. In literary studies, it is often assumed that criticism must follow a tragic mode: that literary works can identify historical conditions but cannot change them. To put this another way, neither literature nor its analysis is understood to be capable of adhering to the Romantic trajectory of heroic overcoming. And yet in the legal arena, just as in *The God of Small Things*, both of these modes of emplotment necessarily operate in conjunction, with neither of them fully implemented and neither of them successful on their own. While historical conditions limit what can be done — and while legal change occurs only slowly because the law corresponds to entrenched social practices — reforms can be achieved through concerted efforts. In both its tragic narrative mode and egalitarian aesthetic form, *The God of Small Things* confronts and reworks Indian women's substantial exclusion from property rights as well as Indian law's tragically gendered constraints. Roy produces a model of gender-equitable property law and a share in society's material resources that at once echoes feminist legal reforms that had already been won by the date of this novel's publication and insists on the need for further reforms for which activists likewise continued to fight. Through its own aesthetic impropriety, in other words, *The God of Small Things* holds out the promise of literature's capacity to engage in the extended discursive process of establishing necessary legal reforms.

3
Accretion
Decolonizing Intellectual Property Law

South Africa's famous elections of 1994 ushered in an era of intense debate over property rights—and not just in the frequently discussed terms of land redistribution after Black and brown people's systematic territorial dispossession over the course of nearly four centuries of white supremacist rule.[1] The ending of apartheid and securing of South Africa's multiracial democracy also coincided with a movement across the Global South for substantive intellectual property protections from Global North profiteering. Since at least the 1960s, Indigenous peoples and minoritized ethnic groups have continuously argued that intellectual property (IP) laws have effectively sanctioned the Global North's intellectual plunder of the Global South. As this book has already shown, the Anglo-American property regime regulates far more than land ownership and personal property. With its proprietary modes of possession and their racialized and gendered consequences, European-derived property law has facilitated dispossession of natural resources, gendered economic security, and racialized subjectivities. Stemming from this same proprietary and exclusionary conception of property, including its values and logical structure, extant IP law likewise allows for the continued siphoning of resources—namely creative products and inherited knowledge—from colonized or formerly colonized peoples. As such, efforts to regain economic and ownership rights over cultural practices and systems of knowledge production not only coincide with struggles to decolonize land ownership but form part of the same material and discursive process.

As has been widely recognized over the last several decades, IP law was implemented around the world as a colonial tool and sustains neocolonial structures of power.[2] This particular legal regime developed out of European conceptions of copyright in particular and private property in general, both of which uphold exclusionary property rights as a crucial tenet of individual freedom. Copyright largely took its current form in eighteenth-century England while IP was formalized in the early nineteenth century. These two methods of knowledge protection gained their subsequent global reach as a result of late nineteenth-century colonial powers insisting on international standardization in order to buttress domestic protections that were rendered largely ineffectual when not enforced abroad. The signing of 1883's Paris Convention, which regulates industrial property, followed by the 1886 Berne Convention, which governs copyright, not only enforced a culturally specific conception of intellectual and creative labor all over the world but was made possible by the depth and spread of European colonial power in the late nineteenth century.[3] Indeed, it is no coincidence that these discussions about IP law took place either side of the infamous Berlin conference of 1884–1885, during which European states divided up Africa to extract resources and accumulate wealth. The capitalist-colonial system of property ownership structures knowledge as much as land and its proprietary predicates always entail resource depletion.

Under the forceful imposition of colonial legislation, as well as through contemporary neoliberal leveraging of international protocols, especially Trade-Related Intellectual Property Rights (TRIPs), the North has profited from an IP regime that has cast collaborative creativity and inherited knowledge practices as insufficiently original and undeserving of copyright protection. The existing proprietary model of IP law largely refuses to recognize the necessarily cumulative social processes of artistic labor and knowledge production that are widely practiced throughout the world.[4] As a consequence of legally formalizing protections for intellectual and creative production from a culturally specific model, Europe and the United States have effectively facilitated the ongoing extraction of knowledge and creativity from the Global South. Data on patent ownership, for instance, reveals that "97% of the world's intellectual property is held by the industrialized countries in the north," and that, of the 3 percent of patents deriving from the Global South, 80 percent are held by noncitizens.[5] Given colonial and neocolonial distributions of power, IP law's systematic appropriation of knowledge inevitably involves racialized dispossession.

The spread of political independence in the 1960s coincided with an anticolonial movement to interrogate IP law's founding presumptions, challenging the uneven global distribution of cultural and intellectual protections and the ongoing colonial practice of knowledge extraction by the Global North from the Global South. Under the principle of national sovereignty, early postcolonial nation-states sought to resist historical patterns of exploitative resource extraction by protecting their intellectual resources and cultural practices for national use. India fought to defend oral traditions by granting rights to unknown authors under a modified Berne Convention in 1967, while Tunisia led the development of more robust protections with the signing of the Tunis Model Law in 1976.[6] Yet, the most significant challenges to IP law's predicates and consequences have been generated not by postcolonial governments but by Indigenous peoples.

Particularly since the 1980s, when multinational corporations started patenting plant and animal species at accelerating rates, Indigenous peoples have mobilized against IP law's legalized dispossessions and have proposed alternate models that are, in this book's terms, constitutively improper.[7] Indigenous activists and authorities have argued, with increasing success, that IP law facilitates biopiracy: that is, the widescale plunder of Indigenous knowledge about biological materials by pharmaceutical companies who trademark inherited knowledge for corporate gain.[8] Over this same period, Indigenous peoples and minoritized ethnic groups have demonstrated that the system of IP law also enables cultural theft, whether of Maori haka,[9] South African folk songs,[10] Asante textiles,[11] or Quecha agricultural practices.[12] Yet, it was only well into the twenty-first century that Indigenous and local claims to inherited knowledge gained any sort of widespread traction. Early advocacy efforts met with substantial resistance and were further slowed by the formation of the World Trade Organization (WTO) in 1994. The WTO's foundational legal agreement, TRIPs, is broadly understood by postcolonialist legal scholars to undermine Indigenous and Global South creative and intellectual protections. As Chidi Oguamanam explains, TRIPs reveals a fundamental "disregard for local knowledge" by protecting developments in biotechnologies and life sciences in the Global North while failing to protect historically significant knowledge in the South.[13] Some of the damage effected by TRIPs was ameliorated in 2007 when, after sustained pressure, and with the signing of the UN Declaration on the Rights of Indigenous Peoples, the World Intellectual Property Organization (WIPO) finally started to seek greater protections for Indigenous intellectual and cultural property. With new support from the UN, Indigenous peoples and other colonized populations have begun to win necessary legal protections to prevent neocolonial resource extraction of their creative and intellectual assets.[14]

Indigenous-led, anti-colonial critiques of IP law condemn the existing legal regime on three counts: for exalting individual efforts over collaborative processes; for placing undue faith in clear narratives of origin; and for making permanence a requirement for protecting creative work or intellectual production. By contrast, Indigenous models of art and knowledge broadly understand creative and intellectual processes to operate through continuity, collaboration, and ephemerality. Unlike the individualist mandate in European-derived IP traditions, Indigenous peoples frequently affirm that ideas and creative works are produced intergenerationally and collectively. Indeed, across the Global South, and not only among Indigenous groups, creative practices as well as systems of knowledge are understood to be accretional and are carefully maintained and curated over time, whether they involve the Hoodia plant's curative properties or oral narratives that are passed down over generations.

While these coordinated challenges to IP law are framed as protecting Indigenous resources, they have been taken up more broadly across the Global South by states and organizations that recognize the usefulness or relevance of Indigeneity for describing their own ethnicities, including throughout Africa. In 1985, Ghana introduced increased legal protections for Indigenous or traditional knowledge, securing it still further in 2005;[15] in 1994, South Africa introduced the Indigenous Knowledge Systems Program, which was finally passed by Parliament in August 2019 as the Protection, Promotion, Development and Management of Indigenous Knowledge Act; and since 2002, the African Regional Intellectual Property Organization (ARIPO) has been working to protect traditional knowledge and cultural production among English-speaking member nations.[16] ARIPO's paradigmatic Swakopmund Protocol of 2010, for example, recognizes that traditional stories, or what it names "folklore," take a particular form, which the agreement identifies as their "collective or community context; the intergenerational nature of their development; their preservation and transmission, and their link to a community's cultural and social identity, integrity, and beliefs."[17] Such practices of inherited knowledge, intergenerational collaboration, or oral production are typical outside the European context, particularly among many Indigenous people as well as among what WIPO sometimes terms "local" populations.[18] These widely recognized practices of creative and intellectual production operate improperly, in this book's terms, because they preclude proprietary ownership and corresponding methods of property protection.

In the context of this worldwide push to protect Indigenous or traditional knowledge systems and creative practice, the newly independent South Africa sought to tackle IP law's colonialist underpinnings and dispossessive effects. Postapartheid South Africa's most famous and immediate legal initiative was the Truth and Reconciliation Commission (TRC), which used oral testimony shared in public settings to engage in a national process of restorative justice and reckon with the atrocities that had been legislated under apartheid. In meeting to hear spoken accounts of systemic racism, the TRC affirmed the value of oral narratives even as it faced criticism for prioritizing spectacular accounts of male violence, effectively dispossessing women of narratively owning their traumatic experiences. Less conspicuously, and at the same time as the TRC's famous hearings, the newly elected African National Congress (ANC) government was likewise endorsing orality in early discussions about reforming the country's IP laws. From its initial policy discussions in 1996 through to the August 2019 signing of the Protection, Promotion, Development and Management of Indigenous Knowledge Act, South Africa has sought to revise its legal code to protect systems of knowledge that have been vulnerable to exploitation under the current IP regime.[19] In doing so, it has recognized that finding adequate measures for protecting Indigenous and localized forms of knowledge and creativity is a vital part of redressing colonial subjugation and racialized subordination.

"Accretion: Decolonizing Intellectual Property Law" analyzes South Africa's efforts to expand IP protections in and through Zoë Wicomb's critically acclaimed postapartheid novel *David's Story* to show how thinkers across the Global South have at once engaged with the strictures of IP law and theorized alternative models for protecting localized forms of cultural practice and inherited knowledge. Set in 1991, in the interregnum between apartheid's promised demise and its official end, and published in 2000, six years into a very public and painful reckoning with the white supremacist apartheid state, *David's Story* assesses a long regional history of erasing Black and brown women's achievements from the historical record. Wicomb's novel mounts markedly similar critiques as have been established by Indigenous-led coalitions and it makes very similar demands. Much like the coordinated legislative and policy complaints directed at governments and international bodies by Indigenous and Global South actors, *David's Story* criticizes IP law's proprietary formulations and proposes contradistinctively improper methods to inclusively protect creative work and intellectual production. Both *David's Story* and anti-colonial challenges to IP law operate according to this book's model of aesthetic impropriety: they respond to proprietary structures or logics — in this case, to IP law; they configure alternatives that are improper, in the sense of bearing open, expansively inclusionary contours rather than the closed, exclusionary tenets of proprietary systems; and, in their robust criticism of the legal regime, they refuse to follow norms of propriety that require largely unquestioning acceptance of existing social formations.

Using the model of aesthetic impropriety to identify shared structures of thought across legal and literary venues, this chapter argues that *David's Story* offers an early example of retheorizing South Africa's IP laws according to Indigenous principles of collective, inherited, and ephemeral creative production. I identify these three tenets of anti-colonial IP law as accretive, contending that, as a form of aesthetic impropriety, accretion engages with capitalist-colonial property laws in general and IP laws in particular. *David's Story*'s accretional aesthetics are evidenced in its complex narrative temporality, distributed focalization, plural plotting, embedded texts, and multiform oral narratives. By interpreting Wicomb's account of the systemic silencing of Black and multiracial women as engaging with IP law's significant limitations, I not only offer a new reading of this novel but I also provide a clear example of how a literary work's aesthetic engagement with complex legal ideas has preempted significant reform. Wicomb's early theorizing of what would become a concerted effort by South African politicians, legal theorists, and activists to expand IP law's purview, culminating in the Indigenous Knowledge Act (2019), extends the argument that *Aesthetic Impropriety*'s first two chapters have been developing: that new legal ideas circulate discursively, and often through aesthetic means, well before they are signed into law.

Narrative Production and Intellectual Property in South Africa

In South Africa, a region that is famous for apartheid's legislated racial hierarchies and extreme violence but whose racist legal and political systems stretch back to settler-colonizers' arrival in the seventeenth century, Black and brown writers have long fought to have their voices heard. Scholarship that addresses representations of racialized silencing in South African literature have tended to address material conditions of publication, typically examining the publishing industry broadly conceived, including prestige book publishers, newspaper and magazine companies, and underground networks which, during apartheid, published Black writing that was otherwise excluded from the public sphere.[20] These analyses of South Africa's publishing scene are important: the industry remains overwhelmingly white, despite white people constituting only approximately 7 percent of the South African population, and this significant racial imbalance limits the stories that are told about the nation and its history.[21] Complementing existing sociological studies, the model of aesthetic impropriety clarifies that South African publishing's racial exclusions also derive from normative assumptions about what kind of creative work is valued and how that work ought to be produced: that is, the core features of IP law. Only a very small amount of work currently exists on IP law's operations in literature from the Global South, with two innovative and foundational exceptions being Matthew Eatough's reading of South African novelist Zakes Mda's *Heart of Redness* and Joseph Slaughter's analysis of Nigerian novelist Chris Abani's *Graceland*. For Eatough and Slaughter, these novels respectively examine the entrenchment of neoliberal economic values across Africa: in Eatough's analysis, *Heart of Redness* thematizes the concerning monetization of heritage through patent law; for Slaughter, *Graceland* deploys IP law's parody exception to assess African literature's commodity value in the global marketplace.[22]

Building on Eatough and Slaughter's scholarship, this chapter makes an unusual case for *David's Story*'s significance, contending that Wicomb's novel addresses the consequences of a legal system that fails to protect Black and Indigenous women's creative and intellectual labor: the stories that are left untold; the work that goes unrecognized; the structures of power that remain unchanged. *David's Story* tells the interconnected stories of David, Sally, and Dulcie, all of whom are trained anti-apartheid guerillas but only one of whom — David — receives any public recognition for their work. David and Dulcie had been senior militants for over a decade and are emotionally, if not sexually, involved. Sally resents having been forced to leave the movement upon marrying David, and her professional frustrations are compounded by realizing her husband's intimacy with Dulcie. All three characters are haunted: Sally by her lost career and sense of purpose; Dulcie by the trauma of repeated torture; and David by his guilt over his actions during the course of guerilla warfare and his viable fear of imminent death. Alongside these triangulated narratives, Wicomb's novel traces the coming-into-being of the Griqua, an Indigenous, multiracial people whose history David researches in a misguided attempt to secure his racial origins. *David's Story*'s historical plotline, which concerns Griqua demands for political recognition and land restitution, also addresses a pattern of male appropriation of female narrative labor and creative expertise. These two narrative threads — of the present anti-apartheid struggle and the historical Griqua experience — are brought together by the narrator, whom David hires to compose the narrative that he struggles to arrange, and who performs the labor that David claims as his own. Functioning as a character in her own right, the narrator not only bookends this novel with self-reflexive analyses on the writing process but she also weaves her insights throughout. Despite the novel's wry title, this story is — from a labor perspective — the narrator's rather than David's.

Existing scholarship on *David's Story* frequently engages public discourse about women's testimony in the new South Africa, particularly surrounding the TRC's failure to provide Black and brown women with the opportunity to narratively claim their traumatic ordeals. Aryn Bartley, for instance, interprets *David's Story* as critiquing the TRC's demand for public storytelling as necessary for producing a newly cohesive national community.²³ Dina al-Kassim and Meg Samuelson have persuasively argued that *David's Story* offers a necessary riposte to the typically masculinist accounts of anti-apartheid activism that are not only lauded in South Africa but are constitutive of its contemporary national identity.²⁴ Yet, Wicomb is concerned not just with whether or not women's voices are heard but also with the work of producing and crafting narrative: a process that gets to the heart of the TRC's rationale and practice. As Christopher J. Colvin demonstrates, the TRC participated in a growing global demand for survivors of atrocities to narrate their trauma, not necessarily to their benefit. In response to this new political economy of traumatic storytelling, Colvin finds, female survivors of apartheid violence have begun to assert IP rights over their stories, demanding recompense in place of exploitation.

As well as addressing apartheid-era violence, *David's Story* recognizes that contemporary South Africa's exclusion of Black and brown women's experiences from the historical record remains inextricable from a longer regional history of raced and gendered dispossession. Through diary entries, letters, and imagined histories, *David's Story* spans the early nineteenth century through to the present, including Griqua woman Sarah Baartman's coerced display for white European audiences at the turn of the nineteenth century, Indigenous land dispossession under British colonial rule, and the negation of women's experiences under apartheid and in its aftermath. By integrating multiple technologies of writing, narrating, and recording female experience into its plot, this novel condemns a gendered and racialized history of men passing off women's narrative labor as their own. Like legal theorists of copyright and IP law, Wicomb recognizes that narratives are produced through work and labor; that their shaping is informed by their conditions of production; and that narrative labor can be appropriated by more powerful people and institutions. Through its persistent focus on the arrogation of Black and Indigenous women's narrative labor, *David's Story* prizes open the imperialist, individualist, proprietary structure of globalized IP law. In its place, Wicomb develops an accretive model of intellectual and cultural production that is similarly articulated in anti-colonial challenges to the IP regime.

Intellectual Property's Proprietary Form

The proprietorial form that characterizes IP law as a globalized regulatory system derives from the conditions of copyright's historical emergence in seventeenth- and eighteenth-century England.²⁵ Intellectual property law typically requires a creative work or knowledge practice to meet three main criteria in order to receive protections: originality, individualism, and permanence. These culturally specific principles derive from early modern European conceptions of property ownership, which apply to literature as much as land and largely took their current form in the eighteenth century with the development of copyright law in England, particularly with the famous literary legal case *Pope v. Curll* (1741). As a juridicoliterary formation, copyright reflects a nexus of historicizable beliefs about property rights: these include early modern capitalism's formulation of ownership through the Lockean doctrine of property in the person;[26] late eighteenth-century European ideas about the author as an "originary genius-proprietor";[27] and enduring capitalist commitments to securing property for investment and inheritance.[28] In other words, copyright and its nineteenth-century descendant, IP law, share their motivating logics with the legal and political systems of the European nation-states that are likewise responsible for IP's global implementation.

David's Story demonstrates that IP law's proprietary structure—which involves a demand for identifiable origins that are recorded in permanent form and are generally ascribed to one person alone—helps to facilitate gendered and racialized models of labor exploitation. As the narrator makes clear, *David's Story* is, from a labor perspective, really her own; yet, because David falsely passes off her work as transcriptional rather than substantive, he maintains ownership—as he would maintain copyright—over the text. Mark Rose explains that "the distinguishing characteristic of the modern author . . . is proprietorship," a term that here serves as shorthand for the particular model of property law that has been established over the course of European colonial rule and which persists into the present.[29] In the proprietorial model of creativity, Rose explains, "the author is conceived as the originator and therefore the owner of a special kind of commodity, the work."[30] Significantly, even in the Global North, copyright's originary expectation is naturalized rather than foundational. As Martha Woodmansee and Peter Jaszi explain, prior to the formalizing of copyright in eighteenth-century England, legal protections for a written work were granted to the guild—that is, to the collective members who printed and distributed the work—or to a given project's collaborators.[31] It was only with copyright's propertization that the demand arose for clearly identifiable origins, regardless of the collaborative or cumulative conditions of a work's production.

Copyright's proprietary logic coincides precisely with colonial England's emerging global dominance, as evidenced in the "acquisitive, expansionist, and colonial activity" that Woodmansee and Jaszi identify in late seventeenth-century England's publishing trade.[32] In 1695, threatened by the decline of the patronage system and the lapse of the Licensing Act, members of the

Stationers' Company, which comprised what had been the book trade's only licensed printers and distributers, attempted to maintain their trade monopoly by newly invoking the rhetoric of individual interest.[33] Between 1710 and 1774, the process of what Simon Stern terms "the 'propertization' of copyright"[34] increasingly took shape through a series of statutes and appeals, including the pivotal dispute between writer Alexander Pope and bookseller Edmund Curll. Stern charts two possible legal frameworks that competed for primacy during this period, revealing that while copyright is now understood as a type of property, it has a parallel possible history as a dignitary right. Whereas the property conception justifies copyright in terms of ownership, and specifically the capitalist-colonialist formulation of private property that had, by the eighteenth century, been substantively implemented both in industrial Britain and its colonies, the dignitary conception of copyright affirmed rights based in reputational standing.[35] In other words, the process of understanding creative work in terms of ownership was highly contested and by no means a given; it was only through six decades of litigation that copyright's primary explanatory category became ownership rather than reputation. For Stern, this unearthed history reveals how and why it has been possible for copyright terms and derivative rights to expand so substantially over the last century. Just as significantly, though, Stern's scholarship suggests both that the forms of thought encoded in copyright law are specific and historicizable and that they are distinctly associated with European modernity's proprietary logic and its exclusionary consequences.

Engaging with contemporary debates about copyright and IP's individualist paradigms, *David's Story* reflects on authorial ownership, recognizing that copyright has served, since its inception, to protect the rights of the historicizable figure of the author. Both doctrinally and discursively, the author has been conceptualized as an originary innovator, sole proprietor, and possessive individual.[36] As Woodmansee and Jaszi argue, copyright's "exclusive vision of authorship" is "part of [its] postcolonial legal legacy."[37] *David's Story* exposes the limits of this normative legal model of the author as a proprietary figure through the narrator's repeated reflections on authorial ownership. The novel opens with the narrator's claim that "this is and is not David's story,"[38] signaling both that the titular character's biography appropriates the life stories of several women and that his account was not produced by his labor alone. In similar metacommentary throughout the novel, the narrator describes how she crafts, shapes, and gives meaning to David's biographical account. She recognizes herself as David's "collaborator,"[39] despite his protestations that she is only a channel for his ideas, because, as she explains, she identifies the feelings and motivations behind his words, chooses a temporal framework through which to plot his narrative, and decides how much weight to give each reported episode. By making the narrator a self-reflexive character, Wicomb differentiates between story as personal-life narrative and the labor of crafting a text.

By repeatedly drawing attention to the work involved in composition, Wicomb frames her novel as engaging with IP law's proprietary paradigm. IP law has historically struggled to adequately protect creative labor because both copyright and IP have failed to extricate themselves from the unrealistic model of the author as sole producer. According to the narrator, David appoints her as what he terms his "amanuensis" because "he [is] unwilling or unable to flesh out the narrative" and because hiring a writer would mean that the story "would no longer belong to him. In other words, he both wanted and did not want it to be written."[40] David's inability to order his narrative is typically interpreted as a trauma response that derives from his experience in the armed resistance movement. As critics like Meg Samuelson recognize, survivors of trauma usually narrate their experiences indirectly, finding it too painful to speak directly about what happened to them.[41] While Wicomb encourages this interpretation, in which David exemplifies the difficulties of writing coherently about painful memories, she also presents David as maintaining a masculinist desire to lay claim to the manuscript that recounts his life story even though someone else has shaped it into a cohesive and comprehensive narrative. He had hoped, the narrator complains on several occasions, to "father his text at a distance":[42] to claim ownership without putting in the labor to nurture his textual child into existence. In David's desire to "acknowledge and maintain control over his progeny even if it is fathered from a distance,"[43] Wicomb "displace[s] the patriarchal male author and, implicitly, the patriarchal authority presumed by the author," a trope that Andrew van der Vlies identifies as consistent in all of her work.[44] What's more, I might add, Wicomb also registers the material consequences of an IP regime that distinguishes between narrative originality and narrative labor. In the terms of the IP legal system that this novel confronts, Wicomb indexes the globally acknowledged problem of men requisitioning women's compositional labor while claiming economic benefits and moral rights over a work.

In David's repeated claims to narrative fatherhood, Wicomb invokes copyright's paternity clause, or the moral right to claim authorship.[45] In doing so, she implicitly recognizes, along with many cultural historians, that copyright's foundational metaphors shape its ongoing legal form and consequences. As Rosemary Coombe explains, early eighteenth-century parliamentary debates linked an author's ownership rights to primogeniture:

> The patriarchal notion of a father begetting his book and the book as his child . . . suggests a notion of creation and paternity that goes far beyond a simple notion of property as possession or commodity. A father's child is his own, not because he owns it or has invested in it, but because this child will carry the father's name and likeness. The child is the means by which the father's immortality is to be realized.⁴⁶

Here, Coombe is responding to the 1735 *Letter from an Author to a Member of Parliament*, which proclaimed: "For if there be such a Thing as Property upon Earth, an Author has it in his Work. A Father cannot more justly call his Child, than an Author can his Work, his own."⁴⁷ Glossing Mark Rose's argument in *Authors and Owners: The Invention of Copyright*, Coombe argues that "Rose takes metaphor seriously as the means by which cultural significance is conveyed."⁴⁸ In other words, both Rose and Coombe recognize that metaphor bears material significance: that it shapes literary practice, legal systems, and the production of cultural value.

The metaphor of book as child, which is seen as the means by which the father's immortality is realized, likewise pervades *David's Story*. According to South Africa's Copyright Act of 1978, as Caroline Ncube explains, "the author of [the] work also has the moral rights of integrity and paternity which enable him to object to any distortion or mutilation of the work and to be identified as the author of the work, respectively."⁴⁹ Wicomb stages the violent policing of the author's implicitly male paternity right in the anonymous destruction of the entirety of the narrator's work at the novel's close. This final scene might be read as referencing David's well-documented frustrations with the narrator for "taking liberties with the text"⁵⁰ and instead asserting his moral rights against the aforementioned "distortion[s] or mutilation[s]" to the work. Yet, David can no longer make such objections as he has just died by suicide, coerced into the act after finding his name on a hit list produced by the apartheid state. David's violently thwarted claims to literary fatherhood register two historical moments at once: in the waning days of apartheid South Africa, the state maintains its famed control over written materials;⁵¹ meanwhile, on the late twentieth-century world stage, a movement led by Indigenous communities and spreading across the Global South is mounting an increasingly successful challenge to proprietary models of IP.

Searching for Origins: Race, Gender, & Intellectual Property Law

In identifying the legal conditions of literary publication and their frequently gendered and racialized omissions, Wicomb makes a feminist argument about the systemic exploitation of South African women's labor, particularly but not only in relation to their intellectual production and creative work. Throughout *David's Story*, male characters repeatedly requisition women's labor in order to benefit reputationally. During his genealogical research, for instance, David discovers written accounts of Griqua history that historians attribute to nineteenth-century Griqua chief Andrew Le Fleur but which, the narrator explains, are obviously shaped, molded, and formed by his wife, Rachael Susanna Kok. The letters that Le Fleur had produced in prison, where he had been consigned by the British colonial authorities for sedition, are largely incoherent; by contrast, the early writings to which his name is attached, and which were produced while he was living with his wife, are remarkably clear. David assumes that Le Fleur's prison writings had been written in code, arguing that the incomprehensibility of the Griqua chief's late writing is a marker of sophistication. By contrast, the narrator recognizes her own gendered experiences of compositional exploitation in Le Fleur's archive, "explaining that it was possible to speak well and not be able to write, that Rachael may have been responsible for the earlier well-written pieces."[52] Through the differences between how David and the narrator understand these contested Griqua archives, Wicomb recognizes that women's intellectual work has a long history of devaluation in contemporary and colonial South Africa.

In exposing the concealed labor that is frequently involved in producing a copyrightable product, *David's Story* comments on racialized forms of narrative appropriation, especially under apartheid. *David's Story* begins not with David's account of his life but with the narrator's extradiegetic preface, part of a broader set of paratextual material that also includes a fictionalized Griqua family tree. Within a few pages, *David's Story* opens for a second time with a series of reflections that are seemingly unmediated by the narrator and which are likewise focalized not through David but his mother-in-law, Ouma ("grandmother") Sarie. Reflecting on the social and political transformations in "the mos South Africa,"[53] Ouma Sarie boldly enters her former workplace, the Logan Hotel, which she is now permitted to enter as a guest in advance of racial segregation's coming end. Leaving the hotel, Ouma Sarie enters the workers' neighborhood, remembering somewhat fondly the racialized order of her youth, during which she would wear a "smart black dress with white apron and cap — the Logan Hotel always looked well after its staff" and young girls in her neighborhood would wear "the cut-off ends of stockings . . . to flatten their hair."[54] Her activist daughter had worn a stocking for the same purposes, she remembers, but also — she thinks with disgust — to disguise her face while on guerilla missions. Using the stocking as a cipher for racial anxieties as well as a tool for guerilla warfare, Wicomb raises two of this novel's main concerns: the construction of race in the new political dispensation and Black and brown women's simultaneously racialized and gendered labor. If Ouma Sarie metonymically stands in for the prior political order, her daughter represents the demands of anti-apartheid activists and multiracial democracy.

By tracking the narrative's focalizing perspective from Ouma Sarie to Sally, Wicomb indexes both the historical continuities of the kinds of work that are available to racially marginalized women and the elision of Black and Indigenous women's labor under late twentieth-century IP laws. Like Ouma Sarie, the younger generation of women, represented through Sally and Dulcie, find their labor exploited and their dreams curtailed, even as they have gained a greater liberatory consciousness and were actively involved in bringing about apartheid's end. Sally is introduced analeptically during the middle of a successful guerilla mission, her indirect interior monologue revealing both her expertise and her deep commitment to the movement. Just as quickly, the narrative temporality returns to the present, divulging Sally's lost sense of self and purpose after David forces her to stay home to raise their children. Serving somewhat as a foil for Sally, Dulcie's active militarism both indexes and undercuts masculinist ANC narratives that continue to prevail about the resistance movement. David avoids discussing Dulcie when he tells the narrator about his time in uMkhonto weSizwe (MK), consigning his comrade and lover to a ghostly textual presence; despite her many accomplishments, he confesses to seeing her as "a kind of scream echoing through my story."[55] The narrator pushes back against David's minimizing of Dulcie's labor and her professional skill by granting considerable narrative space to what the narrator can only imagine, without David's input, as Dulcie's extraordinary achievements: her leadership and charisma, her humility and grace, and her assault and torture by fellow guerillas at the infamous Quatro camp. For the narrator, David's reticence reveals his feelings of guilt surrounding Dulcie, both for betraying Sally through their affair and for being unable to prevent her torture. But David's inability to render Dulcie as anything more than a scream might also be understood in relation to the logical presuppositions of proprietary IP law. Just as David forces Sally into undertaking the reproductive labor that enables his biographical achievements and their historical significance, and just as he minimizes the narrator's labor in recounting his life during and after his ANC decommissioning, so too does he write Dulcie out of his narrative. Together, Ouma Sarie, Sally, Dulcie, and the narrator all signify the occlusion of women's labor, and especially Black and multiracial women's labor, under late twentieth-century IP regimes.

The forms of labor exploitation that are facilitated by existing IP laws bear racially inequitable consequences not only because legal systems tend to reinforce hegemonic structures of power within a given society but also because colonial regimes and IP law are similarly obsessed with origins. *David's Story* suggests that IP law's insistence upon demarcating origins derives from imperialist ideas about purity that are themselves embedded in capitalist-colonial property law's founding presumptions. As Indigenous challenges have successfully argued, existing IP law allows for unclaimed or collaboratively produced work to be appropriated for profit. Like the fabricated ownership claims of *terra nullius* which European nations used to justify annexing land around the world, IP law demands verifiable ownership in ways that are often fictional and bound up with racially exclusionary sociopolitical systems. Isabel Hofmeyr's analysis of colonial South Africa's copyright regime reveals that, under Britain's Copyright Act (or the Foreign Reprints Act) of 1847, South Africa could, until 1911, import foreign reprints of works that were subject to British copyright as long as a customs duty was paid. In order to ascertain duties, customs officials had to decide where a work's copyright was held; yet, because origins were often hard to identify, they were frequently fabricated. "Once marked as British," Hofmeyr argues, "the book became a 'white' object trailing a racialized copyright, a mode of commoditized whiteness determined by imperial trade."[56] Consequently, Hofmeyr continues, "copyright became construed as one of these forms of inscription — a sign of manufacture, a mark of origin, and a racial trademark — and could ensure a book safe passage."[57] By requiring a mark of origin on all imported goods, and by associating certain origins with security and unmarked origins with danger, colonial South Africa's customs regime shows how copyright is and was sustained through racialized measures of assessment.

Wicomb most obviously exposes the affiliations between origin narratives, authorship, and racial supremacy in the genealogical research with which David fills his time after his post-revolutionary demobilization. Like Wicomb herself, David belongs to the Griqua, an ethnic group that has Khoisan, Malay-Madagascan, and white European heritage. David's efforts at charting his family tree serve not only as a plot device that helps to clarify this novel's complex temporalities but also to register the resurgence of Griqua nationalism at the turn of the twenty-first century. Under the Population Registration Act (1950), the Griqua had been classified as "Coloured," one of the four racial categories established by the ruling National Party, but the overthrowing of apartheid encouraged many people to affirm their distinct ethnic identities. Whereas some Griqua, including the older generation like David's father, still accept the apartheid-era designation because it had ranked them above Black Africans, younger Griqua, as well as guerillas like David, proudly acknowledge their Indigenous ancestry. (Wicomb shares the same ethnicity as David but herself favors recognizing that she is multiply racially and ethnically located by using the term "coloured," with no capitalization, rather than "Griqua.")[58] While David's genealogical endeavors operate as part of a nationwide rejection of white supremacy, they also register a deep association between origin narratives and myths of racial purity. As Brenna M. Munro argues, postapartheid novels like *David's Story* frequently ironize the monoracial, heterosexual reproduction desired by the settler-colonial state even as they deploy the "narrative of the national family" that apartheid's architects and enforcers, the National Party, promoted. Wicomb, in Munro's words, "reconstitut[es]" the trope of the national family as "complex, extended, multiracial, and perhaps dysfunctional."[59] In its fictionalized and factually impossible family tree, *David's Story*'s at once refuses the unitary racial classifications desired by both David and the apartheid state and, at the same time, recognizes — much like IP law's challengers — that new models can emerge out of existing structures.

David's Story uses its paratextual family tree to metonymically confront new as well as old homogenous nationalisms. Sally takes the part of the loyal ANC cadre, criticizing David's plan to visit the city of Kokstad, a Griqua homeland, not only because she suspects that the trip serves as cover for her husband to meet with Dulcie but also because she questions its ideological implications. Sally rejects the racial separatism that she understands Griqua and Afrikaner nationalism to share, declaring: "There's nothing to reclaim. We are what we are, a mixture of this and that, and a good thing too, so we don't have to behave like Boers, eating braaivleis and potjiekos and re-enacting the Great Trek."[60] Sally's reflection on the dangers of trying to identify singular ethnic origins echoes the ANC's position throughout its decades of apartheid resistance even as it mobilizes a critique of what van der Vlies terms "the new nationalism that followed apartheid's demise — a nationalism not necessarily black, but often uncompromising in its unwillingness to countenance the subtleties of a culturally, racially, and linguistically heterogeneous country."[61] In the context of racially singular nationalisms both during and after apartheid, Sally's critique of David's genealogical efforts echoes the narrator's concerns over the exclusions built into models of originary authorship.

Inasmuch as David's genealogical research is at once part of his personal history and a central element of this novel's plot, it functions metonymically to connect Griqua history to questions of authorship. Through David's research, Wicomb relays the repeated nineteenth-century displacements experienced by the Griqua, who established a sequence of small, independent states in what is now South Africa after being displaced by the Boers and then the British. Mobilizing her novel's temporal expansiveness and its flexibility with archival facts, Wicomb introduces nineteenth-century biologist Georges

Cuvier as Andrew Le Fleur's distant relative, suggesting that Cuvier conceived a son, Eduard, with a Huguenot woman, Madame la Fleur, who had settled in South Africa decades before his own birth. Cuvier and Madame la Fleur's temporally impossible relationship, which Dorothy Driver terms a "genealogical fiction,"[62] ironically recognizes Cuvier's significant role in contemporary Griqua land claims. Cuvier infamously dissected Griqua woman Sarah Baartman's body after her death, drew racist conclusions about her anatomy, and donated her remains to the Musée d'Homme (Museum of Man) in Paris. In pickling her brain and genitalia, Cuvier derived information from her body without her permission—on the faulty premise that Black women's physiology correlates to their sexuality—and profited economically and reputationally as a result. As such, he embodies colonial-racial-capitalist approaches to knowledge, in which figures in the Global North, including individuals like Cuvier as well as cultural institutions like the Musée d'Homme, extract knowledge directly from the bodies, lives, and livelihoods of people in the Global South. As WIPO found when it finally began researching the frequently dispossessive effects of globalized IP law, the current regime allows for local knowledge and creative works to be appropriated without obtaining prior informed consent.[63] Baartman's presence in *David's Story* establishes an extended history of African women's exploitation by European men that is also an account of IP theft.

In drawing attention to the compounding effects of racism and sexism on Black and multiracial women, Wicomb recognizes what decolonial challenges to IP law do not: that gender, as well as race and ethnicity, contributes to the inequities of the existing IP regime. Baartman was of renewed interested at the time of Wicomb's writing this novel because of the newly elected ANC's public efforts to repatriate her remains from France. These attempts at repatriation, which finally succeeded two years after *David's Story*'s publication, aimed not only to return home an African woman who had been exploited by white men throughout the decades of her life and for centuries after her death but also to animate the ANC's nation-building project. As cultural theorist Hershini Bhana Young explains, Baartman's return is of particular significance to the Griqua, who reburied her in an elaborate traditional ceremony that both restored her to her homeland and reinforced Griqua land claims after a long history of white colonial annexation. In Young's terms, "Baartman provided a way to consolidate their long unrecognized and complicated identity, their land claims based on that identity, and their place within the new South Africa."[64] Equally, as both Young and Wicomb recognize, male political leaders use Baartman as a source for their own origin narratives. David's desire to trace his Griqua genealogy is prompted by learning about Baartman, whose large buttocks share similarities with Sally's physique and were pathologized by white European men like Cuvier as *steatopygia*. According to the narrator, it is this term, and the female anatomy to which it corresponds, that had inspired David to trace his Griqua ancestry and which therefore "set the story on its course so to speak."[65] By incorporating Baartman into this novel's plot, Wicomb ties what Young terms "the illegibility of (black) will in the historical archive,"[66] and specifically the illegibility of black women's will, to the broader proprietary system of property ownership, including IP law, that was enforced around the world through European colonialism.

Legal Impropriety: South Africa's Indigenous Knowledge Act

Like the other literary works that this book examines, *David's Story* demonstrates that the process of contesting existing laws always also involves formulating more desirable models of legal protection and social relation. In its simultaneous critique of proprietary approaches to narrative production and its aesthetically produced argument for expansive protections for intellectual work Wicomb's novel is paradigmatically aesthetically improper. *David's Story* offers a complex account of how existing IP law both enables and compounds manifold forms of dispossession throughout and in the aftermath of colonial domination; at the same time, like "What the Tapster Saw" and *The Fishermen* in Chapter 1 and *The God of Small Things* in Chapter 2, it contributes to the broader process of producing equitable, sustainable, and just systems of postcolonial legal relation. Just as Okri and Obioma aesthetically establish the same grounds for protesting petroleum extraction as have been established by lawyers and activists in Nigeria and Europe, and just as Roy contests and reworks Indian marriage and inheritance laws on similar grounds as Indian lawyers and activists, so too does *David's Story* aesthetically advance the same arguments for reconfiguring IP law that have been increasingly leveraged in legal and political venues. Like the advocacy groups that have for decades lobbied states and supranational organizations, Indigenous representatives who have attended WIPO conventions, researchers who have published critical accounts of IP law, plaintiffs who have mounted challenges to IP violations, and Indigenous peoples and similarly affected communities who have established databases of their traditional knowledge,[67] *David's Story* participates in the diffuse yet coordinated process of establishing better protections for cultural practices and knowledge across the Global South.

In robustly theorizing the problems with South Africa's IP regime, *David's Story* predates legislative changes by nearly two decades. In 2019, South Africa extended IP protections beyond originality and individuality mandates, and it did so in ways that formalized indigeneity expansively enough to include all Black and brown South African communities that have been harmed by IP law's proprietary predicates. The Protection, Promotion, Development and Management of Indigenous Knowledge Act (2019) expands IP's protective scope to include inherited, intergenerational, and community-based knowledge. Under this statute, Indigenous knowledge receives property protections if it "a) has been passed on from generation to generation within an indigenous community; b) has been developed within an indigenous community; and c) is associated with the cultural and social identity of that indigenous community."[68] Recognizing the colonialist operations of IP law, the Preamble to the Indigenous Knowledge Act expressly ties its demands to "the liberation of South Africa and its people from centuries of racial discriminatory colonial rule and domination."[69] Not surprisingly, given the challenge it poses to legal norms, the Indigenous Knowledge Act has been subject to substantial criticism: detractors variously argue that Indigenous knowledge and cultural expressions do not fit under IP law but instead require sui generis statutes; that they are not adaptable for commercial purposes nor should they be; that the public domain is threatened by the extension of protections to Indigenous knowledge and cultural expressions; and that the Act does not adequately delimit Indigenous community.[70] This latter argument, unlike the others, is compelling: the Indigenous Knowledge Act allows for Afrikaners to claim themselves as an Indigenous group, despite the twinned histories of settler colonialism and apartheid, and their attendant white supremacy, belying any such claim.[71]

Marking a significant development in global debates about IP law's colonial violence, the Indigenous Knowledge Act extends protections beyond originality and individuality, two of IP law's three core tenets (the other being permanence). As Mikalien du Bois explains, South Africa has taken a relatively progressive approach to expanding IP protections. Whereas conservative attitudes toward protecting Indigenous IP seek either to limit expansions to protect the public domain (what du Bois terms the public domain position) or facilitate Indigenous resource use by international corporations (the appropriation position), South Africa is taking the more substantive moral rights position, which allows rights holders to market their cultural or intellectual products. In du Bois's terms, the Indigenous Knowledge Act "provide[s] property rights to the traditional holders of the knowledge and allow[s] them to share in the benefits of intellectual property products which are based on or derived from traditional knowledge."[72] Notably, South Africa's Indigenous Knowledge Act provides fewer protections for oral or ephemeral practices than other recent anti-colonial legislative or policy measures: whereas the precursor to the 2019 Act allowed for "works that [are] capable of substantiation from the collective memory," the final statute removed this provision.[73] In this way, the Indigenous Knowledge Act is much narrower than the Swakopmund Protocol of a decade earlier, which protects knowledge that is "integral to the cultural identity of a local or traditional community" and whose relationship may be "established formally or informally by customary practices, laws or protocols."[74]

Broadly speaking, though, the Indigenous Knowledge Act upholds a similar commitment to intergenerational creativity and intellectual labor as other anti-colonial challenges to IP law that have been established in both legal and literary form. In Ncube's analysis, the expansion of copyright protections to traditional knowledge means that South Africa's majority Black creators can enjoy fair compensation for their labor and products. More than half of South Africa's creative industries are under Black ownership, Ncube explains, and these industries contribute significantly to the country's GDP: "For a country still working to undo the negative effects of apartheid and colonialism, a sector that is dominated by previously disadvantaged persons becomes of critical importance."[75] Legislation like the Indigenous Knowledge Act is one part of a necessary process of revising South African law to both protect and facilitate cultural production by the country's Black communities and other historically marginalized populations.

Accretion: Wicomb's Improper Aesthetics

Like the fullest anti-colonial reworkings of IP law, *David's Story* recognizes that Indigenous and Global South forms of knowledge and cultural expression tend to uphold heritability, so they are not protected under the doctrine of originality; they often involve collaborative production, which typically does not meet the individualist mandate; and they allow for orality and assume that cultural production takes place over generations, so they are not necessarily recorded and made static. Aesthetically and thematically, *David's Story* reveals the limits of globalized IP law as a result of its proprietary, exclusionary tenets. As well as diagnosing similar problems as those that are found in contemporaneous legal and policy debates, *David's Story* also offers similar solutions. *David's Story* upholds the collective and cumulative process by which practices of knowledge and creativity come into being through its aesthetically improper stylistic features. In its nonlinear and multinarrative plot, its complex focalization, its expansive cast of characters, its incorporation of fictional and historical archival materials, and its valuing of orality, *David's Story* models the kind of intergenerational, collaborative, and ephemeral forms of cultural expression for which Indigenous and Global South communities continue to fight for protections. This novel's aesthetic reworkings are not separate from broader sociopolitical conversations or legal developments but instead operate discursively, registering and generating slow changes to structures of thought as part of the similarly slow process of legal transformation.

First, like challenges to South Africa's IP laws that would only take effect nineteen years after this novel's publication, *David's Story* upholds heritability rather than the doctrine of originality, and it does so primarily through its temporally complex plot. Ostensibly set in 1991, this novel's plot takes place over much of South Africa's white supremacist history, from the seventeenth-century arrival of Huguenot settlers in the Cape Colony to the late-twentieth century transition from apartheid to Black sovereignty. Through the narrator's compositional perspective, *David's Story* charts two principal trajectories: on the one hand, David's traumatized emergence from guerilla combat during a period of increased state violence toward freedom fighters; on the other, the development of Griqua national consciousness in the nineteenth-century in response to persecution and land dispossession. In the temporality of the narrative present, *David's Story* charts the titular protagonist's journey to Kokstad to undertake archival research into his Griqua ancestry and recover from mental ill-health. While in Kokstad, David receives notice that both he and Dulcie are on a paramilitary hit list. Through this plot detail as well as through the novel's narrative construction, Wicomb connects the late-apartheid state's frenzied vengeance against militants to the psychological workings of trauma,[76] whereby historical experience resurfaces in the present to inflict harm. David's research into his family tree also facilitates this novel's parallel plotting of the Griqua's repeated land displacement at the hands first of the British and then the Boers. Like *David's Story*'s contemporary trio, its historical characters also fought for freedom in the face of racist oppression: these figures include Chief Adam Kok III who, in the 1860s, led the Griqua on a two-year trek east after they had been forced off their land; his indirect descendant, Adam Muis Kok, who led a rebellion against the British in 1878; and Chief Andrew Le Fleur, who led the Griqua through the end of British colonial rule into the rise of Afrikaner separatism, and whom the narrator credits with producing much of what has been hailed as his writings

While these two chronologies are important for this novel's assessment of nationalism, dispossession, and freedom, their linear movement is substantially concealed, and in this way, *David's Story* undermines proprietary IP law's insistence that a work's origins can always be accurately located and claimed. In Wicomb's dense novel, the temporal moment shifts frequently, moving regularly between the historical late-eighteenth and early-nineteenth century of the Cape Colony, the mid- to late-nineteenth century of the Griqua archives, the recent history of apartheid resistance in the 1980s and 1990s, the similarly recent history of demobilization on the cusp of multiracial democracy, and the extradiegetic present of this narrative's construction. While it is easy for a reader to feel lost in these multiple temporalities, distinct but submerged plots, and extradiegetic narration, Wicomb facilitates comprehension by linking her episodes associationally rather than chronologically. These associational connections enable understanding while maintaining an expansive — or improper— compositional arrangement. *David's Story* employs many recurrent motifs that serve to connect the narrative across time and space: examples include the pantyhose that both Griqua and militant women wear on their heads (and which echoes the caul with which Andrew Le Fleur was born); the figure of the so-called amanuensis, comprising the narrator (for David), Rachael Susanna Kok (for Andrew le Fleur), and Lady Kok (wife of Adam Kok III), as well as the numerous other women, like Sally, who "ventriloquize" for men;[77] and the many newspaper cuttings of both past and present. Beyond enabling comprehension, these motifs function to chart an alternate way of making sense of the world, whether within this novel or outside it. By connecting South Africa's past and present through recurrent tropes like the pantyhose, amanuensis, and newspaper cuttings, Wicomb rejects the totalizing thrust of origin narratives and their demand for narrative or racial purity, instead demonstrating, through her non-chronological plot, the viability and desirability of understanding our place in the world as always multiply connected.

What's more, in its challenge to IP law's insistence that a work's origins can and must always be accurately located and claimed, *David's Story* similarly undermines the racial and cultural supremacy of colonial rule, and yet it does so while recognizing the risks of a postcolonial polity, like postapartheid South Africa, lauding homogeneity. By telling two stories at once — by offering accounts of both militant demobilization at the cusp of multiracial democracy and the Griqua's endurance against white supremacy in the preceding century — *David's Story* takes up the genre of the postcolonial epic while troubling its faith in new beginnings. Wicomb stylistically and thematically references James Joyce's national epic *Ulysses*, which is similarly set at the dawn of independence after centuries of colonial rule and which likewise engages with property, whether in terms of copyright law, as Paul Saint-Amour has argued, or inheritance, as Ravit Reichman contends.[78] Both *Ulysses* and *David's Story* are committed to literature's radical potential, as the narrator of Wicomb's novel excitedly explains: "Youth Day — Soweto Day, the sixteenth of June — that's also Joyce's Bloomsday . . . Day of the Revolution of the Word. Imagine, black children revolting against Afrikaans, the language of oppressors, on the very anniversary of the day that Leopold Bloom started with a hearty breakfast."[79] Yet, Wicomb improperly undercuts the epic's claims to narrate an origin story, even as she recognizes the historic significance of apartheid's end. Her own novel starts fitfully: first with a pictorial family tree, which connects a largely factual account of nineteenth- and twentieth-century Griqua ruling families to the obviously fictional David; then with a preface, albeit one that is focalized not through the copyrighted author, Wicomb, but through the unnamed narrator; then with an introduction to Sally by way of her mother, whose recollection of her daughter's birth offers a female family tree that counters the opening image; and finally with David himself, or Comrade Dadzo, as he was known while serving in MK. These faltering starts are at once decried and endorsed by the narrator, who observes, after Ouma Sarie's introductory musings: "This is no place to start. But let us not claim a beginning for this mixed-up tale. Beginnings are too redolent of origins."[80] Through these four separate openings, which affirm a logic of impropriety or constitutive openness by offering multiple ways into this novel's world, Wicomb establishes an aesthetic challenge to the white supremacist belief in narrativizing racialized origins, as well as to the demand made by most IP laws for clearly demarcated origins if a creative work is to receive protections against appropriation.

David's Story's accretive plotting likewise affirms the second tenet of Indigenous and Global South challenges to IP law: that cultural and knowledge production often develops through collaboration rather than being the product of a sole individual. In its vast historical sweep, and in shifting its narrative focalization every few pages if not every few lines, this novel aesthetically recognizes the Indigenous legal position that knowledge and narratives are often produced collaboratively rather than originating with a single author. Through the metafictional device of the narrator as an unnamed amanuensis, Wicomb facilitates multiple and variable focalization, allowing the narrator to at once comment on the diegetic conditions of this narrative's fictional production and observe the actions of a huge cast of characters. This novel's sophisticated use of free indirect discourse likewise pushes back against IP law's individualist mandate. Describing Dulcie's regular torture, at night in her home, the narration is first omniscient and then profoundly intimate:

> The men in balaclavas come like privileged guests into her bedroom, in the early hours, always entering the house by different routes, ridiculing her reinforced bolts and locks, the secret code of her Securilarm system. She wakes up and with every sense aquiver, mentally

follows them over the fence, along the garden path, through the chosen window. . . . Now they come without a sound, but the singing in the bridge of her nose precedes conscious knowledge of their arrival.[81]

The shift into Dulcie's consciousness, as she awakes "with every sense aquiver," registers not only the capacity for skillful narrative technique to evoke distinct characters' affective and cognitive experiences but also the ethical necessity of this process. Typically, postapartheid ethics are understood within the framework of trauma: the difficulty of telling stories about other people's suffering; the raced and gendered dynamics that complicate storytelling in a region emerging from centuries of oppression; and the power of stories in facilitating healing.[82] Even as these accounts of narrative ethics are vital, and even as they are legible, too, in *David's Story*, Wicomb's aesthetic strategies also invoke the collective and ephemeral conditions of narrative production.

David's Story challenges the individualist propertization of narrative even at the smallest aesthetic scale, refusing the type of punctuation whose legal history is directly tied to Anglo-American practices of enclosure and proprietary ownership. Quotation marks once signaled the parts of a text that were considered common to all; as Margreta de Grazia explains, in medieval and early modern manuscripts, they "pointed to or indicated an authoritative saying like a proverb, commonplace, or statement of consensual truth."[83] Over the course of the eighteenth century, however, and during the same period as the propertization of copyright, quotation marks underwent a significant transformation. With the cementing of copyright's proprietary conceptual structure and juridical form, they became a way to register private ownership over individually produced language: that is, to enclose words within a textual fence or boundary marker. By the late eighteenth century, legal doctrine and literary practice had aligned to "reconceptualiz[e] language as a discursive field capable of being portioned into assignable private tracts or lots over which proprietary and usufructuary rights prevail."[84] Quotation marks' textual history, in other words, materially aligns with copyright's juridical history.

Wicomb's decision to not use quotation marks sustains her critique of the colonialist, white supremacist consequences of eighteenth-century Britain's models of individualist ownership. As both *David's Story* and archival documents reveal, apartheid's separatist logic of racially exclusionary territorial sovereignty was also endorsed by Le Fleur in his later years. In a scene that is recounted by a horrified Rachael and mediated through the narrator (and presented in Wicomb's novel without the quotation marks that this chapter is legally required to include), Le Fleur declares to a Griqua crowd: "Here good people, is the solution for God's stepchildren: absolute separation. From white and from black. We shall have our own territory, land in which we as a people can live and develop separately. Let us work together as one nation in our own homeland."[85] Affirming Rachael's narrated distress at her husband's racial separatism, *David's Story* renounces Le Fleur's political philosophy of "absolute separation" that he shared with apartheid's early architects, including the Union of South Africa's first prime minister, Louis Botha. Wicomb identifies the convergence of Afrikaner and Griqua nationalisms in the plot device of Le Fleur's ostensibly having written to Botha about his ideas, his letters apparently going unanswered only because "that great politician was too busy thinking up good, workable schemes for relieving real black people of the burden of land, so that only after three years in office did he pass the Natives' Land Act."[86] By registering speech without quotation marks, whose legal and grammatical history reveals the development of capitalist-colonialist property ownership, Wicomb also rejects the proprietary logic that underpins the apartheid policy of separate homelands for separate races.

Just as this novel refuses individualist ownership through its lack of quotation marks, so too does it recognize, through its mediated narration, that many creative or intellectual works are collectively produced and that women's labor in these collaborative endeavors often remains unacknowledged. The narrator and her predecessor, Rachael Susanna Kok, provide the narrative cohesion that is demanded by Griqua men who ignore the extent of their labor and dismiss the skillfulness of their contributions. Whereas the male characters see the women as scribes, Rachael and the narrator recognize their work as at once collaborative and cumulative, much like Indigenous challenges to IP law. In Kenya's Protection of Traditional Knowledge and Traditional Cultural Expressions Act (2016), for instance, works are protected "if the traditional cultural expressions are the products of creative and cumulative intellectual activity, such as collective creativity or individual creativity where the identity of the individual is unknown."[87] In this vein, Rachael Susanna Kok's and the narrator's compositional work is cumulative not only because it is produced in collaboration with their male counterparts but also because it builds on the work of previous generations. The narrator inherits Rachael's role and both women construct a Griqua history that gains its meaning accretively over time.

In demanding that their work be recognized, Rachael and the narrator do not make claims for individualist ownership. Instead, they resist the extraction of their intellectual resources and exploitation of their labor. Both characters know how easy it is for their creative output to be stolen; David even plagiarizes Dulcie when he finally tells his family of his resistance work after she has appeared at a public meeting to recruit supporters: "The atmosphere in the school hall was electric. Her words, of course, but then Ant Mietjie was hardly likely to question him on a matter of style, indeed, hardly likely to know that they were hers, the new woman's — Dulcie's — words."[88] Wicomb's accretive aesthetic strategies — including her lack of quotation marks, slippery focalization, and multiply compounded sentences — serve to reject David's act of appropriation, and the nominal protagonist finds himself consumed by Dulcie's words: "from his own mouth, wrapping themselves around his own tongue, her words came tumbling into the old-fashioned house to perch on the things he had known all his life."[89] Wicomb stages the accretional process of knowledge production through Dulcie's words being heard by David, reconstructed by the narrator, and ultimately taking up place in Ant Mietjie's home. In affirming the moral position that men should stop claiming women's intellectual labor as their own, Wicomb does not accede to masculinist appropriation but moves beyond the logic of possession, demanding an alternate method of knowledge protection to that of IP law: one that is normatively improper in that it accepts and enables accretive collaboration.

It is in *David's Story*'s insistence on the ephemerality of collaborative knowledge that is created over time and across generations that it rebuts IP law's third stipulation: that an individually or jointly authored work must exist in recorded form in order for it to reveal its requisite origins and be worthy of protections. Tertia Behari and Tshepo Shabangu explain that one of South Africa's issues in developing the Indigenous Knowledge Act was that "it is very difficult, if not impossible, to identify an author in the case of traditional works as such works have been preserved and passed on from generation to generation, with the result that the author is usually unknown."[90] Similarly, Justin Hughes argues that "the intergenerational premise of [Indigenous Knowledge] means that we will also have to resolve a question that labor theory does not usually confront: who is the *laborer* across time?"[91] This legal problem of authorial knowability and cross-temporal labor is addressed in Wicomb's novel, just as it is in Indigenous and Global South communities, by recognizing collectively produced, ephemeral narratives as equally worthy of protection as their singularly claimed, permanently recorded variants. The narrator constructs much of David's story through archival materials: their collaboration begins when he arrives at her home "with fragments of Le Fleur's writings, a faded copy of *Griqua and Coloured People's Opinion* as well as photocopies of several dense, poorly typed or handwritten pages."[92] Much of the labor of collecting and archiving nineteenth-century Griqua materials is attributed to Rachael: she spent her evenings "reading the *Kokstad Advertiser* in lamplight," collecting "the vulgar writings of the Reverend Dower . . . ; the devious arguments against retrocession; or the vicious misrepresentation of Andrew's words and actions. These were her task to collect and relay to her good man."⁹³ While "the task of collecting and filing struck her as an odd thing to do," she dutifully clips newspaper reports on Griqua demands for sovereignty, including the *Eastern Province Herald*'s reporting on Andrew's arrest for sedition.⁹⁴ In selecting stories that seem relevant, Rachael shapes the historical narrative about the Griqua as a cultural and political body; she does so, moreover, by building on existing stories just as the narrator in turn builds on Rachael's archived cuttings. While Chief Le Fleur understands his wife to be merely following his orders and collecting stories written by other people — to be completing her "task" for her "good man" — Wicomb recognizes that Rachael's curatorial activities are part of a larger collective project of producing a historical narrative and shaping how we understand South Africa's past and present.

Wicomb is as interested in orality as in material culture, and these oral narratives provide the narrator with the bulk of her material, including meetings with David, reports of his formal and informal interviews in Kokstad, and family lore passed down through generations. Indeed, much of what David knows about the Griqua, and about his own Griqua identity, comes from listening to his Ouma Ragel as a child. It is Ragel who tells David about the economic hardships of her youth and about Le Fleur's attempts to make the Griqua prosperous despite centuries of dispossession and their displacement onto arid land. Through Ragel's stories, mediated as they are through David, the narrator concludes that David is descended from Le Fleur, who, despite being married to Rachael, seems to have conceived Ragel with David's great-grandmother Antjie. (Like David's desired narratorial process, and in a similarly fictional manner, Le Fleur fathered Ragel at a distance.) Some of David's most significant findings in Kokstad come not from the archives but from oral interviews, especially with people of his Ouma Ragel's generation, including a woman named Ouma Rhodes who recalls one of Le Fleur's slogans just moments before she dies: "East Griqualand for the Griquas and the Natives! That's it, she says."⁹⁵ As Ouma Rhodes's statement was not immediately recorded, and because her death means it cannot be verified, this significant detail about Griqua life under Le Fleur's leadership is ephemeral and part only of collective memory. Yet, Le Fleur's slogan — which is spoken by Ouma Rhodes, repeated by David, and written down by the narrator — forms a crucial part of Griqua oral history. Above all, this slogan helps to establish the Griqua as a cohesive ethnic group, which is required for making corresponding land claims in the postapartheid state after a history of colonial dispossession.⁹⁶

The necessity of not only protecting exploited people's labor and intellectual resources but also recognizing collective and ephemeral narratives that accrete over time as similarly worthy of protection underpins both *David's Story* and anti-colonial challenges to IP law. The narrator's telling of David's story, while ostensibly built from scraps of paper and oral interviews, more broadly recounts orally transmitted Indigenous knowledge. As Rachael explains to Andrew: "[W]hat do we know of our [Khoisan] ancestors?... Only that which is passed down by word of mouth, for there was no one to record those momentous times."[97] Wicomb does not romanticize Indigeneity; she cannot be read in an uncomplicated way as simply upholding Indigenous IP rights.[98] For instance, in the fictional story of the Rain Sisters, a group of women whom Le Fleur commands to undertake a pilgrimage to make the rains come, Wicomb reveals her skepticism about Griqua claims to Indigenous heritage, at least when these claims are built upon troubling assertions of racial and cultural purity.[99] Whereas Le Fleur argues, according to the narrator, that his theory of "radical moisture" that underpins the Rain Sisters' pilgrimage is a "memory of a lapsed tradition,"[100] the narrator points out (incorrectly — a joke that confirms Wicomb's taste for irony) that this concept comes from Laurence Sterne's eighteenth-century novel, *A Sentimental Journey through France and Italy*, which Le Fleur had heard passed down in oral stories from his grandfather Eduard la Fleur — himself a character in Sterne's *Tristram Shandy*.[101] In remaining exceedingly skeptical of origin narratives, *David's Story* offers a challenge to those exclusionary accounts of racialization that have inflicted such violence in what is now South Africa, as well as to the IP laws which, as Indigenous activists have likewise demonstrated, facilitate ongoing racialized dispossession.

Preceding the Law: On the Aesthetic's Sense-Making Capacities

David's Story offers a clear example of how literary works discursively engage in the same kinds of transformational processes that are ordinarily understood to be law's domain. Wicomb's accretive aesthetics not only share the temporality of recent legislative changes but they also aesthetically encode the same commitments to collectivity, heritability, and ephemerality as South Africa's Indigenous Knowledge Act (2019). As this chapter has established, *David's Story* significantly precedes not only the Indigenous Knowledge Act but also the state's very first discussions about protecting Indigenous knowledge and culture. The ponderous pace of anti-colonial reforms to South African IP law, which themselves came on the back of decades of sustained anti-imperialist work, mainly by Indigenous peoples but also by postcolonial nations including Tunisia and India, demonstrates that changing the legal landscape is frequently slow and laborious. While legal scholarship has reasonably suggested that the anti-colonial process of restructuring IP law has taken place solely in the legal or political domain, *David's Story* suggests that creative writers also engage in the discursive process of critiquing and reformulating the law. As this novel's publication history suggests, the epistemological change that is both a precondition for legal transformation and intrinsically part of the same process necessarily also occurs in extralegal venues, including in literary works and their engagement by readers and critics.

To recognize both legal activities and literary work as participating only slowly in producing social change is to acknowledge that emerging practices unfurl over time and space: that the law is as accretive as Wicomb's aesthetics. The process by which structures of thought gradually shift and take shape can be identified aesthetically and these emerging logics themselves take an aesthetic form. For Jacques Rancière, as this book's Introduction discussed, politics is aesthetic because of how it organizes space and distributes subjects. Law, too, is similarly predicated on organization and distribution; in its mandate to fairly organize social systems and distribute justice, the law is also aesthetic. The process of forming new laws and legal ideas in response to changing social demands is effectively one of redistributing component parts: of adapting law's constitutive shape. Or, to put this another way, the complex and extended process of transforming the laws that structure our daily lives is necessarily aesthetic, as it involves changing the relationships between a given area of law's constitutive parts. Understanding legal systems as aesthetic is illuminating as well as liberatory: illuminating because recognizing specific areas of law, like IP law, as arranging space in particular ways clarifies their subtending logics; and liberatory because being able to identify those logics makes it easier to see their failures and recognize possible modes of transformation.

In the narrator's self-confessed "weakness for patterns,"[102] Wicomb recognizes the aesthetic object's capacity to construct meaning. While David and Sally both see reading as frivolous and as detached from their work as revolutionaries, the narrator understands the aesthetic's powerful potential. According to the narrator, "David knows nothing of the art of inferencing,"[103] but the narrator, like Wicomb, understands just how much can be deduced from aesthetic forms. Inferencing is itself a basic facet of legal practice, one that is fundamental to building a case and achieving justice and one that involves deducing logical consequences from presented facts. As I have argued in this chapter, the aesthetic contours of a legal regime (like IP law) or a literary text (like *David's Story*) contribute to producing a given set of principles, laws, and logics that structure our daily lives. These logics gain their power over time; their strength comes from the cumulative nature of their repetition. In other words, like the Indigenous Knowledge Act, which came into being between

1996 and 2019, Wicomb recognizes what David cannot: "how truth, far from being ready-made, takes time to be born, slowly takes shape in the very act of repetition" (103). Legal reforms similarly "tak[e] time to be born"; they, and the new structures of thought that they represent, "tak[e] shape in the very act of repetition."[104]

Unlike David, then, who argues that "aesthetics . . . should be left to the so-called artists, to the writers and readers of fiction,"[105] this chapter contends that aesthetics cannot be separated from the social world in which they operate: that they absolutely should not be left to readers, writers, and artists. David's proprietary demands over the narrative that bears his name derive from his refusal to acknowledge its collective shaping and his desire to lay claim to it all himself. And yet, David's refusal offers a cautionary tale. Just because lines of creative or intellectual influence are difficult to identify, *David's Story* contends, does not mean that they should be denied or that art or knowledge should be devalued as a result. The current proprietary model of IP law entails many exclusions, particularly along racialized, colonial, and gendered lines. The improper, accretive methods of protecting Indigenous and other collectively, intergenerationally, or ephemerally produced art and knowledge that are theorized in both *David's Story* and anti-colonial challenges to IP law provide more accurate, more inclusionary ways of honoring other people's work.

4
Dispersal
Admiralty Law and Raising the Dead

Whereas prior chapters of this book have examined various types of extant property law alongside contemporary literary works, this chapter addresses not current legislation but historical legal regimes and their ongoing shaping of the present. Having begun this book's narrative arc by analyzing in-process litigation that seeks recompense for the multinational petroleum industry's infliction of environmental and human harms in the Niger Delta, I end by turning to the ex post facto case of mid-Atlantic murder and sexual assault that M. NourbeSe Philip outlines in her 2008 epic poem *Zong!*. One way of reading *Aesthetic Impropriety*'s analytic trajectory, then, is of its moving from the present into the past. As this chapter reveals, the infamous 1781 *Zong* massacre was made possible not by exclusions that were built into maritime insurance law, as analyses of both the event and Philip's rendition of it typically contend, but by a doctrine that developed in the earlier field of admiralty law, as legal historians have demonstrated. Yet, considered in terms of impropriety's propulsive capacities, another, quite different way of reading this book's narrative trajectory is of its traveling from the present into the future. Analyzing Philip's dispersively improper aesthetics, this chapter argues that *Zong!* breaks apart English admiralty law's enabling logic of racial propertization to make space for the dead to rise. Engaging in an act of legal restitution, Philip breathes figurative life into the raised spirits of the *Zong* massacre and introduces the possibility of a new legal doctrine: that legal personality might be granted to ghosts.

Philip's poem participates in a wave of renewed literary and historicist attention to an infamous 1781 massacre on board the British slave ship *Zong*, during which the ship's English captain, Luke Collingwood, ordered his crew to throw 150 enslaved Africans to their deaths as if they were spoiled and damaged goods.¹ Adhering to the logic of what Katherine McKittrick terms the "mathematics of black life,"² Collingwood made the lawful but horrific calculation that because the enslaved Africans were chattel and lacked legal personality, they could be discarded in order to save the rest of the ship's crew and human cargo. After a voyage that had taken five weeks longer than average,³ the ship's rations were substantially depleted; consequently, the enslaved Africans on board the Zong would be so emaciated upon arrival in Jamaica that they would command lower prices than would typically be expected if they were sold at market. In a bloody and heartless calculation, Collingwood decided to throw the most infirm captives overboard to increase the ratio of remaining supplies per person, making the rest of the journey more comfortable for the approximately ten European crew on board and providing more rations for the 200 Africans who would remain.⁴ Most significantly, Collingwood's direction would allow the Zong's owners, William Gregson and partners, to file an insurance claim for the drowned victims under the maritime insurance clause of goods lost to the perils of the sea. As Collingwood knew, maritime insurance policies covered enslaved people at £30 each, which is more than would be received by selling malnourished or sick people at market, so Collingwood's navigational errors would not cause his employers to lose profits.⁵

Zong! is a scathing critique of both the 1781 massacre and the subsequent Gregson v. Gilbert case, which assessed whether the insurance underwriter, Thomas Gilbert, owed insurance monies to the Gregson syndicate for goods lost to the perils of the sea — for throwing living people to their deaths. Zong! condemns the enslaved victims' transformation into commodities to be bought, assaulted, murdered, and sold; the stripping away of their legal personalities in order to accrue inordinate wealth for slave traders in particular and Britain more generally; and the significant role played by English law in authorizing the slave trade's incalculable cruelties. Not surprisingly, most readings of Zong! are deeply attentive to its poetic denunciation of both chattel slavery and English law. Critics recognize Philip as variously condemning legal discourse and the law's "ostensibly rational terms" that enable and sanction extreme violence;⁶ as denouncing "the differential distribution of personhood imposed by the law" whereby enslaved people broadly lacked legal personality;⁷ and as "expos[ing] the limitations of the law in protecting human flourishing" by causing harm rather than achieving justice.⁸ These analyses of Zong! are all correct, and yet they also "reinforc[e] what has been a common view for law and literature scholars: that law primarily demands censure and critique."⁹ In recognizing as unjust the eighteenth-century English laws that permitted slavery, many accounts of Zong! end up suggesting that law, in general, is irredeemably harmful. As Elizabeth Anker cautions, scholarship that engages with literary explorations of legal questions, like those that are raised in Zong!, risks positing literature as a domain that can grant a belated if insufficient form of justice that the law necessarily always precludes. As this book has shown, however, the law can be a space for justice, however limited and circumscribed.

Certainly, racial justice remains an urgent need in the enduring temporalities of colonial racial capitalism and in chattel slavery's wake. A significant body of scholarship confirms that the regime that sanctioned chattel slavery and negated enslaved people's legal personhood continues to shape Black life to this day. While Zong! is an account of a historical massacre, it is also a record of colonial racial capitalism's enduring consequences, whether in routine police brutality in North America and Western Europe, as Laurie Lambert notices in response to an oral performance of "Zong! #15,"[10] or in migrant drownings in the Mediterranean Sea, among many other forms of globalized anti-Blackness, as Christina Sharpe identifies in her groundbreaking study In the Wake: On Blackness and Being.[11] For Sharpe, the consequences of systemic anti-Black racism can be usefully identified through her concept of "the wake," an expansive term that at once denotes the process by which "the past that is not past reappears, always, to rupture the present," "the unfinished project of emancipation," and "[a] frame of and for living blackness in the diaspora in the still unfolding aftermaths of Atlantic chattel slavery."[12] Sharpe describes "wake work" as both a method of critique and an affirmative practice: as "a mode of inhabiting *and* rupturing this episteme with our known lived and un/imaginable lives."[13] Tiffany Lethabo King engages in a similar process of simultaneous denunciation and transformation in The Black Shoals, both in the analytic category of the shoal and the concept of fungibility that she extends from Saidiya Hartman. Analyzing Black and Indigenous dehumanization under liberal humanism, King argues that "Black fungibility — rather than Black labor — represents the unfettered use of Black bodies for the self-actualization of the human and for the attendant humanist project of the production and expansion of space."[14] For King, fungibility indexes the wholesale propertization of Black and Indigenous peoples' lives, well beyond the remit of capital and its concomitant logics of property and labor, to produce a regime of white cultural ascendency. At the same time, King notes, fungibility offers a conceptual tool for disrupting modern liberal humanism's ongoing shaping of the present. Sharpe's and King's respective analytic frameworks operate similarly to my paired concepts of property and impropriety, in that they simultaneously register constraint and possibility, violence and hope. Impropriety, like wake work and fungibility, identifies at once a system of extreme historical violence that endures into the present and a conceptual method for envisaging and producing a contradistinctively better future.

Examined through the lens of aesthetic impropriety, *Zong!* offers a more constructive response to the massacre than can be sustained through mere critique. In a much-discussed literary technique, Philip disassembles the text of the short, two-paged *Gregson v. Gilbert* decision and builds the entirety of her text upon its words, whether they appear in full, are rearranged into anagrams, or broken into phonemes. This process of first taking apart an extant text and its underpinning logics, then reassembling its pieces into a new structure that fundamentally contradicts the prior system, exemplifies the improper aesthetic strategies that this book has identified in work by Ben Okri, Chigozie Obioma, Arundhati Roy, and Zoë Wicomb. Philip's impropriety takes the form of dispersal: graphically and sonically stretching letters across the page; visually separating and spreading words into new phonemes; scattering prepositions that register possession; fully displacing possessive apostrophes; and integrating negative space into the body of her poem through innovative lineation. By dispersing the logic of racial propertization that is evidenced in the Gregson v. Gilbert decision and which derives from admiralty case law, Philip clears visual, conceptual, and juridical space for Collingwood and company's long-dead victims. In an extended process of incantation, Philip reanimates the dead, making use of this poem's dispersed text to increasingly introduce the breathiness of aspiration, egression, and enunciation into her extended work. Drawing implicitly on Virgil's *The Aeneid* as well as on elegiac poetry, Philip rewrites this English tragedy as a Black epic, raising the dead in an act of mourning that is also an act of legal restitution.

It is through this poem's aesthetic dispersal and its extended act of mournful yet generative incantation that Philip breathes life into the victims of the Zong massacre, granting their ghosts legal personality that might have standing to file suit for sexual assault and murder. Philip's process of aesthetic resurrection and her conferral of spectral personality is not entirely without precedent: the Anglo-American legal system has long made space for ghosts, as both English and U.S. case law reveals, so bestowing personhood on spectral beings should be understood as more than an act of imaginative significance. In opening up imaginative space to not only mourn the dead but also demand redress, *Zong!* prefigures the forms of justice that might yet be established in an English court. If prior chapters of *Aesthetic Impropriety* have shown the extent to which literary works can shape the legal imagination, this chapter argues that Philip's granting of legal personality to the dead makes thinkable a novel, ex post facto lawsuit with Collingwood's victims as its spectral litigants.

Admiralty Law and Racial Propertization

In the extensive welcome return to assessing the *Zong* massacre's causes and consequences, historians have consistently addressed the role played by maritime insurance in enabling Collingwood and his crew's act of calculated mass murder.[15] Analyses of Philip's poetic account of the tragedy typically frame Collingwood's actions and the ensuing court case in relation to maritime insurance, which both sustained and derived riches from the industry of enslavement.[16] Offering a much-needed process of historical reckoning, historians and legal scholars have revealed how important the system of underwriting financial risk was to enabling chattel slavery and the extensive triangular trade that operated across the Atlantic.[17] Such scholarship has been vital for calling to account wealthy financial institutions that benefited economically from chattel slavery and made trading in enslaved Black people a lucrative industry. In the aftermath of research into the financing of chattel slavery, companies including Lloyds of London, Barclays Bank, and the Bank of England have been forced to publicly acknowledge their financial involvement in the centuries-long trade,[18] while cultural institutions such as Britain's National Trust have been compelled to acknowledge that many of their large estates were built only because their original owners enslaved Africans and people of African descent in the Caribbean.[19] Philip's work acknowledges the extent to which the insurance industry, in particular, made the *Zong* massacre possible, and *Zong!* makes explicit the wealth amassed in Britain by those who enslaved people in the Americas. Ian Baucom's magisterial *Specters of the Atlantic: Finance Capital, Slavery, and the Philosophy of History* develops an extended analysis of the speculative financial system that provided the *Zong* massacre's conditions of possibility. Subsequent analyses of *Zong!* routinely draw attention to insurance law, likely due not only to excellent existing research but also because this is the reading that Philip provides in her own afterword, or "Notanda." And yet, as this chapter reveals, it was, in fact, seventeenth-century admiralty law that made it possible for white British sailors like Luke Collingwood — and for slave traders like the Gregson syndicate, and insurance providers like Gilbert and company — to see enslaved Black people as commodities that could legally be considered goods lost to the perils of the sea and could therefore be disposed of as if they were spoiled grain or beef. It was admiralty law that effectively codified slavery as legal in England.

When English admiralty law expanded significantly in the mid-seventeenth century, it was to protect the nation's growing empire, which was being built upon chattel slavery and the goods that enslaved people were forced to produce in the Americas. Admiralty law had operated in England from at least 1340, established by royal prerogative and finessed through statute, and it served throughout the fourteenth and fifteenth centuries as a frequently inadequate check on piracy and privateering and as a way to forestall European contests over territorial expansion.[20] In the sixteenth century, under Henry VIII, the admiralty court gained greater adjudicatory powers and methods for civil restitution and criminal justice,[21] and by the seventeenth century, with jurisdiction over international waters, this now robust area of law both facilitated and bolstered the rapid growth of England's violently mercantilist colonial empire. As Renisa Mawani argues in her groundbreaking analysis of the ship as a racialized juridical form, seventeenth-century English admiralty law built a substantial legal arsenal in order to advantageously adjudicate disputes at sea: these measures included English statutes, international treaties, industry regulations, and bestowing legal personality upon ships in order to more clearly demarcate a nation's jurisdictional powers in the legally uncharted space of the seas. England's "new legal mechanisms would address the pressures of maritime commerce and imperial expansion," Mawani explains, "including piracy, prizes, contracts, liens, and eventually slavery."[22] Just as Hugo Grotius's field-defining treatise *Mare Liberum*, or *The Free Sea* (1609), drew upon the law of nations and the law of nature to vest the sea with legal standing, so English admiralty law "transformed oceans into juridical spaces"[23] by bestowing legal personality upon ships, a process that would help control piracy, assert maritime prowess, and maintain primacy in the lucrative and growing business of forcibly transporting enslaved people across the Atlantic.

One of the earliest mechanisms that England employed in its efforts to establish legal jurisdiction at sea and global economic dominance were the Navigation Acts of the 1650s: the acts that first articulated Britain's growing trade in enslaved people. Africanist legal scholar V. C. D. Mtubani explains that in their "strict, monopolistic, mercantilist principles," the Navigation Acts "demanded that all goods for trade should be carried by English ships. The problem was whether African slaves should be regarded as goods in conformity with the Navigation Acts regulating maritime trade."[24] In an era of rapid imperial expansion and intense competition with the Dutch, the Navigation Acts sought to protect England's colonial enterprise by strictly controlling entry of foreign goods into the country and its territories. The first such law, An Act for Increase of Shipping, and Encouragement of the Navigation of this Nation, signed by Oliver Cromwell on October 9, 1651, stipulates:

> No Goods or Commodities whatsoever, of the Growth, Production or Manufacture of Asia, Africa or America, or of any part thereof; . . . as

well of the English Plantations as others, shall be Imported or brought into this Commonwealth of England, or into Ireland . . . but onely [sic] in such as do truly and without fraud belong onely [sic] to the People of this Commonwealth, or the Plantations thereof.[25]

In tying property to nationality, and "Goods or Commodities" to that which does "truly and without fraud belong onely to the People of this Commonwealth, or the Plantations thereof," the Navigation Acts articulated the significance of property ownership to imperial expansion. As Susan Staves identifies in her overview of chattel property's relationship to nation-building, "'England' and 'Englishness' were themselves invented through rules of ownership and through the state's use of rules of ownership to project and to enforce certain ideas of desirable Englishness."[26] From the start, capitalist-colonialist expansion operated by enacting strict customs controls that limited trading operations to English citizens and enforced rigid national boundaries in the fluid space of the sea.

The Navigation Acts' ethnonationalism implicitly introduces the racial calculus that transfigured Black Africans into forms of property. Twenty-five years after the first Navigation Act, and under significant pressure from merchants, jurists clarified the racialized scope of the Navigation Acts' "Goods or Commodities," first in the common-law suit *Butts v. Penny* (1677) and, a month later, in a judicial opinion from the solicitor general. In *Butts v. Penny* (1677), a trover case to recover the value of damage to personal property, the King's Bench returned to the ethnonationalist, empire-building mercantilism of the Navigation Acts to adjudicate whether enslaved Africans constituted commodities under the law. The suit was brought by a slave trader, Thomas Butts, who was employed by the Royal African Company and who sought compensation for the alleged theft of enslaved people over whom he claimed ownership. The case hinged not on the question of whether the defendant, a Barbadian enslaver by the last name of Penny, had taken the enslaved people whom Butts claimed as his own, but on their ontological status: if, as Butts averred, they were chattel, he could claim compensation for lost property; if they had legal personality, he could not. Sir Creswell Levinz's report summarizing the case recounts: "the Court held, that *negroes* being usually bought and sold among merchants, as merchandise, and also being infidels, there might be a property in them sufficient to maintain trover."[27] In other words, Butts was entitled to compensation, or trover, for the wrongful taking of his personal possessions. The following month, on July 17, 1677, Solicitor General Sir Francis Winnington similarly opined that "negroes ought to be esteemed goods and commodities within the Acts of Trade and Navigation, and so it hath been admited [sic] upon debate before the Lords Committees of Plantations."[28] While slavery had been found illegal in England during the Cartwright case of 1569, as scholarship commonly identifies, both *Butts v. Penny* and the solicitor general's 1677 opinion determined that enslaved people were moveable property.[29]

The casting of enslaved people as commodities coincided with the emergence of a peculiar juridical fiction in English admiralty law, and later in US maritime law, that a ship maintained a legal personality. At the same time as enslaved Africans had their personhood conjured away, inanimate objects had personality bestowed upon them. The fiction of legal personality was, in other words, deployed simultaneously to humanize ships and dehumanize people in order to protect the interests of racial capital. In an influential essay, Bryant Smith defines legal personality as "the capacity for legal relations," including both rights and responsibilities under the law.[30] By granting personhood to ships, admiralty courts could respond to civil and criminal actions that occurred on the high seas and otherwise outside their jurisdiction.[31] Similarly, by interpreting enslaved Africans as commodities rather than people, English admiralty law and its common-law counterparts could justify chattel slavery and the enrichment of white enslavers at enslaved Black people's expense. In Mawani's account of ships that transported enslaved people and racially subjugated laborers as "colonial-legal laboratories," she draws closely on Colin Dayan's analysis of racialized legal personality to observe that "in British and U.S. admiralty law, the 'positive personhood' ascribed to the ship was tightly tethered to the 'negative personhood' imposed on the slave."[32] In other words, Mawani implicitly recognizes that one legal fiction — of an inanimate object's legal personality — provided the imaginative model for another, far more violent form: racialized legal nonpersonality.

While England's juridical and economic commodification of enslaved people was not absolute, in that captive Africans maintained legal personality in certain circumstances, it was strictly circumscribed, operating only if they were to be charged for murder or another criminal offence.[33] In what Dayan terms this "fitful valuation of persons and things,"[34] admiralty law swapped object status between ships and Black captives to best suit English economic interests. Mtubani likewise notes this "ambivalence in English law," explaining that even though enslaved Africans were granted civil rights in 1679 under the doctrine of habeas corpus, "[i]n the fundamental conflict between the Habeas Corpus Act and the Navigation Acts, the latter won."[35] As a juridical mechanism, legal personality was leveraged to buttress the economic system of chattel slavery, and it was employed most particularly in admiralty law rather than in common-law courts.

Since the seventeenth century, then, legal personhood has been a constitutively racialized and exclusionary concept whose primary engine of distribution was admiralty law.[36] Under capitalist colonialism's racialized operations, Europeans used the concept of legal personality to metaphorically convert African people into commodities, extract significant value from their forced labor, and assert brutal fantasies of domination. In Fred Moten's analysis of how the black radical tradition offers a necessary amendment to Karl Marx's failure to account for chattel slavery, enslavement constitutes "the historical reality of commodities who spoke."[37] By recognizing capitalism's foundations in racial domination, Moten clarifies that chattel slavery was at once a significant force in capitalist-colonial wealth generation and a transformative fiction of horrific power. Yet, racialized commodification was not merely an economic sleight of hand that demonstrated chattel slavery's extractive ambitions or European people's racism but also a distinction between natural and legal personhood that animates both English law and slave codes in the Americas. As Mawani compellingly argues, the role played by the doctrine of legal personality in shaping laws at sea and on land derives from the antiquated English concept of the deodand, which names an inanimate object or nonhuman being that is found guilty of causing death or harm to humans and is surrendered to the Crown or state as recompense.[38] The doctrine of the deodand effectively granted legal personality to nonhuman entities and was used in US maritime law (which has jurisdiction over the high seas) and English common law (whose aquatic jurisdiction covers only fresh water) to pursue legal proceedings. While US maritime law typically takes action against a ship, pursuing proceedings in rem (against a thing), English admiralty law almost always takes action against a person (in personam). Instead of prosecuting an inanimate object, English admiralty law brings to trial a ship's representative rather than the ship itself.[39] The fictive bestowal or retraction of seemingly human capacities that deodands and legal personality share coalesce in the juridical space of the slave ship. Just as a deodand is effectively a mechanism for granting what Mawani terms "legal liveliness" to nonhuman entities,[40] so too can legal personhood be a means to achieve a certain kind of judicial remedy by figuratively and temporarily bestowing human status upon objects or animate beings.

If English law took legal personality away from enslaved people at the same time as transforming them into commodities, it effectively eradicated their subjectivity and human status in the eyes of the law. Yet, as the case of the deodand demonstrates, negating legal personality does not necessarily bestow object status: just as a ship can have a legal personality, so can an enslaved person lack personhood under the law while still remaining human. The consequences for this legal distinction are significant not just philosophically, especially for the Black people who lived and died through chattel slavery, but also for contemporary reckonings with historical injustice. As Angela Naimou observes in her analysis of salvage poetics, "the figure of the legal slave ... continues to animate, in partial ways, categories of personhood that continue to be marked as exceptions to ideal abstract personhood."[41] Similarly, Stephen Best's analysis of fugitive slaves in the nineteenth-century United States explains that "the law's figuration of the fugitive as pilfered property and indebted person, object of property and subject of contract, bears distinct consequences for the practice of jurisprudence and for legal and aesthetic representation."[42] Long after the ending of chattel slavery, Black personhood remains beholden to the logics of propertization, as Best elucidates through the rhetorical analysis of aesthetic forms, like turn-of-the-century silent film, and legal forms, such as *Plessy v. Ferguson* and the Fourteenth Amendment.[43] In meticulously revealing a "continuity between the structures of equivalence in property law and the counterfactual exchanges that underlay the doctrine of 'formal equality,'" Best reveals that the judicial system which has inflicted so much violence on Black Americans is built upon those most figurative of processes: metaphor, analogy, and rhetorical hypothesis.[44] For Best, the study of form and rhetoric can bear significant moral valence; in legal practice, by contrast, formal analysis forgoes ethical questions for an attention to precedent. Left only implicit in Best's vital monograph and its argument that the United States' persistent subordination of Black personhood to property can be exposed through literary formalist analysis is a central detail: his work lays the foundation for understanding how the law's reliance upon the literary process of figuration makes not only the law but also literary works generative, or capable of creating new modes of being.

Figuring the Law: Property as Trope

Like Best, Philip acknowledges that Blackness imagined as commodity form endures both juridically and aesthetically as one of slavery's afterlives, even as she recognizes that retractable personhood, to use Colin Dayan's coinage, does not equate to object status either in material or legal terms.[45] Philip identifies this metaphorical slippage between human commodification and object status throughout *Zong!*, frequently registering enslaved Africans' negated legal personalities through the shorthand of property ownership. In "Os," which *Zong!* criticism typically translates as Latin for *bone* but which, as this chapter later identifies, bears significant additional meanings, Philip establishes the facts of the case and the philosophical conditions that enabled the *Zong* massacre, offering twenty-six poems that together construct an alphabet of violence and cruelty. "Os" is the first of *Zong!*'s ten sections, which together comprise six books, two spectrally paratextual poetic sections, and two explanatory paratexts. "Os" establishes Philip's searing indictment of eighteenth-century English law, which held—through a series of statutes and decisions—that enslaved people were chattel. More than all of the poems in "Os," "Zong! #8" assesses the consequences of juridically casting "fellow creatures" as "property":[46]

   the good of overboard

   justified a throwing

                      of property

                          fellow

creatures

        become

                  our portion

                      of

                  mortality

        provision

                a bad market

negroes

                    want

        for dying

                                        (Philip, *Zong!*, 16)

In its vertical columns, "Zong! #8" traces the movement of falling bodies by pulling the eye downward. It juxtaposes, on the right-hand side, England's codifying people as "property" who are traded on the "market" with, on the left, the falling weight of enslaved people whom this system reduces first to basic human form ("creatures") then racialized existence ("negroes"). Meanwhile, as the middle column reveals, the Africans who were thrown overboard "become/provision/for dying": they are killed to leave a larger supply of rations to be distributed among the remaining passengers and crew; through dying, they themselves become provisions. In its vertical lineation, "Zong! #8" identifies distinct conceptual categories — people, provisions, property — that sequentially register the sleight of juridical hand by which English admiralty law commodified Black Africans. In "Os" more than in other sections, Philip aligns English admiralty law's encoded logics with her poems' own aesthetic shaping, laying out the terms of Lord Mansfield's decision in *Gregson v. Gilbert* and its strict reading of the laws under which Collingwood's enslaved cargo were rendered mere property.

While the majority of Philip's poem formally and aesthetically repudiates slavery's racially proprietary system of legal nonpersonhood, it takes racialized ownership as a trope, or organizational figuration, just as it was in English law prior to abolition. In *Zong!*'s third section, "*Ventus*" (the wind), Philip anagrammatically reveals the violence embedded within eighteenth-century England's structuring logic of racialized ownership, where *rope*, *troy*, and *pope* are all partial anagrams of *property*:

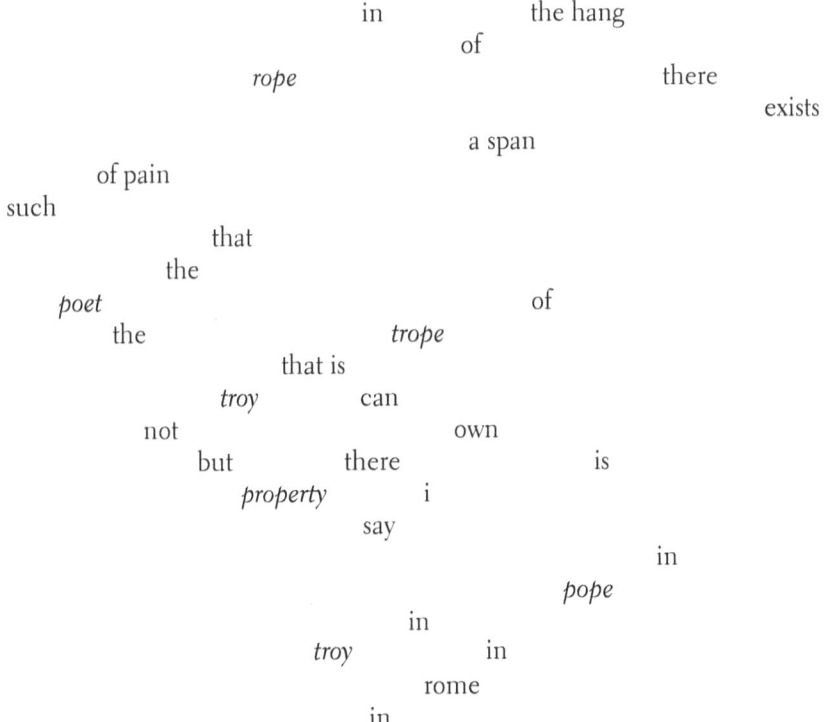

                              negro
                           in
          guns
                       (Philip, *Zong!*, 87; emphasis added)

In this verse that again draws the eye outwards and downwards, as if tracking the movement of Africans thrown to their deaths, Philip at once recounts the *Zong* massacre's violence ("in the hang of rope/there exists a span of pain") and its origins in the racialized exclusions and accumulative ambitions of Western Europe ("But there is property, I say, in/Pope, in Troy, in Rome, in/negro, in guns"). Inasmuch as this verse is representationally constellated around the word *property*, which lies prominently at its heart, it registers the extent to which the system of chattel slavery generated significant financial accumulation by means of racial commodification. Further, in anagrammatically acknowledging the conceptual relationships between rope, poet, trope, troy, property, and pope, Philip recognizes property ownership's shaping effects on seventeenth- and eighteenth-century English jurisprudence and the slave trade that was thereby legitimized. Just as property anagrammatically bears the word *trope* within its own linguistic structure, so too do *Zong!* and English slave codes both take the commodification of Black people as their central motif, whether as a trope to uphold or one to dismantle.

Zong! employs a conceptual architecture and aesthetic configuring that registers the extent to which Captain Collingwood and his crew employed "an entire apparatus of racial and gendered violence" to convince themselves that the people whom they had enslaved were property rather than people both in fact and under the law.[47] Most readings of *Zong!* primarily address the crew's racialized physical violence toward the people whom they eventually murdered for the sake of extra buckets of water and anticipated profits, but Philip's poem is also unusually attentive to the endemic sexual violence that the sailors surely inflicted prior to the massacre. *Zong!* repeatedly recounts sailors' assaulting enslaved Black women, as in the speaker's description of Sade, whom he rapes and renames Dido: "a/queen/once, now/my whore; to the crew/too."[48] In imposing on the West African Sade the name of a legendary East African queen, the speaker engages in the common practice whereby white enslavers renamed the women they enslaved. As Saidiya Hartman explains in *Lose Your Mother*, "[t]he pet name licensed debauchery and made it sound agreeable."[49] Similarly, in "*Ratio*," Philip registers the relationship between enslavement and sexual assault in the speaker's pivoting between figurations of sexual predation and gambling: "I won her, was/wont to bed her, bet/ten, then forty/guineas, first, an/ace/of spades; the deuce, it was, that/got me her forty/days, nights, forty times, forty/sins."[50] In the visual and aural correlation between *won* and *wont, bed* and *bet, ten* and *then*, Philip elucidates the simultaneously raced and gendered violence that was constitutive of chattel slavery. In *Zong!*'s penultimate section, "*Ferrum*," when the speaker has become increasingly frantic and incoherent, Philip communicates Sade's despair: "we sip port: she lay inert,/weals on the skin, no garment to cover her/or my sin: we/shared her."[51] Sade's silent distress as multiple men repeatedly rape her, while she "lay[s] inert" and covered in syphilitic sores, contrasts with their nonchalantly sipping liquor. In repeatedly treating Black women as commodities to be consumed and traded for white male sexual gratification, Collingwood and the crew both produce and reinforce the enslaved women's legal status as objects of property and exchange.

In legal regimes as much as in literary works, as Chapter 3 concluded in its discussion of anti-colonial challenges to intellectual property law, ideas gain structuring import through repetition. If, in literary studies, repeated ideas are identified as tropes, in case law they are identified as guiding principles that justify a court's decision: its *ratio decidendi*. Much like *Zong!*, *Gregson v. Gilbert* took property as its *ratio decidendi*. Courts base their decisions on existing law, and in 1783, enslaved Black people were commodities, as Justice Lee and Justice Chambre explained at the initial hearing: "It has been decided, whether wisely or unwisely is not now the question, that a portion of our fellow-creatures may become the subject of property. This, therefore, was a throwing overboard of goods, and of part to save the residue."[52] The people whom Collingwood and his crew threw to their deaths had been juridically transformed into objects of property, so there could be no indictment for murder; instead, the case turned on whether the drowned people constituted goods lost to the perils of the sea or goods that had been recklessly discarded. Appellate court decided on the latter: as Lord Mansfield explains: "the evidence does not support the statement of the loss made in the declaration," to which Justice Buller adds, "The argument drawn from the law respecting indictments for murder does not apply."[53] Based upon the *ratio decidendi* of the enslaved victims' commodity status, the appellate court decided that the goods (the people) were discarded without due necessity, meaning that the insurance company was not required to pay compensation.

Legal documents like *Gregson v. Gilbert*, as well as their earlier counterparts like the Navigation Acts and *Butts v. Penny*, show that racialized propertization functioned as a trope in eighteenth-century English thought; it was both an idea and a practice that came into being through figurative repetition. In their persistent figuration, juridical tropes like racial propertization shape both social behavior and legal decisions because repetition is necessarily generative: it can reinforce existing ideas and bring new categories into being. When Best explains that "the enforcement of trope is the very work of the law," he recognizes that both the legal and the literary operate through repetition and figuration.[54] In the literary sense, tropes are repeated patterns of figurative language whose coherence and repetition establish a particular set of ideas as important to a text. The juridical norm that enslaved people were chattel similarly gained power through its repetition in legal decisions, opinions, and statutes, as well as in its widespread social acceptance. In addition to the force accrued through repetition, Black commodification was established figuratively: enslaved Africans became legal nonpersons through a metaphorical transformation that was discursively reproduced and juridically enforced. In other words, tropes are enforced in the law not only through judicial mechanisms and law enforcement agencies but also through their structuring repetition that grants them their own internal dynamism. The logic of racial propertization that was established throughout the sixteenth to nineteenth centuries was both juridically enforced and forceful in its very existence.

Inasmuch as the process of tropologically producing racial propertization, or turning African people into enslavable commodities, was made possible by both rhetorically and legally unmaking legal personhood, law's figurations can be seen to bear real impact. In other words, the concept of legal personality offers a striking example of law's aesthetically generative capacities because the act of turning people into commodities by negating their legal personhood is as metaphorical as the contradistinctive process of turning objects into legal personalities. As Smith argues in his 1928 essay, the language of the law is fundamentally figurative, much like everyday speech: "[t]he legal personality of a corporation is just as real as and no more real than the legal personality of a normal human being. In either case it is an abstraction, one of the major abstractions of legal science, like title, possession, right and duty."[55] Yet, the granting and withholding of legal personality—the very concept of personality as juridically separable from human being—bears particularly violent consequences in English admiralty law and associated slave codes. For Dayan, "nowhere is the artifice [of the law] as compelling as in the creation of legal persons, entities that have nothing to do with 'human personality.'"[56] For Mawani, meanwhile, "Questions of legal personhood . . . were nowhere more salient than in the transatlantic slave trade. Just as the law could bestow a lively existence to inanimate objects through the concept of legal personhood, it could transform sentient human beings into things, by denying their personhood."[57] In their analyses of American and Canadian case law, Dayan and Mawani demonstrate that figuration is not only an imaginative process of conceptually transforming one thing into another, but one with real juridical power and material force.

Zong! is concerned with precisely the act of figurative transfer that is involved in the making and unmaking of legal persons: with an imaginative act of legal figuration that bears material consequences. English law has long muddled the categories of fact and fiction, at least insofar as these categories are understood in everyday language, whether by conferring legal personality upon ships, horses, or other nonhuman entities under the device of the deodand or by withdrawing personhood from humans like monks, nuns, and felons under the legal fiction of civil death. Indeed, the law is fundamentally creative, as Simon Stern contends in his analysis of legal fictions, both because it is "thoroughly artificial" and because it bears extralegal effects.[58] Stern notes that many legal doctrines are imaginative or fictional, including estoppels and patent abuse, but doctrines like legal personhood, corporate personhood, and civil death are more likely to be recognized as such: "[l]egal persons overlap with, and merge into, persons in the vernacular, finding attachments outside the legal domain."[59] Philip evokes the doctrine of legal personality in *"Ratio"* when the speaker declares "the sea is now a bod y/pond; I am ex-man."[60] In describing the sea as "a body pond," an aquatic expanse so filled with the dead that it seemingly shrinks to the size of a small pool, the speaker grapples with his guilt about having participated in mass murder. In lamenting his status as "ex-man," moreover, he recognizes personhood's retractability under admiralty law. Figuration is as much a legal characteristic as a literary one and it bears that most transformative of properties: it can both bestow life and take it away.

If legal personality can be revoked, *Zong!* proposes, and in doing so legitimize physical and sexual violence, enslavement, and murder, it might also be conjured back for the sake of justice, however belated: it might also be granted to ghosts. This claim is less outrageous than it might first appear. Not only does the law employ legal doctrines and mechanisms that are at once fictional and generative, but also, as Dayan's analysis of legal personhood in the Americas demonstrates, law's imaginative capacities extend to the spectral. Racialized exclusions in the United States and the Caribbean are not only grounded in racist formulations of the Black person as other-than-human, Dayan contends, but they are also made possible by a long history of permitting ghosts into Anglo-American law. Analyzing the infamous US case *Stambovsky v. Ackley* (1991), which determined whether a couple who had bought a haunted home were obliged to continue with the sale, Dayan argues that Judge Israel Rubin "gives law the power to make ghosts count."[61] Admittedly, Dayan's claim is based on a misreading of Stambovsky, a case that Rubin heard on appeal after plaintiffs Jeffrey and Patrice Stambovsky had purchased a mansion in Nyack, New York without knowing that the vendee, Helen Ackley, had long declared it to be possessed by poltergeists. According to Dayan, Rubin found the terms of the contract to have been broken because the Nyack property was not vacant, per real estate contract, but haunted by Civil War ghosts, so the Stambovskys were not obliged to continue with the purchase. Rubin makes no claim that the house was haunted; instead, he decides in favor of the Stambovkys by applying the principle of estoppel, under which a person cannot assert a claim that contradicts an earlier statement that either they or a court of law has established as true.[62]

Significantly, though, Rubin's ruling does accept the supernatural's legal existence and it does so for doctrinal reasons. His decision is based on a legal finding, not a factual one, and it is at once imaginative and evidentiary: "Whether the source of the spectral apparitions seen by defendant seller are parapsychic or psychogenic, having reported their presence in both a national publication (*Readers' Digest*) and the local press (in 1977 and 1982, respectively), defendant is estopped to deny their existence and, as a matter of law, the house is haunted."[63] A legal fact is constitutively different than its extralegal variety: it needs only to exist within the logic of the law, not as an objective truth. As Ackley had invoked the existence of a poltergeist in print, that poltergeist also bears a legal existence. As such, it is irrelevant whether the house is haunted in fact because it is haunted under the law. Dayan is, therefore, correct in concluding that Rubin's decision reveals that "judicial speculation owe[s] a great deal to the dead as well as the unreal," despite her misreading of his rationale.[64] *Stambovsky v. Ackley* exemplifies a long legal history: despite a seeming hyperfixation on facts and rationality, the law has long accounted for ghosts.

Zong! confronts the infamous massacre whose story it tells by raising the dead and granting them spectral legal personality. When the poem's speaker dies by suicide, bereft at Sade's death, Philip symbolically rectifies a historical wrong; a sailor who had engaged in repeated sexual assault and mass murder suffers a self-imposed, extrajudicial death sentence. Yet, the kind of restitution that *Zong!* offers is more than symbolic. Over the course of this long, experimental poem, Philip allows the dead to tell their stories, centering their subjectivities in an exemplary yet entirely representative account of sexual and physical violence in the Middle Passage. What's more, *Zong!* engages in an extended process of transforming the dead from their historic status as racial nonpersons to legal persons with standing to make a claim. *Zong!*'s transformative aesthetics operate improperly, against both rational norms and proprietary logics, to disperse eighteenth-century admiralty law's dehumanizing suppositions to make space for the dead to rise. Legal personality is a figuration as much as a material fact — a metaphorical condition that can be both bestowed or withdrawn — and Philip appropriately restores its materiality by figurative means. More than granting literary space to stories that have for too long gone untold, *Zong!* grants legal personality to the raised dead.

Laying the Ground for a Legal Challenge: Zong!'s Dispersive Poetics

Formally, grammatically, and rhetorically, Zong! rejects pre-abolition English law's metaphysical act of turning living people into exchangeable commodities, instead transforming property back into being. Over the course of Zong!'s several hundred dense pages, Philip slowly raises Collingwood's victims from the dead, and she does so in two ways: first, by breaking apart and dispersing the logic of racial propertization that upheld and was exemplified in enslaved people's racial nonpersonhood and which made the Zong massacre both thinkable and legal; and second, by establishing an incantatory poetics that reanimates the dead in the form of underwater spirits. As a preparatory act to raising the dead from the ocean's depths, Philip breaks apart chattel slavery's juridical and epistemological structures of racialized possession: of white people owning Black people; of enslaved Africans' retractable personhood; and of ships bearing legal personality while enslaved people did not. In its aesthetically improper poetics of dispersal, Zong! fundamentally reworks chattel slavery's globalized system of white property ownership and of Black legal, economic, material, and spiritual dispossession. Philip formally disperses these structures of racial propertization through Zong!'s visual and aural distribution, its breaking apart of tropes of ownership, and its elegiac narrative trajectory. Literally and figuratively dismantling the *Gregson v. Gilbert* decision over the course of its 182 pages of poetry, Philip uses vocabulary taken only from Lord Mansfield's judgment, at first repurposing whole words and then anagrammatically rearranging these borrowed idioms into a new dictionary of European and African terms. Offering a partial list of these words in "Glossary," a poetic paratext that appears after Zong!'s six primary books, Philip theorizes her creative method. "Glossary"'s subtitle, "Words and Phrases Overheard on Board the Zong," acknowledges the oral and aural techniques by which Philip introduces new terms into discursive circulation about this tragedy. In "overhear[ing]" the dead, Philip at once honors their experience and introduces new ways of thinking about English law's historical negation of African legal personality. Philip likewise disperses the Gregson decision's affective coldness and brevity by instead registering powerful emotions: this work is pained, angry, sad, fearful, wry, melancholic, and hopeful.[65] Zong!'s dispersive poetics are most particularly established through its internal elements, including its extreme enjambment, extending to words and phonemes; its visual and aural spatialization, with stanzas that need to be pieced together by the reader or listener; and its recursive plotting, involving the regular repetition and reworking of story elements and phrases. By dismantling existing syntactical structures, Philip clears space for the dead to rise.

Philip's conspicuous experimentation with grammatical formulations of possession refuses pre-abolition English law's codifying of racialized ownership and accompanying profit motivations. *Zong!*'s formal practice and aesthetic effects recall Hortense Spillers's argument, in her formative essay "Mama's Baby, Papa's Maybe: An American Grammar Book," that the way to establish a racially just society is "1) to break apart, to rupture violently the laws of American behavior that make such *syntax* possible; 2) to introduce a new *semantic* field/fold more appropriate to his/her own historic movement."[66] Like this book's model of aesthetic impropriety, Spiller's formulation for achieving racial justice recognizes the need to at once dismantle the prior system and build a radically new model in its place. In using the metaphor of *grammar* to describe the normative process by which racialized subjectivities are produced and reproduced, Spillers recognizes not only discursive structures' material power and the very real violence they inflict but also the necessity of intervening in structures of thought ("syntax" and "semantics") in order to establish racial justice and Black freedom. Philip self-consciously echoes Spillers's formulation throughout *Zong!*, from "*Os*"'s concrete poetry, to the visual and grammatical dispersal of "*Ratio*," to the typographical density of "*Ebora*"'s raised underwater spirits. In a literalization of Spillers's structural analysis, Philip grammatically breaks apart slavery's logic of racialized possession. With one crucial exception, names in *Zong!* are only ever recorded in lower case, indicating a nonpossessive relationship to all states of being: examples include anachronistically named sailors like dan, hans, and roy; a female collective whom Philip identifies as "women who wait," meaning the sailors' wives, including eve and clara; and a small West African family consisting of a father, wale, a mother, sade, and a son, ade. As with "Glossary," these names are all itemized in a second poetic paratext, "Manifest," which subverts the traditional ship's document by providing entries not only on the people aboard the *Zong*, including both the crew and the white women whom they leave behind while they rape Black women at sea, but also of the body parts identified throughout Philip's elegiac reckoning, including "arm," "*ongle*," and "cunt." The only exception to Philip's improper or nonproprietary naming practice is the litany of the imagined dead who appear in "*Os*," which bestows possible West African names onto Collingwood's victims, identifying them in an extended act of under-writing — of writing under the body of each poem — that finally, belatedly, honors the dead.

In its grammatical dispersal, *Zong!* not only rejects the logic of racialized propertization and its doctrinal corollary, retractable legal personality, but it also clarifies that enslaved Africans always held full personhood in fact, if not under the law. In "*Zong! #5*," Philip visually decouples ownership's subject and object by scattering prepositions that register possession:

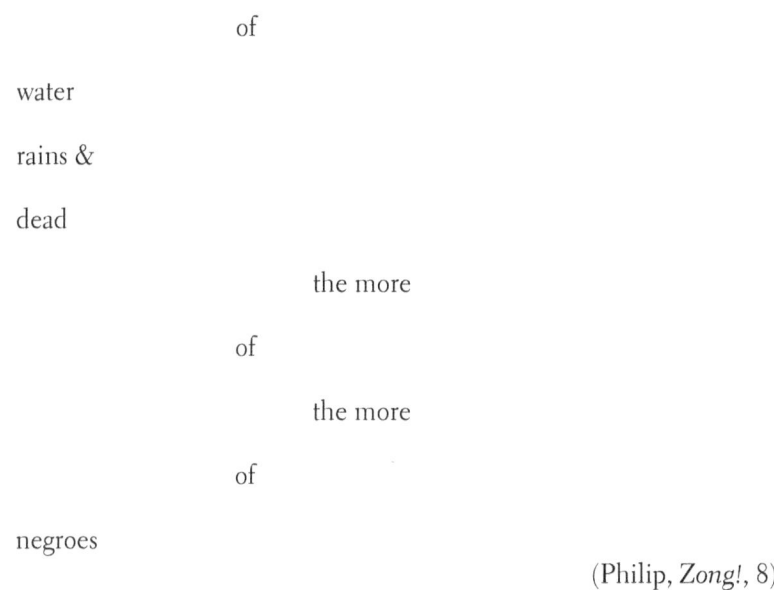

(Philip, Zong!, 8)

In granting a single, central column to the preposition signaling ownership, and in placing the capitalist desire for profit accumulation on the right and the effects of racial capitalism on the left, Philip visually and conceptually undercuts chattel slavery's enabling logic. Similarly, Philip never uses an apostrophe with the possessive "of" but instead introduces negative space between the noun and the "s": in "*Sal*," for example, the white British speaker declares, "I write to you of mortality s lien on l ife."[67] By decoupling *mortality* from its "lien on life," Philip alters the grammatical structure whereby one element can possess another. While a *lien* grants an investor the legal right to possess a debtor's property until their loan is paid off, chattel slavery permitted a white person to own an enslaved person in perpetuity. Erupting into the space of uncoupled possession is the grapheme "ife," providing a visual reminder of Ilé Ifè, the Yoruba holy city that stands metonymically for the homeland from which the enslaved Africans on board Philip's rendition of the *Zong* are separated. When the trope of the lien recurs later in "*Ratio*," the speaker tells Ruth "there is now a lien / on my soul,"[68] figuratively transferring the moral failing of his enslaving humans, or owning chattel, onto his eternal existence.

Elsewhere, Philip replaces nouns that register juridical violence with their verb form, creating a poem that grammatically turns property back into being. In "*Zong! #16*," Philip addresses the lower court's reasoning when it ruled that the Gregson syndicate should receive compensation for the goods (people) who were lost (murdered) to the perils of the sea. Discussing the court's decision, "Zong! #16" uses verbs where nouns would make more immediate grammatical sense:

should they have

found being

                sufficient

                a necessity

(portion that question)

should they have

                found the justify

for exist

                a rule for new

                the policy with the loss

(portion that question etc)

                              (Philip, *Zong!*, 27)

By conjugating both "justify" and "exist" as verbs, instead of the noun forms "justification" and "existence," Philip turns the grammatical object into the ontological subject, the commodity into the person; she reverses chattel slavery's juridical sorcery by instead bestowing legal personality on the Africans from whom it had been taken away. Beginning by asking the most fundamental philosophical question about eighteenth-century English law, "Zong! #16" recognizes that the conditions of possibility undergirding both chattel slavery and admiralty law lie in the conjuring away of Africans' legal personality and their fully human status: "should they have found being/sufficient," the poem asks, in an incomplete counterfactual statement, and then trails away.[69] In a disconsolate rhetorical echo, the poem goes on to pose another statement that is also a question: "should they have found the justify/for exist."[70] The modal "should" operates in two registers at once: in legal discourse, meaning "this is how things are," and in moral discourse, meaning "this is how things ought to be." Offered as a sentence fragment and structured through the modal verb "should," these lines at once make a moral claim and articulate the possibility of a different outcome.

In playing with nouns and verbs to signal that the question of being is at stake in *Gregson v. Gilbert*, Philip participates in a long tradition of Black writing in the Americas, as both Evie Shockley and Nathaniel Mackey have observed. If verbs suggest "action and the ability to act," Mackey explains, nouns imply "hypostasis, paralysis, and arrest."[71] Shockley similarly acknowledges verbs' potentially agentive significations when she reveals that the verb *to be* plays a significant role in *Zong!*, much as it does in the law. Shockley associates the prevalence of "to be" in *Zong!* with this verb's usefulness to juridical processes, arguing that "[it] is so informative to the law because of its transformative quality."[72] Whereas the legal variant of *to be* is associated with the stillness of evidence, facts, and existing norms, its use in *Zong!* invokes the victims' personhood: their subjectivities; their ability to think, move, and engage in self-reflection; their status as living beings. In place of the racial nonpersonhood bestowed on the captive Africans by English law, *Zong!* grammatically grants them the legal personality that they had been denied.

Philip's dispersive aesthetic strategies contribute to her poetic project of not only critiquing England's de facto slave laws but also actively pursuing justice. *Zong!*'s extensive syllabic and phonemic enjambment functions to contest the *Gregson v. Gilbert* decision, as well as the statutes and case laws upon which it was based, by visually and aurally dispersing the logic of racial propertization. The following extract from *"Sal,"* which seems relatively easy to read only because it has been excerpted from a much denser rendition on a page filled with text, exemplifies *Zong!*'s method of graphically and sonically dispersing juridical norms:

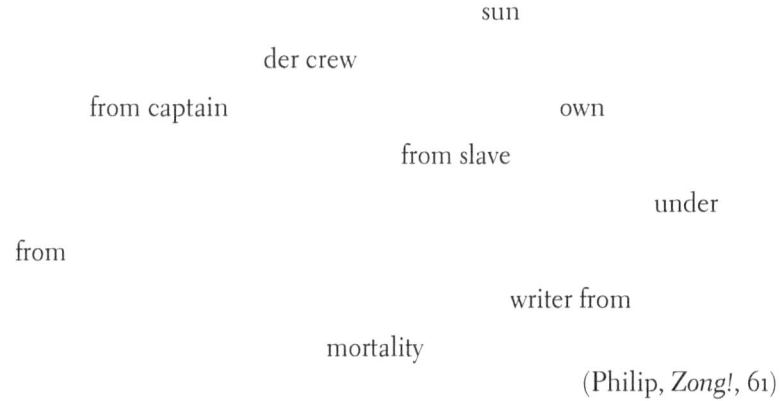

(Philip, *Zong!*, 61)

Effectively offering a metacommentary on her process throughout *Zong!*, Philip here "sund/der[s] crew/from captain . . . under/from/writer" through enjambment and negative space. In place of the Gregson decision's reference to "owners," and the historical legal fact that British people could own Africans as property, Philip separates "own" from "slave," symbolically returning self-possession to the enslaved person. She also undercuts maritime insurance's structuring premise of underwriting the pecuniary risks involved in shipping millions of people across vast oceans in cruel, cramped, and unhygienic conditions.[73] In place of the "underwriter," who synecdochically stands in for the profession that both bolstered and profited from chattel slavery, Philip makes the insurgent creative "writer" a distinct and generative entity, one who is no longer bound by the rules of "mortality" but who can instead travel "under" the oceans to raise the dead.

Zong!'s dispersive version of improper aesthetics becomes more insistent over the temporal and spatial dimension of this long work, establishing a narrative tension that echoes the extended temporality of a court case and the heightened anxieties in the build-up to a decision. Examined visually, *Zong!* modulates from a relatively modest mode of reassembly in book 1 ("*Os*") to a more substantial remodeling in "*Sal*" and "*Ventus*" (books two and three, respectively), moving to what appears, in the third and fourth books of "*Ratio*" and "*Ferrum*," to be so broken as to be largely illegible, and ending, ultimately, with "*Ebora*," whose greyed-out font and overlaid typeface make it impossible to fully comprehend. *Zong!*'s proliferating, dispersive, spatializing, and restructuring aesthetic process becomes clear only over this work's long arc. During the solemn and venerational process of listening to or reading *Zong!*, Philip's reader or listener witnesses a process that epitomizes the workings of what this book terms aesthetic impropriety: of taking apart an extant structure, engaging in an extended process of reorganization, and building a very different model out of the bones of that which had previously existed. Over the course of nearly two hundred pages, Philip takes a short, two-paged judgment and turns it into a voluminous meditation on racial violence, sexual assault, and the possibilities for belated justice. Beyond its complexly formed lines and verses, *Zong!*'s narrative and aesthetic trajectory disperses and redistributes colonial England's de facto slave codes.

By dismantling the text of the *Gregson v. Gilbert* decision, and by symbolically breaking apart the racially proprietary logic embedded in its associated statutes, judgments, and opinions, Philip produces an account of the *Zong* massacre that reckons with its historical violence. To use Fred Moten's theorizing of experimental black aesthetics, *Zong!*'s grammatically and syntactically produced spatialization functions to "anarrange" colonial racial capitalism's legal logics.[74] For Moten, black radical aesthetics participate in producing the political system its creators wish to inhabit. Conscious blackness, he argues, is disruptive and agentive, functioning as a verb to change rather than name the state of things: "Blackness—the extended movement of a specific upheaval, an ongoing irruption that anarranges every line — is a strain that pressures the assumption of the equivalence of personhood and subjectivity."[75] As Moten's analysis makes clear, *Zong!*'s extended grammatical, syllabic, visual, and aural disassembly of *Gregson v. Gilbert* is more generative than the critically commonplace language of fragmentation, breaking apart, and dismantling might suggest.[76] While *Zong!*'s extended textual disassembly does seem to replicate the chaos and distress caused by Collingwood's actions and the laws that legitimized them, and while the immediacy offered by such an interpretation might seem to be poetically apt, *Zong!*'s visual and aural spacing is significant less because of what it might signify mimetically and more because of what it generates.

Despite critical temptation to associate Philip's poetic techniques with the violence that Collingwood's crew and chattel slavery inflicted upon the 150 murdered Africans, *Zong!*'s aesthetic strategies operate to reorganize thought, not to reproduce it, doing so more than any of the other literary works examined in this book. As Anthony Reed explains, *Zong!*'s visual spatialization serves to extend temporality rather than to duplicate affective experience or replicate political forms: "The orphaned syllables adrift across the surface of *Zong!*'s pages ... may recall bodies drowning at sea and the drift of histories that have refused to claim their dead, but that resemblance on its own allows readers the false comfort of a history and historiography the poem deconstructs."[77] Reed cautions against too easily imagining the experiences of the dead given a long transatlantic white supremacist history of equating blackness with immediacy and materiality: of accessing a timeless essence that defies the more complex subjectivity of historical white self-possession. As Reed provocatively asks, "How does one recover the drowned Africans into a notion of life at once within but also transcendent of those notions that foreclosed black humanity?"[78] Jenny Sharpe offers a compelling answer to Reed's question, arguing that Philip's aesthetic process creates an affective experience with political consequences: "In cutting up the text of a document that designates slaves as cargo to be disposed of at will, Philip's poems open up wide spaces between words and even the letters of words to suggest that silence is not an empty space even if it does not deliver language as such."[79] For Sharpe, *Zong!*'s constitutive pauses acknowledge the irrecuperable narratives contained in archival occlusions. While the politics of witnessing embedded in Sharpe's analysis is ethically compelling, I want also to suggest that *Zong!* is generative as well as respectful; it honors the dead not only by acknowledging their trauma but by working to make conditions better for the living. Instead of attempting to recover Collingwood's victims, *Zong!* poetically establishes the epistemological conditions — the structures of thought —

that would help to create belated justice. *Zong!* works to achieve justice by raising the dead.

Raising the Dead: Oration, Incantation, and Reanimation

Throughout this book, I have been building an argument for literature's material force that recognizes how aesthetics function to reconfigure thought. My reading of *Zong!* extends this argument that an aesthetic work can forcefully produce new legal conditions — that poetry can be a generative act — because instead of simply critiquing the *Zong* massacre and aesthetically dismantling its conditions of possibility, Philip engages in an act of restitution in a juridically literal sense: she reanimates the dead and restores them to ghostly legal personality. If, as Walt Hunter argues, "[p]oets creatively intervene in global processes by remaking their poetry's repertoire of forms,"[80] *Zong!*'s own juridical intervention in the global process of chattel slavery and its afterlives occurs in its raising the dead through incantation and oration. Philip draws the reader or listener into her dispersive, incantatory poetics, resuscitating the *Zong* massacre's victims through breath's propulsive capacities. As performances of *Zong!* demonstrate, this poem is constructed as much through judicious pauses, emphatic articulations, carefully regulated breath, and improvisatory lineation as it is built upon the cut-up and reorganized text of the *Gregson v. Gilbert* decision. For Christina Sharpe, Philip's activation of breath in this poem is transformational: Sharpe argues, "Philip aspirates those submerged lives and brings them back to the text from which they were ejected."[81] Indeed, Sharpe theorizes "wake work" as aspiration, both as intention or ambition and as the work of breathing and producing breath: of "keeping breath in the Black body."[82] *Zong!*'s visually and aurally spaced graphemes and phonemes make space for the dead to rise from the ocean's depths and from the racially proprietary logics of English legal history.

To listen to Philip recite this work, and to hear the musicians that often accompany her, is to recognize how much *Zong!* works with sound as with sense, sonically submerging the listener into a poem that recalls the captives' immersion first into an affective atmosphere of fear and violence and then into the ocean's depths. Yet, it would be a mistake to think of *Zong!* as aesthetically mimetic. When Philip produces sensory intensity, it is as much to create forward propulsion and temporal dispersal as it is to replicate emotional distress. As a result of *Zong!*'s extreme enjambment, the reader or performer is forced to pause as they figure out the sound of a word and its future direction from what is usually only a partial rendering on the page: in "*Ferrum*," for instance, the reader would enunciate lines that describe drowning and lost souls:

ADMIRALTY LAW AND RAISING THE DEAD

"ash . . . . .es and sa . . . . lt for the bo . . . . die..s . . . . .of kin un . . . . der the sk . . . . .in of s . . . . ea; whe . . . . .re repo . . . . se the bo . . . . .ne sou . . . . .ls of kin."[83] As is common throughout Philip's poem, this excerpt sprawls its words across the space of the page or the room: "ashhhhhhhhhhhhhes and saaaaaaaaaalt. . . . . wheeeeeeeeeeeere repoooooooooooooooose the booooooooooooooooooones." In these extended vowel sounds, Philip introduces the sound of breath, as well as of words, into her poem. As such, Zong!'s elaborate lineation does more than visually break apart the speaking sailor's narrative in order to figuratively dismantle the Zong massacre's narrativization by white men in history and the law (and, as it might at first seem, in this collection), and it does more than visually register Philip's insistence that chattel slavery's historically racially violent logics must be broken apart in order to achieve justice in the present. By inserting the sounds of enunciation into Zong!, Philip breathes metaphorical life into the dead.

Operating juridically and poetically, Zong! functions not just to speak about the dead but to raise them. Philip's process of oratorical revival is most visually obvious in "*Ferrum*," the final section before the dead rise as underwater spirits, because it is here that Philip engages in this poem's most substantial forms of enjambment, splitting words at the level of syllables or even phonemes:

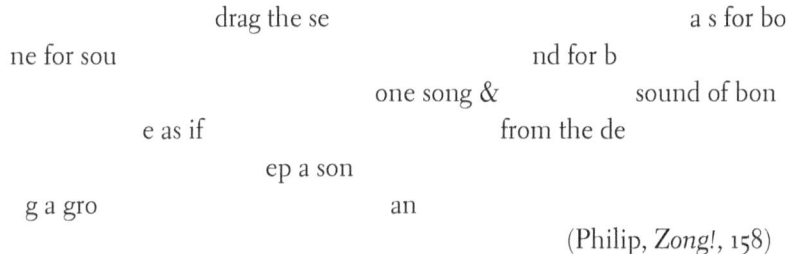

(Philip, Zong!, 158)

Read as if each clump of words were a line, this excerpted verse communicates in halting, stuttering language, seeming to evoke an imagined speaker who is sounding out words phonically as if just starting to read English, or perhaps someone who cannot bring themselves to describe what they know: "drag the se," "nd for b," "from the de." In each of these sonic excerpts, Philip requires the reader to repeatedly start and stop their utterances, and in the process, she creates a sense of psychological stultification or loss. In separating out the vowels of "se————a-s" and "sou————nd," Philip extends the process of articulating these long vowels, emphasizing the act of egression, or breathing out, and making the lines sound like sighs. "Drag the se————a-s,"

Philip writes, forcing the reader's internal narration, or a performing orator's voice, to elongate the word *sea*, bringing the breathiness of aspiration into this word's extended vowels and resurrecting metaphorical breath from the bones that have been called upon "as if from the deep."

In resuscitating the dead through poetic means, Philip operates within a long elegiac tradition. When the prior excerpt from *"Ferrum"* is read as an extended, enjambed verse, temporarily erasing Philip's extensive use of negative space, it scans as follows:

> drag the seas for bone, for
> sound, for bone song & sound of
> bone, as if from the deep, a
> song, a groan
>
> (Philip, *Zong!*, 158)

Adapting Philip's lineation reveals *Zong!*'s recuperative efforts and its desire to honor the dead: to "drag the seas for bone, for/sound" and to pull from the ocean's depths "a/song, a groan." In this sense, *Zong!* is demonstrably elegiac; as Jahan Ramazani argues, modern elegy works "not to achieve but to resist consolation, not to override but to sustain anger, not to heal but to reopen the wounds of loss."[84] In dragging the seas for both bone and sound, Philip revives the dead from their resting places after an act of historical violence, and in doing so, she rightly sustains their anger: they respond both in honor and distress. At the same time, these lines suggest that Philip, too, is singing as well as moaning; detached from a named subject, the lines "as if from the deep, a/song, a groan" hover on the page, emanating from Philip as much as from the *Zong*'s ghosts. If, as Anne Carson suggests of the epitaphic contract, "a poet is someone who saves and is saved by the dead,"[85] Philip writes not only for Collingwood's victims but also for herself. Furthermore, because the chorus that is sung and moaned by the dead is likewise intoned by the reader, Philip insists that the community of the present should likewise respond to their anger and their sorrow; she insists that the living should rise, like the dead, to address an act of historical violence.

While in elegy, raising the dead is an act of mourning, in *Zong!* it is also an act of legal restitution. Repeated throughout *Zong!* is the sonic proximity between *ius*, us, and *os*: between justice, collectivity, and bone. In one of the early iterations of the speaker's referencing Sade's murder, an event that he recounts over and over, he acknowledges that her death "proved justice dangerous; the law: a crime."[86] In this account of Sade's killing, Philip scatters the letters "SOS," first recombining them into the Latin *"os"* and then translating them back to the English word "bone":

(Philip, Zong!, 63)

By breaking apart the letters of an acronym and writing them out phonemically, Philip forces the reader or orator to linger over the sounds, emphasizing their sibilance. Drifting from "es oh es" to "SOS," from "os" to "bone," from "us us os" to "save us os," Philip embeds violence into the victims' pleas: their bones, their "os," synecdochically stand in for the lives they beg to keep. Similarly, in the proximity between "us" and "os," the victims' appeals for help are necessarily collective, both then and now: they ask that they are saved; they ask that their bones be resurrected. Playing on the sonic continuity between us, os, and ius, Philip suggests that restitution for mass murder remains possible: "for ius, for us, for os"[87] — for justice, for the victims, for the African diaspora — and to rectify "the loss in os in us in ius."[88] The sibilance produced through these slow, synecdochic modulations between justice, community, and buried bones sonically evokes the Sibyl of Cumae, whose prophetic capacities Philip recalls throughout this work, along with "circe the crone"[89] and the sirens of Greco-Roman mythology who "call, t/empt with son/g."[90] Hissing, groaning, and singing beneath Zong!'s waves are echoes of ancient European empires' epic poems, which both articulated a chauvinistic pride for their historical publics and bolstered early modern Europe's imperial dreams.

Drawing loosely but distinctively on *The Aeneid*, Philip makes os a central motif, using its double meaning of *bone* and *mouth* to register this poem's efforts to find justice for Collingwood's victims. As a figurative device that functions both referentially and generatively, *os* establishes Philip's interest in raising the dead, or recuperating their bones, through oratorical means. Her poet's mouth narrates the victims' stories, including their possible lives and histories, the West African communities from which they were forcibly taken, the physical and sexual violence they suffered on board the *Zong*, their horrific deaths, and their desires for justice. *Zong!* honors the dead by bestowing a name on each person who would otherwise remain nameless: on people who had been turned, through chattel slavery's dehumanizing mechanisms, into the single racialized term "he negro" or "she negro" in the *Zong*'s manifest: "Thandiwe, Lukman, Sabah, Liu, Sikumbuzo," this poem instead intones, offering names for the massacre's dead at the bottom of each page in "*Os*." Similarly, Philip brings to imaginative life Wale, Sade, and Ade, who stand in for the millions of families broken apart by chattel slavery. Taking increasing prominence in this poem's visual and narrative space, their love for one another and their distant home offers a tender portrait of ordinary life destroyed: "wh/ere is *wa/le, sa/de* too a/nd *a/de*; whe/re the hu/t of ru/sh ree/d and red mud."[91] By introducing this small family in "*Ventus*," and through continual references to West African life, especially the grief of the *oba* or king, Philip increasingly interrupts the *Zong* tragedy's historically white narration, registered in *Zong!*'s focalizing through a British sailor.[92] In place of a narrative about white violence followed by white abolition, Philip visually, aurally, narratively, and conceptually augments this history's West African presence, counteracting Britain's racially proprietary logics by improperly dispersing and disrupting the speaker's lyric voice:

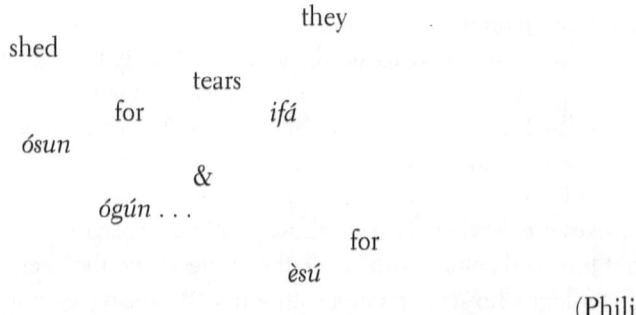

(Philip, *Zong!*, 82)

In this recitation of Yoruba regions and gods — Ifá is a city and Ósun a state, while Ógùn is a spirit and Èsú a religion — *Zong!* orally and aurally presents testimony not of the Gregson syndicate or the Gilbert insurance company but of the West African dead. Zong!'s lineation not only mimetically evokes the victims' drowning, as critics have frequently suggested,[93] but it also visually and aurally implies that they and the rich lives they led will rise again.

In its literary, mythological, and spiritual references, Philip transforms an English tragedy into a Black Atlantic epic. When Zong! — and the poem's anxious speaker — repeatedly assures the reader (and himself) that "This is but an oration," the phrase's auricular unruliness evokes narration, oratory, and erasure all at once: "this is but an oration"; "this is but a narration"; "this is but an erasure." Philip's oratory offers a necessary rejoinder to the *Gregson v. Gilbert* decision that the killings on board the Zong did not constitute murder. Zong!'s retelling of the massacre narrates and orates a court ruling that was based not on the victims' human status but on their enslaved legal personalities: on the juridical erasure of their human liveliness. In one of this phrase's many repeated occurrences, which serve aurally and musically as variations on a theme, "*Sal*" recounts: "this is but an o/ration; time sands/the loss within; how many/days?"[94] Visually duplicitous, this line presents itself as an honorific funeral speech — "this is but an oration," the speaker proclaims — even as it embeds a reference to the limited rations that supposedly provided justification for the killings. Through this line's duplicity and the epic device of apostrophe, Philip ironizes the speaker's putative sorrow: "O! Ration time," he laments, as though differently distributing time would have changed the consequences of the Africans' negated personhood. Similarly, when the speaker makes his repeated claims to mournful oratory, Philip ironizes his position: "Dave asks — this is but an oration — he asks that I (these words come) that I write from his lips, though my hand shapes: 'why are we here?'"[95] The sailor's slew of embedded subclauses signify anxious knowledge of his own moral culpability. While the act of oratory is associated with attempts to persuade a crowd of the justness of one's case, the speaker's rhetorical attempts in *Zong!* merely confirm the crew's guilt.

In place of historical erasure, both archivally — in the victims' substantive absence from maritime records — and juridically — in the negation of African legal personality — Philip's *Zong!* employs an incantatory poetics whose repetitious solemnity raises the dead from the ocean floor. *Zong!*'s effects are achieved through an almost liturgical repetition of phrases and stories: about the *oba*'s sobs; about Wale and Sade; about profit and sin. These rhetorical acts of circular repetition are evidenced even at the level of phrasing; toward the end of "*Ferrum*," for instance, the speaker narrates: "They ask for water; we give them sea./They ask for bread; we give them sea/They ask for life; we give them only the sea."[96] Intensifying earlier figures of repetition, Philip here employs the rhetorical device of symploce, where a phrase is repeated at both the beginning and ending of a line, and she accompanies this doubled echo with an internal repetition: the sailors' ironized "gift" to their murdered captives. In response to the Africans' requests for water, bread, and life, the sailors "give them sea, . . . give them sea . . . give them only the sea." Exposed in the implied mutuality of the sailors' dreadful gift is chattel slavery's profit-driven motives of juridically sanctioned racial violence. Yet, even as these lines seemingly center the speaking sailor who elaborately confesses his guilt, Philip's acts of repetition, of solemn incantation, are focused more especially on honoring the dead. *"Ferrum"* ends with yet another account of the *oba*'s grief ("over and over the *oba* sobs") along with the last of the speculative names that are missing from the *Zong*'s manifest:

> *Bektemba Agbeke Gbolahan Fasuyi Abifarin Olurun*
> *Fadaira Abiona Nuru Okunade Dolap Moya*
> *Olufunde Olupitan Falana Esi*
> *Wale Sade*
> *Ade*

(Philip, *Zong!*, 173)

After this liturgy of the dead, and the incantatory repetition of words and phrases over the course of five books, and the embodied injection of breath into the very structure of this poem, *Zong!* has speculatively named all of the Africans who were thrown overboard the *Zong* and has offered elegiac recompense.

In its incantatory repetition, *Zong!* raises collective voices from the depths of the Atlantic and grants them ghostly expression. Philip's extended act of elegiac incantation culminates in *"Ebora,"* *Zong!*'s sixth and final book, and it ends at once narratologically, in raising this massacre's ghosts, and symbolically, in restoring Africa to the center of this story. The voices of the dead have been heard throughout this poem, most especially in *"Ferrum,"* but until *"Ebora,"* which is named for Yoruba underwater spirits, their ghostly presence has remained unconfirmed: "sshh, listen," the speaker asks; "can you not hear from the deeps, voices, not sirens?"[97] And he addresses the *oba*, explaining that the spirits beg for help: "Do/you hear a/bove or is it un/der the roar of/water their song, *"aide moi, aide moi*; help/me help me'?" "I can't, it is/late, too late," the *oba* sobs.'"[98] While the *oba* suggests that "it is late, too late" to keep alive the people who are enslaved on board the *Zong*, his extended act of mourning resurrects their ghosts. Through Philip's incantatory oration, their collective voices slowly rise, appearing amid their dispersed propertization and once again granted the status of being heard that is necessary for legal personality. In the typographical and metaphorical overwriting that characterizes *"Ebora,"* oration is at once "over," or finished, and utterly present, constituted by the many *"ora"* (or mouths) of its speakers: the voices of the ancestors who have risen from the depths like the sirens in Virgil's *Aeneid* and who drown out any narrative coherence that the speaker had once possessed.

If the dead respond to incantation, their capacity to rise is made possible only by Philip's dispersing the grammatical, aural, visual, and legal structures that had kept them buried. Indebted to Virgil, she rewrites what will come to be seen as his Eurocentrism, not least in his adoption by colonial elites, to offer an alternative account of the founding of a people: this time, not of Rome, but of the African diaspora. Echoing significant moments in *The Aeneid*, Philip makes the mouth, *os*, a constitutive part of *Zong!*'s dispersive poetics because it functions at once as a trope and as a generative poetic device. Indeed, Philip's visually and aurally experimental poem adapts Virgil's own playful poetic experimentation in his vertical lineation and his embedded acrostics. In volume 6 of *The Aeneid*, as Neil Adkin recounts, Virgil includes the "acrostical a-b-e-o-o-s-o-s," first identified by Joshua Katz.[99] Whereas Katz offers three translations of this acrostic, as "I go away; mouth, mouth," "I — a mouth, a mouth — go away," or "I am transformed: a mouth, a mouth," Adkin instead translates it as *"abeo oso(-u)s*: 'I go away hating.'"[100] As *Zong!* shows, each of these possible translations is viable; thanks to Philip's significant enjambment and extensive spacing, any one line can be read from many directions, whether horizontally, vertically, or diagonally, and a single line can therefore hold many possible interpretations. What's more, as *The Aeneid* suggests, narrating an epic journey involves transformation, hateful departures, and oratory: mouths that are transformed and that effect transformation in turn; mouths that speak legal personhood after centuries of negation.

Remaking the Law: Prophecy and Propulsion

Zong!'s generative poetic aesthetics lay the groundwork for a civil case against Gregson and company by raising the syndicate's victims from the dead. In reanimating the enslaved people who were murdered in the *Zong* massacre, Philip allows the dead to testify and to account for the violence that was done to them. In effect, she grants spectral personhood to the massacre's ghosts: she recognizes their rights and responsibilities under the law; she grants them the capacity for legal relations. This claim is more than just metaphorical; in establishing a forceful case for the dead's capacity to rise and seek justice, *Zong!* produces new legal ideas. By formally dismantling the system of logic that made the enslaved Africans commodities without legal personhood, and by raising the dead through an extended act of incantatory oration, Philip opens space for thinking about granting personhood to ghosts, just as it has long been bestowed upon animate and inanimate nonhuman entities. In other words, *Zong!* participates in a process of establishing the imaginative conditions of possibility for a newly enforceable approach to historical injustice.

As Philip's act of poetically raising the dead is a prophetic gesture, one that speaks to the potential for a future act of justice by granting legal personality to the spirits of the dead, it bears some temporal similarities to the workings of the law. Oliver Wendell Holmes Jr. explains that the law gains its force not from what is written in the past but from how the courts will likely interpret those writings: "The prophecies of what the courts will do in fact, and nothing more pretentious, are what I mean by the law."[101] People who break the law do not care about moral axioms, Holmes contends; they are concerned with how courts are likely to enforce rules that have previously been written down and made known. Law is enforceable because it is prophetic: because it tells constituents how to behave and what the consequences will be for their transgressions. For Holmes, then, legal documents describe the future, not the present or the past, and justice, similarly, is prophetic rather than deductive: it operates less by interpretation than by anticipating future judgments. Referencing *The Aeneid*, the same text that Philip invokes, Holmes describes legal reports, treatises, and statutes as future-oriented documents: "In these sibylline leaves are gathered the scattered prophecies of the past upon the cases in which the axe will fall. These are what properly have been called the oracles of the law."[102] Like scholars of maritime law who preceded him, including Hugo Grotius, who quotes from *The Aeneid* twice in *The Free Sea*'s very first chapter, as well as those who follow, like Philip, Holmes uses Virgil's account of oceanic travel, temporality, and international justice to theorize the workings of the law.[103] Holmes's assessment of modern western law's operations are broadly confirmed in the *Zong* massacre and its ensuing insurance case and appeal. All of the judges involved in *Gregson v. Gilbert* reasoned that statutory law is written in the past and that it forecasts — indeed, forecloses — their future actions. Even those judges who questioned the moral veracity of Collingwood's actions — of identifying people as property who could be thrown overboard as goods lost to the perils of the sea — also reasoned that their decisions were already foretold. If the law seemingly operates retrospectively, it is only because its parameters were previously prophesied.[104]

Yet, for Virgil and for Philip, law's preordaining invites wrongdoing. Virgil's figure of justice, the Sibyl, insists that even as she inevitably foretells the future, she must communicate her prophecies obscurely. In the original Latin, *The Aeneid* offers a rare acrostic about oratory and embodiment — about speeches and mouths, about prophecies and respiration — in which Aeneas attempts to guide the Sibyl. Per Shadi Bartsch's translation, Virgil writes:

> Once I rule, I'll build a great shrine for you too,
> kind Sibyl. I'll include the secret prophecies
> you told my people, and consecrate your priests.
> But don't entrust your oracles to leaves, or they'll
> end up muddled, playthings spun by whirling
> breezes. Chant them yourself, I beg.
> (Vergil, *The Aeneid*, VI, 71–76)[105]

According to Aeneas, oratorical clarity is required for predicting the future and articulating justice; the Sibyl's practice of writing her prophecies on leaves, which become "playthings" for "whirling breezes," risks confusing those who use her predictions for guidance. Yet, as the wise Sibyl realizes, justice requires ambiguity; she must write her oracles in unstable form, on leaves that can be blown around by the wind, so that her followers are required to engage in the act of interpretation: to live in uncertainty rather than knowledge.[106] In a similar fashion, and at once acknowledging its debt to a prior epic poem and refusing eighteenth-century English law's racial exclusions, *Zong!* sets out its analysis of justice on muddled leaves. Echoing *The Aeneid*, *Zong!* anarranges eighteenth-century English admiralty law's racially dispropriative prophecies. Like Virgil's acrostics, Philip's dispersively improper aesthetics function as her own sibylline leaves.

If justice is associated with oratory and breath, with speaking the future while refusing easy codification, both Virgil's acrostics and Philip's dispersive aesthetics bear the generative potential of bringing the future into being. They describe possible futures which, in being granted imaginative possibility, can then be brought into effect. According to Holmes, enforceability is law's most important feature; as he explained in a 1922 tort case, *Western Maid*, "legal obligations that exist but cannot be enforced are ghosts in the law."[107] But as Philip establishes throughout *Zong!*, ghosts are more powerful than Holmes might think: they do not necessarily signal absence; they have long held a place in transatlantic law; and their spectral presence can carry significant ethical and legal weight. In *Zong!*, the spirits who are oratorically raised from the dead through an extended act of incantation newly possess the legal personality that had been stripped from them under seventeenth-century English admiralty law and its pursuant legal decisions. Collingwood's victims haunt English law and the Black Atlantic, and if *Zong!* poetically raises them from the dead, it also raises the possibility of finally restoring their legal personality. Ghosts, too, are entitled to justice.

Conclusion
Hope's Impropriety

To theorize aesthetic force and postcolonial justice is to celebrate hope: to make emancipation, liberation, persistence, and vitality central to literary analysis, critical theory, legal studies, and, above all, the project of generating more just social formations. Faced with colonial racial capitalism's long duration and vast scale, an inclination toward hope is individually life-sustaining as well as collectively life-improving. And yet, hope is a disposition that remains somewhat peripheral in the humanities as well as in much academic scholarship. For those of us whose work is recognizably embedded in political and social contexts, many excellent reasons exist for this general aversion, including enduring global inequalities, climate crisis, entrenched misogyny and racism, and international complicity in genocide.[1] Within academia as an institution, reservations about optimism's viability derive not only from scholarly norms about affective neutrality and disciplinary tendencies toward critique but also from the recent swathe of job losses, funding cuts, and program closures at universities across the Global North, particularly in the United States and the United Kingdom, despite these countries' relative wealth.[2] Confronted with multiple crises and deep and varied modes of structural inequality, identifying harms and diagnosing causes might seem to be the only ethically and politically legitimate course of action. And yet, without hope, diagnosis and critique cause despair. Hope is the disposition that subtends justice.

In this book's terms, hope is improper: in counteracting existing harms, hope works toward emerging futures; in engaging with circumstances that are cause for anguish, hope remains oriented toward potentiality. Unlike the somewhat similar mode of naivety, hope necessitates identifying and analyzing the frequently pernicious conditions that structure everyday life with a commitment to activating liberatory norms and building sustainable social formations. Even as the many instances of racialized, regionalized, and gendered colonial dispossession that this book has analyzed demonstrate that we are very far from achieving the sovereignty, equality, and care that are vital for justice, my analyses of legal and literary engagements with petroleum pollution, female dispossession, cultural appropriation, and racial subordination have shown that significant work is being undertaken to rectify colonially produced forms of privation and create emancipatory futures.

Methodologically, *Aesthetic Impropriety: Property Law and Postcolonial Style* has proceeded by acknowledging harms across distinct postcolonial anglophone jurisdictions and identifying emergent strategies for reforming property law. Juridically, these methods include the Ogale people seeking compensation in England for petroleum pollution in Nigeria, employing the novel legal approach of challenging a subsidiary corporation's parent company in its home jurisdiction on the basis of distributed responsibility. Methods of achieving legal justice include claimants like Mary Roy challenging gender-discriminatory inheritance laws in India's Supreme Court, as well as a loosely associated set of feminist jurists pursuing statutory reform of Indian divorce law. Legal strategies include extensive, coordinated work around the world to force the World Intellectual Property Organization to establish protections for Indigenous intellectual property, leading to the development of regional instruments like the Swakopmund Protocol (2012) among African member nations and the implementation of new statutes within specific jurisdictions, like South Africa's Indigenous Knowledge Protections Act (2019). And legal measures might well include extending legal personality to ghosts to seek restitution for racially motivated killings, as my reading of M. NourbeSe Philip's *Zong!* has suggested. By recognizing existing legal achievements and possible future remedies, *Aesthetic Impropriety* mobilizes hope's propulsive energies.

In addition to the aforementioned legal responses to injustice, this book has shown that aesthetics not only register but also change structures of thought and that aesthetically induced epistemological transformations contribute to legal reform. In revealing the precise conceptual correspondences between Zoë Wicomb's *David's Story* (2000) and South Africa's Indigenous Knowledge Protections Act (2019), I have shown that new approaches to justice circulate discursively and aesthetically before they become law. It is on this basis that Philip's act of raising the dead and restoring their legal personhood might presage future doctrinal reform. In a more modulated version of *David's Story*'s relationship to intellectual property law, Arundhati Roy's *The God of Small Things* (2007) aesthetically establishes a set of ideas about gendered equality that preempted significant challenges to India's divorce laws. While the Marriage Laws (Amendment) Bill (2013) failed to pass the Lok Sabha, India's lower house of parliament, it passed the Rajya Sabha, the upper house: and this not-insignificant achievement opens conceptual space for future, similar efforts that might finally protect women economically upon divorce. More diffusely, the symbiotic modality that Ben Okri and Chigozie Obioma theorize respectively in "What the Tapster Saw" (1986) and *The Fishermen* (2015) is also evidenced in the successful anti-oil activism of groups like the Art Not Oil coalition, whose member organizations' aesthetic interventions have significantly contributed to the ending of multinational oil companies' sponsorships of major cultural institutions around the United Kingdom. Much as these activists recognize that petroleum extraction's risks and harms are unequally and globally distributed, so too does *Aesthetic Impropriety* acknowledge that aesthetically improper engagement with proprietary property law bears diffuse and dispersed effects. While the impact of literary aesthetics on transformational processes that are usually understood to be law's domain are difficult to measure, we would do well to recognize their diffuse force.

In addressing slow processes rather than immediately achievable or readily visible outcomes, *Aesthetic Impropriety* has attended to structural, systemic, and institutional harms. This commitment to addressing large-scale processes through localized instances is shared with *The God of Small Things*: the novel with which this project began. But the process of balancing large and small, abstract and concrete, also matches the law's operations. Statutes and case law provide general rules that are then applied to particular incidents; legal opinions start with general principles then move to the facts of a case; and jurisprudence, or legal theory, makes the mechanics of legal practice possible.[3] Frequently, as Philip so astutely identifies, the law's emphasis on general principles more than specific, human details allows it to sanction grave injustice. Among scholars of race, colonialism, and human rights, whether in a colonial or postcolonial context, the law's responsibility for enabling violence has been rightly castigated. *Aesthetic Impropriety* produces similar critiques, recognizing that continuing to identify the ways that injustice is systematized and institutionalized will remain vital work.

It has also become clear, over the course of writing a book on property law, that postcolonial literature, both in the anglophone tradition and beyond it, can be richly understood through the seemingly mundane legal fields that profoundly structure daily life. For nonlawyers, it can be tempting to attend to horrific, catastrophic, or spectacular events as loci for addressing injustice. And yet, subdued, structural, quotidian forms of domination similarly effect significant harms that deserve scholarly attention. In postcolonial law and literary studies, areas that warrant further examination, and which involve substantial legal and literary overlap, include administrative law, climate law, labor law, and family law. As my own analysis of property law has hopefully shown, these seemingly mundane areas of law shape everyday life in complex and varied ways, bearing the potential both for injury and protection, devastation and happiness.

I began by discussing how Hew Locke's aesthetically experimental visual art shaped public understandings of racial violence and contributed to the toppling of Edward Colston's statue. I want to end by returning to Hew Locke to show how aesthetic impropriety is hopeful, joyful, and propulsive, this time analyzing a much larger and more recent work, *The Procession* (2022). In this dynamic installation of 150 masked figures in a West Indian Carnival parade, Locke provides a visually stunning critique of capitalist colonialism's property regime, a generative production of anti-colonial community, and an enduring commitment to hope. First staged in Tate Britain's Duveen Galleries between March 2022 and January 2023, *The Procession* explicitly identifies property's many forms under colonial racial capitalism, including resource extraction, joint stock investment, chattel slavery, and indentured servitude. Locke's figures are clothed in images of rapacious accumulation and racialized exploitation: these include share certificates from European states and more recent colonial powers like the United States and China; precious metals and gemstones, including strings of pearls, gold medallions, and a crown; a large trunk filled with sugar that has been produced in the West Indies by enslaved Black people and financed by stocks in the defunct British colonial company, Nigerian Gold Mines Limited; a Taíno-Arawak sculpture that was looted and eventually given to the British Museum, where it remains despite calls for repatriation;[4] and large maps, most prominently of Africa, as well as a three-dimensional globe whose surface is constructed from textiles signifying colonial and neocolonial networks of power, including the UN logo and a late eighteenth-century painting of imperialist propaganda by British-American artist John Singleton Copley.[5] In framing *The Procession* as concerned with both property and the world, Locke registers colonial racial capitalism's history and its endurance in our present.

Yet, *The Procession* evokes hopeful transformation as much as urgent critique. *The Procession*'s primary medium is cardboard, through which Locke constructs figures of extraordinary dynamism, their limbs moving stridently or joyfully, dancing in the halls of the Tate Britain despite cardboard's relative stiffness and its usefully tensile properties. As a product upon which long-distance trade depends, cardboard is at once necessary and disposable; in Locke's hands, it serves as a material index of capitalism's dependence upon short-lived, resource-intensive products and our potential to build newly sustainable artistic and ideological practices.[6] The fabric with which Locke drapes his parade's participants and their carnival accessories — their banners, musical instruments, expressive objects, and flags — similarly engages in an act of aesthetic recycling: sourced from stores across London, approximately half of this material was subsequently printed with Locke's own designs.[7] Bright, vibrant, and celebratory, these textiles sharply contrast with the sedate grey of the Tate Britain's marbled halls.

Locke's mixed-media methods are doubly regenerative: much of *The Procession* incorporates his existing work, which itself typically involves modified images of colonial legacies. Most of *The Procession*'s screen-printed images come from Locke's own back catalog, including the *Restoration* series of which his *Colston* piece is a part. Many of Locke's repurposed paintings and multimedia works emphasize British sovereign responsibility for systemic property theft and racialized dispossession across its empire: these works include his 2016 watercolor painting *Sovereign with Spider Monkeys*, a three-quarter profile of Queen Elizabeth II, her face composed of concentric circles of pink, yellow, green, and white that merge with a background of bright green monkeys, and his 2013 acrylic painting *Hinterland*, which itself reworks his 2013 painting *Victoria*, and comprises a painted, photographed statue of Queen Victoria, her stone dress becoming a world map of neon pink and neon green political boundaries that signal British land acquisition. Locke thus exposes the British imperial state's drive for property accumulation by creating beautiful, detailed, vibrant works of art, their neon colors signaling irreverence and reclamation. In at once rejecting colonial Britain's proprietary conception of property ownership and generatively producing new meanings, *The Procession* operates improperly, in this book's definition, to aesthetically produce emancipatory ways of being.

Inasmuch as Locke's improper aesthetics engage in the slow process of redistributing thought even as they immediately inhibit forms of distribution that celebrate violence, they operate materially as much as they do symbolically. In repurposing colonial share certificates, for instance, *The Procession* not only signifies that racialized resource extraction was made possible through a globalized system of speculative finance but it also intervenes in the circulation of colonial memorabilia. In his ongoing *Share* series, many examples of which form part of *The Procession*, Locke uses bright acrylic paint and pen to engage generatively with the ongoing consequences of European profiteering from enslavement and stolen land.[8] His 2012 work *Castara Estates*, for instance, is reproduced in *The Procession* on a large banner, held aloft by a woman dressed as a tiger, and featuring a large skull, its outline prominently contoured and its shading consisting of pink and white concentric circles that look like slabs of ham. The grinning skull covers most of a £100 share certificate in a Tobagonian sugar estate, leaving exposed only a handful of words along with colonialist depictions of a tropical idyll, replete with palm trees, abundant bananas, and a large, plantation owner's building. The fleshiness of this painted skull, leering like a plate of meat that knows it will be devoured even as it rejects the grounds of that consumption, exposes the violence belied by the certificate's depiction of tropical plenty.[9]

While *The Procession*'s many images of colonial stock certificates register European colonialism's conditions of financial possibility, as well as racial capitalism's continuation into the global present, they also index Locke's own act of aesthetic redistribution. In using colonial shares to form carnival costumes that at once expose and resignify the material mechanisms of colonial exploitation, *The Procession* redistributes colonial racial capitalism's economically, culturally, ecologically, and racially dispossessive system, instead constructing a celebration of anti-colonial community in the heart of London: the heart of European empire. Like Carnival itself, which emerged among communities of enslaved Black people in late eighteenth-century French Caribbean colonies as a subversion of plantocrats' pre-Lenten celebrations,[10] Locke repurposes existing material forms to establish new cultural practices that bear their own political and economic consequences. The figures in *The Procession* comprise the many mas, or characters, from carnival, including Pitchy Patchy, Moko Jumbie, and Soumayree.[11] By repurposing his own work for a dynamic, sculptural installation, Locke employs the same methodological practice as carnival: subverting dominant ideological and economic systems to aesthetically produce a racially just community.

The Procession is, above all, a deeply hopeful work. As its title indicates, it remains oriented toward potentiality even as it critiques the present; it celebrates existing joy even as it confronts colonial dispossession. Like the theory of aesthetic impropriety developed in this book, Locke's work engages in the slow process of redistributing our sense of how things are and how they should be. His work operates processually: it is a movement of people, of structures of thought; it moves thought forward. *The Procession*'s figures of West Indian Carnival are beautiful in their poise, their bright clothes, and their ornate decorations; commanding the span of the 300-foot long, high-vaulted Duveen Galleries, they reclaim London's art world for themselves. Designed for the space, swelling to its edges and distributed to allow for smaller models to be seen, the parade's sculptured participants at once encourage the viewer to marvel at their intricate detail while demanding that their audience remain at their outskirts. Recognizing their value, they share space with the museum's visitors, but they take their rightful place at the same time. In their authority and their beauty, their conceptual complexity and their aesthetic allure, the figures of *The Procession* stage the aesthetic's redistributive potential and its force. Locke's regenerative, improper aesthetics engage in acts of epistemological redistribution that bear material consequences, suggesting that art can play a significant role in changing the values that structure our present. In *The Procession*'s perhaps surprising disposition toward hope and joy, it functions improperly, playfully undercutting expectations while redistributing existing structures of thought.

Acknowledgments

A book is never the product of one person alone. I am grateful to the very many people who made this particular book possible.

Several sources of funding provided valuable research time. Chapter 3 was made possible, in part, by a grant from the West Virginia Humanities Council. Funding from West Virginia University came from the Provost's Office, Dean's Office, Humanities Center, Honor's College, and the Department of English. Some of these funds were used to work with Laura Portwood-Stacer on my proposal and envisioning the book as a whole. Attendance at conferences would not have been possible without significant childcare funding from the WVU Family Travel Program and the MLA.

Production costs have been supported by a Helen Tartar First Book Subvention from the American Comparative Literature Association. I am beyond grateful for this honor.

Parts of Chapters 1 and 2 have previously appeared in print. An early version of Chapter 1 appeared in 2019 in a special issue of *The Journal of Global and Postcolonial Studies*, "Law and Literature from the Global South," edited by Peter Leman and David Babcock. An early version of Chapter 2 appeared in *NOVEL: A Forum on Fiction* in 2015. Anonymous peer reviewers at both journals made my work stronger; thank you.

I was grateful for invitations to share work in development. Thank you to Simon Stern for inviting me to share a version of Chapter 3 with the Association for the Study of Law, Culture, and the Humanities (ASLCH) works-in-progress group, and thanks to all who attended and asked such productive questions. At Bard College, I am grateful to Daniel Williams and Elizabeth Holt for the invitation to talk about oil, land law, and Nigerian literature. Thank you to

Nicole Rizzuto for inviting me to talk about *David's Story* and intellectual property law at Georgetown University.

At Fordham University Press, I have been lucky to work with Tom Lay, Kem Crimmins, and Lis Pearson, along with the many others who make a press run smoothly. I want to express significant thanks to the two readers of this manuscript for providing reports whose intellectual generosity and capaciousness made it easy to identify what changes I needed to make.

This book would not have been possible without the thoughtful and dedicated librarians at WVU. A monograph about multiple jurisdictions, literary traditions, and subfields requires a huge amount of reading material: material that far exceeded the holdings at my own institution. Librarians with the interlibrary loans service processed hundreds, perhaps thousands of requests for this project; in doing so, they brought the world closer. Nicholas Stump provided expert guidance on legal citations. Lynne Stahl shared her outstanding librarianship skills on numerous occasions and her friendship on many others. Thank you to all of you.

Teaching inquisitive undergraduate and graduate students is a joy and has shaped what I know. Thanks are due, in particular, to undergraduate students in "Global Feminisms" and "Legal Fictions"; undergraduate and graduate students in "Global Modernities"; and graduate students in "Borders and Refugees" and "Decolonizing Feminisms." I'm especially glad to have worked extensively with Gabriella Pishotti, Jennifer Peedin, and Qazi Arka Rahman. I have learned so much from our conversations.

Above all, I owe thanks to the friends and colleagues who generously read my work in progress. Kate Hallemeier has engaged with the whole manuscript from start to finish and has consistently provided insightful, probing, and encouraging feedback. Our friendship is a true joy. Many others have read one or more chapters and shared similarly invaluable observations: I owe huge thanks to Brian Glavey, Anne Gulick, Sarah Wasserman, Stephanie DeGooyer, Jeff Insko, Jay Shelat, Matt Omelsky, Liz Anker, Walt Hunter, Johanna Winant, Jess Goldberg, and Simon Stern. I count myself incredibly lucky to be in conversation with such brilliant thinkers. Stephanie Foote and Rebecca Colesworthy showed the best of academia's capacity for intellectual generosity, stepping up at the shortest possible notice to make this manuscript possible: thank you.

Writing a book as a single parent far from family makes a robust support network utterly vital. I've been lucky to land somewhere with an exceptionally strong sense of community. I owe thanks to all of you—truly, too many to name—but particularly to the extended Heady family, who welcomed the three of us as their own.

ACKNOWLEDGMENTS

Much of this book has been written while participating in Morgantown's large activist community — a community that is very much part of a broader state network. Being involved in feminist organizing and social justice work has made the law's limits very clear. It has also shown that transforming the law is vital — and that the process is slow and requires patience. To all of you who have done so much: thank you.

My family has been a source of unending love, joy, and support, emotional and material. You give me strength, even from thousands of miles away. To Jackie Hughes, Mike Casey, Sally, Joe, Jack, Olivia, and Euan: thank you. Words are truly not enough.

To Andy: thank you for your deep love. To Ila: I'm so glad that we're family.

And to my darlings, Fynn and Solomon: being your mum is the deepest honor of my life. You have been my company throughout the long years of writing this book. It's dedicated to you both.

Notes

Introduction: An Aesthetic Theory of Law and Literature

1. Colston Four, Attorney General's Reference on a Point of Law [2022] No. 1 of 2022 (EWCA Crim 1259) (appeal taken from Bristol Crown Court 202201151 B3) (England and Wales), §8, §9, and §10.

2. For the precise charges faced by the defendants, see Peter Blair, "Legal Directions: Judge's Handout, R. v Milo Ponsford, Sage Willoughby, Rhian Graham & Jake Skuse," (Hodge Jones & Allen, 2022), 3–6. See also Alex Benn's explanation of the two defenses put to the court: "One defence was the prevention of crime, pursuant to section 3 of the Criminal Law Act 1967 in order to prevent Bristol City Council's public display of indecent matter, contrary to the Indecent Displays (Control) Act 1981. A different submission was that the defendants' conduct had been in exercise of their rights under articles 9, 10 and 11 of the European Convention on Human Rights. The defendants argued that convicting them of the offences would be a disproportionate interference with those rights." Alex Benn, "Criminal Damage: The 'Colston Four,' Proportionality and the Concerns That Linger," *The Journal of Criminal Law* 87, no. 1 (2023): 61.

3. Colston Four, Attorney General's Reference, §2.

4. Colston Four, Attorney General's Reference, §102.

5. Colston Four, Attorney General's Reference, §123.

6. The human rights group Liberty denounced Lord Chief Justice Hamblen's ruling for "put[ting] a threshold on when people can enact their human rights." "Colston Four Ruling 'Puts a Threshold on Our Human Rights' Liberty Warns," Liberty, September 28, 2022, https://www.libertyhumanrights.org.uk/issue/colston-four-ruling-puts-a-threshold-on-our-human-rights-liberty-warns/.

7. "How Statues Are Falling Around the World," *New York Times*, June 24, 2020.

8. For a description of the 2006 show, see Spike Island, "Hew Locke: Restoration."

Spike Island, www.spikeisland.org.uk/programme/exhibitions/hew-locke-restoration, July 2023.

9. A 2021 article in local newspaper the *Bristol Post* provides an extensive list of civic entities named after Colston whose names have been changed in the aftermath of the 2020 protest. See Tristan Cork and Estel Farell Roig, "The Bristol Things Named After Edward Colston That Have Changed Their Name in the Past Year," June 7, 2021, https://www.bristolpost.co.uk/news/bristol-news/bristol-things-named-after-edward-5486550.

10. Jon Wood, "Photography, Painting and Impossible Sculpture: Hew Locke's Natives and Colonials: Jon Wood in Conversation with Hew Locke," *Sculpture Journal* 15, no. 2 (2006): 283.

11. Hew Locke, *Strangers in Paradise*, ed. Stephanie James and Peter Bonnell (London: Black Dog Publishing, 2011), 125.

12. The term is Paul Gilroy's, theorized in his deeply influential 1993 work *The Black Atlantic: Modernity and Double Consciousness* (Cambridge, MA: Harvard University Press, 1993). While the concept has been robustly criticized, it remains useful for characterizing the ocean space that was subject to laws under complex adjudications of jurisdiction as well as for the transhistorical, transatlantic, hemispheric work undertaken by M. NourbeSe Philip in her poetry collection *Zong!*, which this book examines. For early critiques, see the introduction to the 1996 *Research in African Literatures* special issue: Simon Gikandi, "Introduction: Africa, Diaspora, and the Discourse of Modernity," *Research in African Literatures* 27, no. 4 (1996): 1–6. More recently, see the 2014 special issue in that same journal: Yogita Goyal, "Africa and the Black Atlantic," *Research in African Literatures* 45, no. 3 (2014).

13. I am using the British terms that correspond most closely to most postcolonial anglophone regions and whose legal regimes remain significantly shaped by UK law. The corresponding terms in US English are real estate (for immoveable property) and personal property (for moveable property).

14. I adapt this model from the concept of nonreformist reform that is discussed by Corinne Blalock and theorized by Amna Akbar in a special issue on law and political economy. See Blalock, "Introduction: Law and the Critique of Capitalism," *South Atlantic Quarterly* 121, no. 2 (2022): 231.

15. In developing aesthetic impropriety as a simultaneously analytic and political category, I take inspiration from Chandra Talpade Mohanty, who strategically employs the category of "Third World women" to "suggest potential alliances and collaborations across divisive boundaries." Chandra Talpade Mohanty, "Cartographies of Struggle: Third World Women and the Politics of Feminism," in *Feminism without Borders: Decolonizing Theory, Practicing Solidarity* (Durham, NC: Duke University Press, 2003), 46.

16. I take to heart Ann Laura Stoler's claim in *Duress: Imperial Durability in Our Times*, that the colonial era is very much ongoing. As Stoler writes, "One distinctive, troubled feature for those of us whose research and pedagogy revolve

around colonial histories of the past is how to convey how those histories remain present." Stoler's concept of "colonial presence" is useful for recognizing dispersed and differentiated colonial presents (as with Palestine) and presences (as when postcolonial legal systems maintain colonial laws). Ann Laura Stoler, *Duress: Imperial Durability in Our Times* (Durham, NC: Duke University Press, 2016), 24.

    17. Frederick Cooper, *Colonialism in Question: Theory, Knowledge, History* (Berkeley: University of California Press, 2005). See, in particular, 3–32 and 153–203.

    18. C. L. R. James's innovative historical method in *The Black Jacobins* (1938) newly characterizes capitalism's development through racial violence in plantation colonies. See C. L. R. James, *The Black Jacobins: Toussaint L'Ouverture and the San Domingo Revolution*, 2nd ed. (New York: Vintage, 1989). See also Sidney Mintz, *Sweetness and Power: The Place of Sugar in Modern History* (New York: Viking, 1985), esp. 46–52.

    19. Cedric J. Robinson analyzes racial capitalism's operations on a world scale; see his 1983 work *Black Marxism: The Making of the Black Radical Tradition*, 3rd ed. (Chapel Hill: University of North Carolina Press, 2020). Eric Williams provides a significant precursor to Robinson's framework: see *Capitalism & Slavery*, 3rd ed. (Chapel Hill: University of North Carolina Press, 2021). Sylvia Wynter analyzes contemporary, racialized modes of being human as a colonial legacy that remains to be undone; see "Unsettling the Coloniality of Being/Power/Truth/Freedom: Towards the Human After Man, Its Overrepresentation: An Argument," *The New Centennial Review* 3, no. 3 (2003): esp. 257–82 and 315–31.

    20. Most notably, see Aileen Moreton-Robinson, *The White Possessive: Property, Power, and Indigenous Sovereignty* (Minneapolis: University of Minnesota Press, 2015). See also Robert Nichols, *Theft Is Property!: Dispossession & Critical Theory* (Durham, NC: Duke University Press, 2020).

    21. Brenna Bhandar, *The Colonial Lives of Property: Law, Land, and Racial Regimes of Ownership* (Durham, NC: Duke University Press, 2013); C. B. Macpherson, *The Political Theory of Possessive Individualism: Hobbes to Locke* (Oxford: Clarendon Press, 1962).

    22. In comparative legal studies, Lauren Benton addresses property as one of colonialism's motivations and a legal category that it produced; see, in particular, *Law and Colonial Cultures: Legal Regimes in World History, 1400–1900* (Cambridge: Cambridge University Press, 2002). Renisa Mawani's study of colonial maritime law is, at heart, a study of property rights and exclusion, especially one in which the ship transporting racially minoritized migrants has a stronger claim to legal personhood than its human passengers; see *Across Oceans of Law: The Komagata Maru and Jurisdiction in the Time of Empire* (Durham, NC: Duke University Press, 2018).

    23. Moreton-Robinson, *The White Possessive*, 19.

    24. Bhandar, *The Colonial Lives of Property*, 3.

    25. Edward W. Said, *The Question of Palestine* (London: Vintage Books, 1992), 97.

    26. Frantz Fanon, *The Wretched of the Earth*, trans. Richard Philcox (New York: Grove Press, 2011), 68.

27. Cheryl I. Harris, "Whiteness as Property," *Harvard Law Review* 106, no. 8 (1993): 1707–91.
28. Harris, "Whiteness as Property," 1716.
29. Harris, "Whiteness as Property," 1721.
30. Nichols, *Theft is Property!*, 30–31.
31. Harris, "Whiteness as Property," 1720.
32. Harris, "Whiteness as Property," 1721.
33. Bhandar, *Colonial Lives of Property*, 8.
34. Bhandar, *Colonial Lives of Property*, 70.
35. Bhandar, *Colonial Lives of Property*, 4.
36. Bhandar, *Colonial Lives of Property*, 146.
37. Macpherson, *The Political Theory of Possessive Individualism*, 3.
38. Judith Butler and Athena Athanasiou, *Dispossession: The Performative in the Political: Conversations with Athena Athanasiou* (New York: Polity Press, 2013), 7, 99.
39. Moreton-Robinson, *The White Possessive*, 114.
40. Susan Koshy et al., eds., *Colonial Racial Capitalism*, (Durham, NC: Duke University Press, 2022), especially but not only 1–32.
41. "Proprietary (n. & Adj.)," in *Oxford English Dictionary* (Oxford: Oxford University Press, March 2024), https://doi.org/10.1093/OED/1922005579.
42. Moreton-Robinson avers that "[t]he possessive logic of patriarchal white sovereignty is predicated on exclusion" (81) while Harris maintains that "whiteness and property share a common premise — a conceptual nucleus — of a right to exclude." Moreton-Robinson, *The White Possessive*, 1714.
43. Benton argues, "Wherever a group imposed law on newly acquired territories and subordinate peoples, strategic decisions were made about the extent and nature of legal control. The strategies of rule included aggressive attempts to impose legal systems intact. More common, though, were conscious efforts to retain elements of existing institutions and limit legal change as a way of sustaining social order. Conquered and colonized groups sought, in turn, to respond to the imposition of law in ways that included accommodation, advocacy within the system, subtle delegitimation, and outright rebellion." Regarding property law in particular, Benton argues that "transformations in the law of property (including definitions of rights to land and labor) were sometimes perceived by social actors as primarily about changes in the ordering of legal authorities, rather than about property rights per se." Benton, *Law and Colonial Cultures*, 2–3, 11.
44. For this claim and the statutory law and legal analysis on which it is based, see Chapter 1.
45. Flavia Agnes, "Women, Marriage, and the Subordination of Rights," in *Community, Gender and Violence: Subaltern Studies XI*, ed. Partha Chatterjee and Pradeep Jeganathan (London: Hurst, 2000), 106–37.
46. On colonial law's violence, see Nasser Hussain, *The Jurisprudence of Emergency: Colonialism and the Rule of Law* (Ann Arbor: University of Michigan

Press, 2003); Tanya Agathocleous, *Disaffected: Emotion, Sedition, and Colonial Law in the Anglosphere* (Ithaca, NY: Cornell University Press, 2021); Stephen Morton, *States of Emergency: Colonialism, Literature and Law* (Liverpool: Liverpool University Press, 2013).

47. A particularly significant recent study for recognizing how postcolonial legal systems are a vital mode of producing justice is Peter Leman's *Singing the Law: Oral Jurisprudence and the Crisis of Colonial Modernity in East African Literature* (Liverpool: Liverpool University Press, 2020).

48. For a succinct and compelling case, see Blalock, "Law and the Critique of Capitalism," 230. Blalock explains that the Law and Political Economy (LPE) movement, a school of largely socialist and Marxist legal scholars, operates upon three principles: critique; building new imaginaries; and "actively seek[ing] to transform the world around it through constructive projects."

49. See David Lloyd's *Under Representation: The Racial Regime of Aesthetics* (New York: Fordham University Press, 2019), esp. 1–18.

50. I consciously invoke Angela Naimou's conceptualization of "salvage" as a way to reckon with, and emerge from, the ruins of colonial racial violence, and to do so in a way that balances judicious caution with necessary hope. Naimou explains, "Salvage is neither a full nor a failed recuperation; it is not a miracle of reanimation or resurrection; it is not part of the economy of recycling. It is not an inherently liberatory act and may be an exploitative one." Angela Naimou, *Salvage Work: U.S. and Caribbean Literatures Amid the Debris of Legal Personhood* (New York: Fordham University Press, 2015), 9.

51. J. Daniel Elam makes a compelling case for the aesthetic's import to anti-colonialism, arguing that anti-imperial Indian thinkers "invented aesthetic forms necessary to imagine a worldwide egalitarianism rooted in the unlikelihood of any future at all." J. Daniel Elam, *World Literature for the Wretched of the Earth: Anticolonial Aesthetics, Postcolonial Politics* (New York: Fordham University Press, 2020), 4.

52. As well as Caroline Levine and Anna Kornbluh, whose work I discuss at length in this Introduction, a few of the many recent monographs include Walt Hunter's *Forms of a World: Contemporary Poetry and the Making of Globalization* (New York: Fordham University Press, 2019); Jessie Reeder's *The Forms of Informal Empire: Britain, Latin America, and Nineteenth-Century Literature* (Baltimore, MD: Johns Hopkins University Press, 2020); and Nathan Hensley's *Forms of Empire: The Poetics of Victorian Sovereignty* (Oxford: Oxford University Press, 2018).

53. In addition to Kandice Chuh and Jacques Rancière, whose work is discussed in this Introduction, see Sianne Ngai's extensive body of work; Jean-Thomas Tremblay, *Breathing Aesthetics* (Durham, NC: Duke University Press, 2022); Michael Dango, *Crisis Style: The Aesthetics of Repair* (Stanford, CA: Stanford University Press, 2022); and Erica Fretwell, *Sensory Experiments: Psychophysics, Race, and the Aesthetics of Feeling* (Durham, NC: Duke University

Press, 2022). From a slightly different methodological angle but helpfully within postcolonial studies, see Peter Kalliney, *The Aesthetic Cold War: Decolonization and Global Literature* (Princeton, NJ: Princeton University Press, 2022).

54. Joseph Slaughter, *Human Rights, Inc: The World Novel, Narrative Form, and International Law* (New York: Fordham University Press, 2007). Slaughter's monograph was the first major work in postcolonial law and literature studies and has significantly shaped the field since.

55. Caroline Levine, *Forms: Whole, Rhythm, Hierarchy, Network* (Princeton, NJ: Princeton University Press, 2017), 64.

56. Levine, *Forms*, 85.

57. Levine, *Forms*, 94.

58. Levine, *Forms*, 40.

59. Levine, *Forms*, 52.

60. Anna Kornbluh, *The Order of Forms: Realism, Formalism, and Social Space* (Chicago: University of Chicago Press, 2019), 4.

61. Kornbluh, *The Order of Forms*, 81.

62. Kornbluh, *The Order of Forms*, 156.

63. Kornbluh, *The Order of Forms*, 40.

64. Raymond Williams, *Marxism and Literature* (Oxford: Oxford University Press, 1977), 128.

65. Williams, *Marxism and Literature*, 132.

66. Lloyd, *Under Representation*, 105–7.

67. Lloyd, *Under Representation*, 105.

68. Lloyd, *Under Representation*, 107.

69. Lloyd, *Under Representation*, viii.

70. Kandice Chuh, *The Difference Aesthetics Makes: On the Humanities "After Man"* (Durham, NC: Duke University Press, 2019), 121.

71. Chuh, *The Difference Aesthetics Makes*, 22.

72. Chuh, *The Difference Aesthetics Makes*, 51.

73. Chuh, *The Difference Aesthetics Makes*, 15.

74. Chuh, *The Difference Aesthetics Makes*, 62.

75. Sianne Ngai helpfully dissects the process of aesthetic engagement as occurring through the simultaneity of "feeling-based judgment" and "concept-based justification" in the moment of aesthetic encounter. See Sianne Ngai, *Our Aesthetic Categories: Zany, Cute, Interesting* (Cambridge, MA: Harvard University Press, 2012), 46.

76. Pheng Cheah, *What Is a World? On Postcolonial Literature as World Literature* (Durham, NC: Duke University Press, 2016), 108–9.

77. Cheah, *What Is a World?*, 116.

78. Cheah, *What Is a World?*, 211.

79. Cheah, *What Is a World?*, 11.

80. Cheah, *What Is a World?*, 8.

81. Jacques Rancière, "The Distribution of the Sensible: Politics and Aesthetics," in *The Politics of Aesthetics*, ed. Gabriel Rockhill (London: Bloomsbury, 2004), 7–14.

82. Rancière, "The Distribution of the Sensible," 7.

83. Rancière, "The Distribution of the Sensible," 8.

84. Rancière, "The Distribution of the Sensible," 8.

85. Rancière, "The Distribution of the Sensible," 10.

86. Rancière, "The Distribution of the Sensible," 12.

87. Rancière, "The Distribution of the Sensible," 9.

88. Jacques Derrida, "Force of Law: The 'Mystical Foundation of Authority,'" in *Acts of Religion*, ed. Gil Anidjar (New York: Routledge, 2002), 230–98.

1. Symbiosis: Oil Extraction in the Racial Capitalocene

1. Chidumeje Ndidi Patience Okonkwo, Lalit Kumar, and Subhashni Taylor, "The Niger Delta Wetland Ecosystem: What Threatens It and Why Should We Protect It?," *African Journal of Environmental Science and Technology* 9, no. 5 (2015): 451–63, 452.

2. Rob Nixon identifies the disproportionate impact of petroleum extraction on the Niger Delta, contending that "Shell's racism is manifest . . . in Africa," where "the company waives onshore drilling standards that it routinely upholds elsewhere. Indeed, 40 percent of all Shell oil spills worldwide have occurred in Nigeria." Rob Nixon, *Slow Violence and the Environmentalism of the Poor* (Cambridge, MA: Harvard University Press, 2011), 113.

3. Barisere Rachel Konne, "Inadequate Monitoring and Enforcement in the Nigerian Oil Industry: The Case of Shell and Ogoniland," *Cornell International Law Journal* 47, no. 1 (2014): 184–85.

4. Konne, "Inadequate Monitoring and Enforcement," 188.

5. On fishing as historically plentiful in the region, see Omolade Adunbi, *Oil Wealth and Insurgency in Nigeria* (Bloomington: Indiana University Press, 2015), 99–101.

6. Rhuks T. Ako and Patrick Okonmah, "Minority Rights Issues in Nigeria: A Theoretical Analysis of Historical and Contemporary Conflicts in the Oil-Rich Niger Delta Region," *International Journal on Minority and Group Rights* 16, no. 1 (2009): 64–65.

7. Nixon defines slow violence as something that "occurs gradually and out of sight, a violence of delayed destruction that is dispersed across time and space, an attritional violence that is typically not viewed as violence at all. Violence is customarily conceived as an event or action that is immediate in time, explosive and spectacular in space, and as erupting into instant sensational visibility. We need, I believe, to engage a different kind of violence, a violence that is neither spectacular nor instantaneous, but rather incremental and accretive, its calamitous repercussions playing out across a range of temporal scales." Nixon, *Slow Violence*, 2.

8. For a concise summary of *Four Nigerian Farmers v. Shell* and its consequences, see Samantha Hopkins et al., "Okpabi and Others v Royal Dutch Shell Plc and Another [2021] UKSC 3," *Northern Ireland Legal Quarterly* 72, no. 1 (2021): 148–59.

9. On the case history of the duty of care principle in English common law, especially in relation to foreign liability and duty of care in transnational tortious claims, see Lucas Roorda and Daniel Leader, "*Okpabi v Shell* and *Four Nigerian Farmers v Shell*: Parent Company Liability Back in Court," *Business and Human Rights Journal*, no. 6 (2021): 368–76.

10. Lucas Roorda, "Broken English: A Critique of the Dutch Court of Appeal Decision in *Four Nigerian Farmers and Milieudefensie v Shell*," *Transnational Legal Theory* 12, no. 1 (2021): 146.

11. *Okpabi & Ors. v. Royal Dutch Shell Plc & Anor.* (2021), UKSC 3 (appeal taken from [2018] EWCA Civ 191) (UK), §7.

12. *Okpabi v. Shell*, §127.

13. Christopher Riley and Oludara Akanmidu explain that "although the Supreme Court disagreed with the Court of Appeal's understanding of the principles governing a parent company's duty of care, these disagreements were not in fact relied on by the Supreme Court to justify its decision to allow the appeal. Rather, the Supreme Court allowed the appeal because it felt that the Court of Appeal (like the High Court before it) had conducted a 'mini-trial', in the interlocutory proceedings." Christopher Riley and Oludara Akanmidu, "Examining and Evaluating Transnational Tortious Actions Against Parent Companies: Lessons from Shell and Nigeria," *African Journal of International and Comparative Law* 30, no. 2 (2022): 237.

14. *Okpabi v. Shell*, § 137. See also Roorda and Leader, "Parent Company Liability Back in Court," 370–71.

15. Hopkins et al. compare *Okpabi v. Shell* to similar cases concerning parent company liability for human injuries due to industrial mineral extraction; as they argue, "judgments have begun to fall in favour of the victims rather than corporate defendants, marking what may represent the emergence of a more victim-centred approach to corporate liability." Hopkins et al., "Okpabi & Others," 148–49.

16. Tara Van Ho, "*Vedanta Resources Plc and Another v. Lungowe and Others*," *American Journal of International Law* 114, no. 1 (2020): 110–16.

17. Roorda and Leader identify this history as beginning with the 2000 case *Lubbe v. Cape*. See Roorda and Leader, "Parent Company Liability Back in Court," 369.

18. Much of this work builds on Cedric Robinson's concept of racial capitalism and is a burgeoning and vital part of climate crisis scholarship. For an overview of the emerging field and its histories, see Françoise Vergès, "Racial Capitalocene," in *Futures of Black Radicalism*, ed. Gaye Theresa Johnson and Alex Lubin (New York: Verso, 2017), 72–82. For a robust body of essays, see Anna M. Agathangelous and Kyle D. Killian, eds., *Time, Climate Change, Global Racial Capitalism and Decolonial Planetary Ecologies* (London: Routledge, 2022). Earlier scholarship

recognized the uneven global distribution of climate crisis but typically did so with reference to colonialism rather than race; see, for instance, Amitav Ghosh, *The Great Derangement: Climate Change and the Unthinkable* (Chicago: University of Chicago Press, 2016).

19. Sheena Wilson, Imre Szeman, and Adam Carlson follow the expository model of the energy humanities; see their introductory chapter, "On Petrocultures: Or, Why We Need to Understand Oil to Understand Everything Else," in *Petrocultures: Oil, Politics, Culture*, ed. Sheena Wilson et al. (Montréal: McGill-Queen's University Press, 2017), 3–19.

20. Jennifer Wenzel and Patricia Yaeger, "Introduction," in *Fueling Culture: 101 Words for Energy and Environment*, ed. Imre Szeman (New York: Fordham University Press, 2017), 15.

21. *Okpabi v. Shell*, §7.

22. Van Ho, "Vedanta Resources Plc," 113–14.

23. In her thorough history of the search for oil in twentieth-century Nigeria, Phia Steyn explains that "[t]he search for oil in Nigeria officially started in 1903 when two companies, Nigeria Properties (Limited) and the Nigeria and West African Development Syndicate (Limited) commenced exploration for bitumen, coal and oil." Phia Steyn, "Oil Exploration in Colonial Nigeria, c. 1903–58," *The Journal of Imperial and Commonwealth History* 37, no. 2 (2009): 252. On the searches conducted by the Nigerian Bitumen Corporation, see Chilenye Nwapi, "A Legislative Proposal for Public Participation in Oil and Gas Decision-Making in Nigeria," *Journal of African Law* 54, no. 2 (2010): 188.

24. Steyn, "Oil Exploration," 256.

25. On the political consequences of this history of speculation, see Jennifer Wenzel's discussion of "the long history of trade in commodities like slaves, palm oil, and petroleum in successive resource frontiers that produced new ethnic polities and new modes of governmentality, political subjectivity, and citizenship." Jennifer Wenzel, *The Disposition of Nature: Environmental Crisis and World Literature* (New York: Fordham University Press, 2019), 107.

26. Commercial transactions within the Delta region depended heavily on slave trading until 1807. Ekanade Olumide, "Minorities and Resource Allocation in a Transitional State: The Nigerian Experience," in *Horror in Paradise: Frameworks for Understanding the Crises of the Niger Delta Region of Nigeria*, ed. Christopher LaMonica and J. Shola Omotola (Durham, NC: Carolina Academic Press, 2014), 68.

27. Olumide notes that "Up to 1870, the East/Niger Delta river area was the primary source of production for the whole of the Niger Delta, accounting for over three quarters of the entire African export of palm oil to Europe." "Minorities and Resource Allocation," 68; see also Ako and Okonmah, "Minority Rights Issues in Nigeria," 59.

28. Inge Van Hulle, *Britain and International Law in West Africa* (Oxford: Oxford University Press, 2020), 23.

29. Van Hulle, *Britain and International Law*, 9.

30. R. K. Udo, "The National Land Policy of Nigeria," Research Report (Ibadan: Development Policy Center, 1999), 15.

31. Ako & Okonmah, "Minority Rights Issues in Nigeria," 55.

32. Cyril Obi, "The Geopolitical Consequences of Oil in Africa: The Case of Nigeria," *The Brown Journal of World Affairs* 26, no. 2 (2020): 7.

33. Obi, "The Geopolitical Consequences of Oil in Africa," 7.

34. Udo, "The National Land Policy of Nigeria," 15.

35. Enyinna S. Nwauche, "The Constitutional Challenge of the Integration and Interaction of Customary and the Received English Common Law in Nigeria and Ghana," *Tulane European & Civil Law Forum* 25, no. 4 (2010): 38–39.

36. Udo, "The National Land Policy of Nigeria," 18–19.

37. Udo, "The National Land Policy of Nigeria," 19.

38. Obi, "The Geopolitical Consequences of Oil," 7.

39. Cited in Olumide, "Minorities and Resource Allocation," 70.

40. Olumide, "Minorities and Resource Allocation," 70.

41. Van Hulle, *Britain and International Law*, 5.

42. On the Nigerian Civil War as a resource conflict, at least in part, see Toyin Falola and Matthew Heaton, *A History of Nigeria* (Cambridge: Cambridge University Press, 2008), 157–58. See also Michael Watts, "Resource Curse? Governmentality, Oil and Power in the Niger Delta, Nigeria," *Geopolitics* 9, no. 1 (2004): 59–60, 66–67.

43. See Adefi Olong, *Land Law in Nigeria*, 2nd ed. (Lagos, Nigeria: Malthouse Press, 2012), 14.

44. Petroleum Act (1969) Cap. P10 (Cap. 350 Laws of the Federation of Nigeria 1990), §1.1.

45. Land Use Act (1978) Cap. L5, Laws of the Federation of Nigeria 2004, §5(28).

46. T. O. Elias, *Nigerian Land Law*, 4th ed. (London: Sweet & Maxwell, 1971), 54–68.

47. Muhammed Tawfiq Ladan, "Status of Environmental Law and Sustainable Land Use in Nigeria," in *Land Use Law for Sustainable Development*, ed. Natalie J. Chalifour et al. (Cambridge: Cambridge University Press, 2007), 247.

48. Uche Jack-Osimiri, "Repeal Land Use Act 1978 or Amendment of Its Provisions Governing Compensation for Compulsory Acquisition?," in *Critical Issues in Nigerian Property Law*, ed. Agbe Utuama (Lagos, Nigeria: Malthouse Press, 2016), 153.

49. Constitution of Nigeria, 1999, §44 (3).

50. Amitav Ghosh coined the term "petrofiction" in 1992 in a review of literary representations of oil that has since been named one of the first literary assessments of the field and of climate change fiction more generally. Amitav Ghosh, "Petrofiction," *The New Republic*, March 2, 1992.

51. In *Living Oil: Petroleum Culture in the American Century*, Stephanie LeMenager uses the term "petroleum aesthetics" to name oil's cultural import in US national narratives. Stephanie LeMenager, *Living Oil: Petroleum Culture in the American Century* (Oxford: Oxford University Press, 2014).

52. Wenzel's influential term originates in her 2006 article "Petro-Magic-Realism: Toward a Political Ecology of Nigerian Literature" and refers to magical realist Nigerian texts, including "What the Tapster Saw," that engage somewhat fantastically with petroleum production's material conditions. Jennifer Wenzel, "Petro-Magic-Realism: Toward a Political Ecology of Nigerian Literature," *Postcolonial Studies* 9, no. 4 (2006).

53. Ben Okri, "What the Tapster Saw," in *Stars of the New Curfew* (London: Vintage, 1999), 184; emphasis in original.

54. Okri, "What the Tapster Saw," 184.

55. Okri, "What the Tapster Saw," 184.

56. Okri, "What the Tapster Saw," 185.

57. Andrew Apter, *The Pan-African Nation: Oil and the Spectacle of Culture in Nigeria* (Chicago: University of Chicago Press, 2014), 8, 16.

58. Okri, "What the Tapster Saw," 185.

59. Okri, "What the Tapster Saw," 185.

60. In 2023, 19,162.504 gallons of oil were spilled in the Niger Delta. The year before, 47,708.98 gallons were spilled. NOSDRA, "Nigerian Oil Spill Monitor. NOSDRA, National Oil Spill Detection and Response Agency," n.d., https://nosdra.oilspillmonitor.ng/.

61. Okri, "What the Tapster Saw," 189.

62. Okri, "What the Tapster Saw," 189.

63. Watts, "Resource Curse?," 67; Wenzel, *The Disposition of Nature*, 92.

64. Rob Nixon writes that "A 1995 World Bank report noted that 76 percent of the natural gas resulting from petroleum production in Nigeria was flared (at temperatures of 14,000 degrees Celsius), while in Britain only 4.3 percent and in the United States a mere 0.6 percent was flared." Nixon, *Slow Violence*, 113. More recent reports confirm that the United States has substantially increased its own gas flaring practices, now flaring more gas than Nigeria each year. "Global Gas Flaring Tracker Report" (World Bank, 2023), www.worldbank.org/en/programs/gasflaringreduction/global-flaring-data, 5–6, 12.

65. Okri, "What the Tapster Saw," 186.

66. Okri, "What the Tapster Saw," 191.

67. Okri, "What the Tapster Saw," 186.

68. Nixon, *Slow Violence*, 113.

69. Nigeria secured independence from Britain in 1960. Oil was discovered by the Shell-BP Development Company, a colonial consortium owned by Royal Dutch Shell and British Petroleum, in 1956. Royal Dutch Shell remains the dominant oil company in the region. Falola and Heaton, *A History of Nigeria*, 181.

70. Lisa Stephens, "The Illusion of Sustainable Development: How Nigeria's Environmental Laws Are Failing the Niger Delta," *Vermont Law Review* 36, no. 2 (2011): 394–95.

71. Environmental Impact Assessment Decree No. (86) (1992), Cap 2 §20 (Nigeria).

72. Stephens describes Nigeria's environmental laws as "weak and underenforced" and as "providing only the illusion of environmental protection and sustainable development." Stephens, "The Illusion of Sustainable Development," 387, 406–7. Likewise, Konne argues that Nigeria's environmental laws typically fail because of a lack of independent monitoring and because fines for breaking existing regulations are too low to prove a deterrent. Konne, "Inadequate Monitoring and Enforcement," 190–96.

73. Falola and Heaton, *A History of Nigeria*, 184.

74. During the latter quarter of the twentieth century, oil and gas generated around 95 percent of Nigeria's export revenue and approximately 80 percent of all government revenues: Nixon, *Slow Violence*, 106; Stephens, "The Illusion of Sustainable Development," 390; and The World Bank, "Nigeria Economic Report: Report no. 101751," *Nigeria Economic Report*, no. 3 (November 2015), 21. Only since the global economic crash of 2008 has Nigeria's dependence on oil diminished, with the majority of the country's GDP deriving today from the service sector. World Bank, "Nigeria Economic Report," 2014, 2.

75. Rhuks T. Ako, "Nigeria's Land Use Act: An Anti-Thesis to Environmental Justice," *Journal of African Law* 53, no. 2 (2009): 297.

76. Ako, "Nigeria's Land Use Act," 290.

77. Olumide observes that decree no. 27 of 1967 had the "effect of denying minorities of their rights to their land and resources derived therefrom." Olumide, "Minorities and Resource Allocation," 70.

78. Chigozie Obioma, *The Fishermen* (London: Little, Brown & Company, 2016), 15, 21, 35.

79. Obioma, *The Fishermen*, 15.

80. Obioma, *The Fishermen*, 15

81. Obioma, *The Fishermen*, 13.

82. Kate Harlin, "'How Can a River Be Red?' Violent Petroculture in Chigozie Obioma's *The Fishermen*," *Journal of Postcolonial Writing* 55, no. 5 (n.d.): 690.

83. Obioma, *The Fishermen*, 13.

84. Obioma, *The Fishermen*, 84, 87.

85. Obioma, *The Fishermen*, 84.

86. Nnimmo Bassey, *Oil Politics: Echoes of Ecological Wars* (Montréal: Daraja Press, 2016), 14.

87. Nnimmo Bassey, *The Secure and the Dispossessed: How the Military and Corporations Are Shaping a Climate-Changed World* (London: Pluto Press, 2015), 3.

88. Obioma, *The Fishermen*, 142.

89. W. B. Yeats, "The Second Coming," *The Collected Poems of W. B. Yeats*, 2nd edition, ed. Richard J. Finneran (New York: Scribner, 1996), 200, line 1.

90. Obioma, *The Fishermen*, 8.

91. Obioma, *The Fishermen*, 84.

92. Yeats, "The Second Coming," lines 5–6.

93. Wenzel, *The Disposition of Nature*, 89.

94. David Chandler and Julian Reid provide an excellent overview of these processes in their scathing analysis of anthropology's ontological turn, rebuking theorists including Viveiros de Castro, Bruno Latour, Donna Haraway, and Isabelle Stengers for at once exoticizing and objectifying Indigenous knowledge. David Chandler and Julian Reid, "Becoming Indigenous: The 'Speculative Turn' in Anthropology and the (Re)Colonisation of Indigeneity," *Postcolonial Studies: Culture* 23, no. 4 (2020).

95. Kyle Whyte, "Settler Colonialism, Ecology, and Environmental Justice," *Environment and Society: Advances in Research* 9 (2018): 126.

96. Whyte, "Settler Colonialism," 128.

97. Whyte, "Settler Colonialism," 137, 140.

98. Cajetan Iheka, *Naturalizing Africa: Ecological Violence, Agency, and Postcolonial Resistance in African Literature* (Cambridge: Cambridge University Press, 2018), 8, 3.

99. Iheka, *Naturalizing Africa*, 30, 104.

100. Iheka, *Naturalizing Africa*, 104, 30.

101. Iheka, *Naturalizing Africa*, 29.

102. Whyte, "Settler Colonialism," 140.

103. Some legal theorists identify Niger Delta peoples like the Ogoni as Indigenous (Konne, "Inadequate Monitoring and Enforcement," 82–83) while others argue that they are not (Nwapi, "A Legislative Proposal," 187). The former position is becoming more widely accepted. Greater interdisciplinary analysis and engagement between postcolonial studies, area studies, and Indigenous studies will likely clarify some of the political stakes in continuing to parse these categories and form alliances.

104. Kristen A. Carpenter, Sonia K. Katyal, and Angela R. Riley, "In Defense of Property," *The Yale Law Journal* 118, no. 6 (2009): 1028.

105. The "bundle of sticks" theory of property as a relative right derives from Wesley Hohfeld's early twentieth-century work. Carpenter, Katyal, and Riley, "In Defense of Property," 1066–67. Yet, as David B. Schorr explains, the conception of property as involving a bundle of relative rights has a much longer history than is usually acknowledged. Schorr writes, "the 'bundle of rights' approach to property permeated early-modern English property law, especially land law, to its core. The disintegration of property into a multitude of sticks was . . . the product of the common law's medieval origins." David B. Schorr, "How Blackstone Became a Blackstonian," *Theoretical Inquiries in Law* 10 (2009): 108.

106. Carpenter, Katyal, and Riley, "In Defense of Property," 1082.

107. Lin Heng Lye, "Land Law and the Environment: Re-Examining the Concept of Ownership and Forging New Rights and Obligations in a Changed World," *Land Law and the Environment* 22 (2010): 198.

108. English common law was imposed on Singapore in 1826. Lye, "Land Law and the Environment," 190.

109. Lye, "Land Law and the Environment," 193.

110. Lye, "Land Law and the Environment," 212–17.
111. Okri, "What the Tapster Saw," 184, 185.
112. Okri, "What the Tapster Saw," 186.
113. Okri, "What the Tapster Saw," 188.
114. Okri, "What the Tapster Saw," 189.
115. Obioma, *The Fishermen*, 175.
116. Obioma, *The Fishermen*, 183.
117. Obioma, *The Fishermen*, 178.
118. Obioma, *The Fishermen*, 182.
119. Obioma, *The Fishermen*, 182.
120. Obioma, *The Fishermen*, 183.
121. Wenzel, *The Disposition of Nature*, 84.
122. Wenzel, *The Disposition of Nature*, 115.
123. Wenzel, *The Disposition of Nature*, 88, 116.
124. Okri, "What the Tapster Saw," 186.
125. Abiola Irele, *The African Experience in Literature and Ideology* (London: Heinemann, 1981), 174–97; Ato Quayson, *Strategic Transformations: Orality and History in the Work of Rev. Samuel Johnson, Amos Tutuola, Wole Soyinka, and Ben Okri* (Oxford: Currey, 1997), 44–64, 101–56.
126. Obioma, *The Fishermen*, 144.
127. Obioma, *The Fishermen*, 155.
128. Udo, "The National Land Policy of Nigeria," 21.
129. Elias, *Nigerian Land Law*, 74.
130. Udo, "The National Land Policy of Nigeria," 19.
131. *Amodu Tijani v. the Secretary*, Southern Provinces. Nigeria Supreme Court (1921) (Nigeria).
132. Obioma, *The Fishermen*, 155.
133. Minerals Act (1946) Cap. 121. *Federal Republic of Nigeria: Mines Manual*, 9th ed. (Govt. of Nigeria 1965), §3 (1).
134. Okri, "What the Tapster Saw," 192–93.
135. Okri, "What the Tapster Saw," 193.
136. Okri, "What the Tapster Saw," 194.
137. Obioma, *The Fishermen*, 295.
138. Obioma, *The Fishermen*, 295.
139. Obioma, *The Fishermen*, 295.
140. Obioma, *The Fishermen*, 295.
141. Okri, "What the Tapster Saw," 188–89.
142. For an overview of activist actions against oil sponsorship in London in the 2010s, see Mel Evans, *Art Wash: Big Oil and the Arts* (London: Pluto Press, 2015), 140–65.
143. Riley and Akanmidu, "Examining and Evaluating Transnational Tortious Actions Against Parent Companies," 247.

144. Iheka, *Naturalizing Africa*, 2.
145. Iheka, *Naturalizing Africa*, 2.

2. Reciprocity: Female Dispossession in Inheritance and Divorce

1. After Britain began codifying India's vast and flexible laws, in the process removing women's customary property rights along with other legal protections, women took legal action and organized themselves politically to demand access to property. For a discussion of nineteenth-century actions, see Bina Agarwal, *A Field of One's Own: Gender and Land Rights in South Asia* (Cambridge: Cambridge University Press, 1994), 202–3. For a detailed discussion of twentieth-century actions, especially from the 1930s and the "intense contestation" from the 1930s to the 1950s, see Agarwal, *A Field of One's Own*, 205–10. More broadly, see Ratna Kapur, "Hecklers to Power? The Waning of Liberal Rights and Challenges to Feminism in India," in *South Asian Feminisms*, ed. Ania Loomba and Ritty A. Lukose (Durham, NC: Duke University Press, 2012), 334–35.

2. Srila Roy argues that the 2012 gang rape and murder of Jyothi Singh Pandey in Delhi newly brought together establishment feminists, represented by academics and NGO workers, and young feminist activists, outraged by spectacular violence, to challenge visible forms of misogyny; see Srila Roy, *Changing the Subject: Feminist and Queer Politics in Neoliberal India* (Durham, NC: Duke University Press, 2022), 1–3 and 13–14. More generally, see Kapur, "Hecklers to Power?," 335.

3. Roy, *Changing the Subject*, 3–4.

4. *Madhu Kishwar v. State of Bihar*, AIR 1826 SCC (3) 644 (India), 8.

5. *Madhu Kishwar v. State of Bihar*, 1. And yet, as Nandita Haksar explains, Kishwar's action caused significant harms. Haksar decries feminists like Kishwar who have been "insensitive to the problems of tribal peoples in the Northeast," noting that "their patronizing attitude can be used by the state to justify the breaking up of the Northeast societies." More than a case of competing interests between tribal rights and women's rights, the Kishwar action against the Chota Nagpur Tenancy Act failed to recognize that establishing gender equitable inheritance rights for northeast Adivasi communities would mean both that "the government and other vested interests would use it to break common property into private property" and that tribal women would have fewer protections as both women and Adivasi people. Nandita Haksar, "Human Rights Lawyering: A Feminist Perspective," in *Women's Studies in India: A Reader*, ed. Mary E. John (New Delhi: Penguin, 2008), 282, 283.

6. I have not been able to locate the Act itself. The closest document I have found to the original is a 1916 discussion by Travancore state legislators, recorded in the Keralan legislature's archives: Travancore Christian Succession Act, Abstract Proceedings of the Travancore Legislative Council (TLC), (TLC 9) December 20, 1916, (India), *Kerala Legislative Assembly: Proceedings*, http://klaproceedings.niyamasabha.org/index.php.

7. Travancore Christian Succession Act, quoted in *Mrs. Mary Roy Etc. Etc v. State of Kerala & Ors*, AIR, 1011, SCR 1–371 (1986) (India), headnote.

8. This latter case, *Bahadur v. Bratiya* (2015), assessed female inheritance rights among the Gaddis tribe in Himachal Pradesh. The state's high court overturned tribal jurisprudence, holding that "daughters in the tribal areas in the State of Himachal Pradesh shall inherit the property in accordance with the Hindu Succession Act, 1956 and not as per customs and usages in order to prevent the women from social injustice and prevention of all forms of exploitation. The laws must evolve with the times if societies are to progress." *Bahadur v. Bratiya & Others*, HP 1555 High Court of Himachal Pradesh (2015) (India), §63.

9. *Solomon v. Muthiah* (1974) was heard in the Madras High Court and is cited twice in *Mary Roy v. Kerala*, including quoting its decision directly. In his decision, Mr. Justice Ismail concluded that "the Travancore Christian Succession Regulation II of 1902 is a law corresponding to the provisions contained in Part V of the Indian Succession Act, 1925 so far as Christians are concerned," meaning that "the Travancore Christian Succession Act, 1092 was wholly repealed by virtue of sec. 6 of Part States (Laws) Act, 1951." *Solomon & Ors. v. Muthiah & Ors*, *Madras Law Journal* (1974) (India): 1–53.

10. Thomas John, "Succession Law in India and Obstacles in the Road to Gender Equality: The Experience of Mary Roy. State of Kerala," *Student Bar Review* 18, no. 2 (2006): 46 n. 28.

11. For a detailed discussion of the bill and its rationale, see John, "Succession Law in India," 44.

12. Section 3 of the 2002 Indian Succession Amendment Act altered section 213, subsection 2 of the 1925 Act to extend its jurisdiction to "Indian Christians," i.e., to Kerala's Syrian Christian community. See Indian Succession (Amendment) Act, 2002 (Act No. 26 of 2002) (India); and compare with Indian Succession Act, 1925, (Act No. 39 of 1925).

13. The 2013 version of the Marriage Laws Amendment Bill 2010 went further than its first iteration. Whereas the bill that was presented in 2010 sought simply to make divorce more accessible, allowing only one spouse to present a petition for divorce rather than requiring both spouses to agree (per the Hindu Marriage Act of 1955), the 2013 amendment also sought to protect female economic security upon divorce. Section 13F of the 2013 Amendment stipulates that "the court may, at the time of passing of the decree under section 13C on a petition made by the wife, order that the husband shall give for her and children as defined in section 13E, such compensation which shall include a share in his share of the immovable property (other than inherited or inheritable immovable property) and such amount by way of share in movable property, if any, towards the settlement of her claim, as the court may deem just and equitable, and while determining such compensation the court shall take into account the value of inherited or inheritable property of the husband." See Marriage Laws Amendment Bill, 2013 (Bill No. 41 of 2010 as passed by

Rajya Sabha) (lapsed), §13F; see also Marriage Laws Amendment Bill, 2010 (Bill No. 41 of 2010) (lapsed) (India).

14. Lotika Sarkar offers a comprehensive account of wide-ranging feminist legislative achievements — and less successful efforts — from the 1970s to the 1990s: Lotika Sarkar, "Women's Movement and the Legal Process," CWDS: *Occasional Paper*, no. 24 (1995).

15. Kapur, "Hecklers to Power?," 334.

16. Kapur, "Hecklers to Power?," 335.

17. Rajeswari Sunder Rajan, *The Scandal of the State: Women, Law, and Citizenship in Postcolonial India* (Durham, NC: Duke University Press, 2003), 159.

18. Kapur argues that the autonomous women's movement is too focused on commonality but Indian feminists' composite approach to establishing gender-just legal reform since the mid-1990s offers a more granular understanding of female subjectivity, patriarchal forces, and gender discrimination than in prior periods. Kapur, "Hecklers to Power?, 338.

19. Rajan, *The Scandal of the State*, 148.

20. Menon explains that "[t]he ... personal laws of each of these religions that are being defended today in the name of tradition and religious freedom are, thus, colonial constructions of the late nineteenth and early twentieth centuries. . . . [T]he gender discriminatory provisions of the personal laws are based on the same logic of exclusions that characterize the coming-into-being of the Indian nation itself." Nivedita Menon, "A Uniform Civil Code in India: The State of the Debate in 2014," *Feminist Studies* 40, no. 2 (2014): 483. See also Rajan, whose account of personal laws in relation to the UCC is frequently repeated in recent feminist scholarship: Rajan, *The Scandal of the State*, 147–48.

21. For a detailed analysis of the *Shah Bano* case, including its context, the conflicts that arose and their relevance for Indian politics, and the way in which the Muslim Women (Protection on Divorce) Act was in fact used by the judiciary to protect women's rights far more than before its passing, see Flavia Agnes, "From Shah Bano to Kausar Bano: Contextualizing the 'Muslim Woman' with a Communalized Polity," in *South Asian Feminisms*, ed. Ania Loomba and Ritty A. Lukose (Durham, NC: Duke University Press, 2012), esp. 33–41. On the *Shah Bano* case in relation to legal history as a distinct discourse and mode of knowledge production, see Mitra Sharafi, "South Asian Legal History," *Annual Review of Law and Social Science* 11 (2015): 314.

22. Flavia Agnes, *Law and Gender Inequality: The Politics of Women's Rights in India* (Oxford: Oxford University Press, 1999), 193.

23. For a thorough overview of the various possible positions taken by both liberal and communitarian feminists, see Rajan, *The Scandal of the State*, 158–62. For an account that broadly contextualizes feminists' rejection of a UCC since the 1990s, see Menon, "A Uniform Civil Code," esp. 484–86. For a theoretical proposition of how Indian feminism might develop a more radical response to legal progress that follows neither liberalism nor communalism, the two current main approaches,

see Kapur, "Hecklers to Power?," esp. 348–52. See also Agnes, *Law and Gender Inequality*, 192–200.

24. Menon, "A Uniform Civil Code," 485–86.

25. Archana Mishra, "Towards Women's Equal Right to Property," *Property Law Review* 5, no. 3 (2016): 15.

26. Law Commission of India, "Consultation Paper on Reform of Family Law" (Government of India, August 31, 2018), https://archive.pib.gov.in/documents/rlink/2018/aug/p201883101.pdf, (1, §1.1), (30, §2.38).

27. For a historical account of the legal category of woman as worker, and of colonial legislation's deleterious effect on women laborers, see Janaki Nair, *Women and Law in Colonial India: A Social History* (Kali for Women, 1996), 95–121.

28. See Kapur on sex workers' mobilization and specifically on actions by Mumbai dancers: Kapur, "Hecklers to Power?," 340, 342. For a lengthy account that argues that sex worker mobilization has transformed the meaning of India's Constitution, see Rohit De, *A People's Constitution: The Everyday Life of Law in the Indian Republic* (Princeton, NJ: Princeton University Press, 2018), 169–214. The edited collection *South Asian Feminisms* contains multiple relevant essays in two sections: section II, on "Feminism, Labor, and Globalization" and section IV, "Feminism, Sex Work, and the Politics of Sexuality." Ania Loomba and Ritty A. Lukose, eds., *South Asian Feminisms* (Durham, NC: Duke University Press, 2012). See also "Women in Sex Work," written on behalf of sex worker collective Veshya Anyay Mukti Parishad (VAMP): Meena Sarawathi Seshu, "Women in Sex Work," in *Negotiating Spaces: Legal Domains, Gender Concerns, and Community Constructs*, ed. Flavia Agnes and Shoba Venkatesh Ghosh (Delhi: Oxford University Press, 2012), 29–58.

29. Rajan proposes that "work might serve as a possible locus of women's collectivization and identity" in the early twenty-first century, in the face of fractured feminist solidarity, which she attributes to increased recognition of intersecting identities and gradations of difference among the category of woman. Rajan, *The Scandal of the State*, 170. For her account of the female worker as a contemporary political subject, see 170–73.

30. De, *A People's Constitution*, 9.

31. As De explains, the Constitution permits citizens "to petition the Supreme Court for the enforcement of fundamental rights" and empowers appellate courts "to issue remedies in forms of writs against the state." De, *A People's Constitution*, 10.

32. De, *A People's Constitution*, 3.

33. In an essay that is quite clearly a response to *The God of Small Things*, Mary Roy sets out the similarities between her own life and the events of her daughter's first novel. After chronicling the biographical convergences, Mary Roy writes, "*The God of Small Things* is a chronicle of what Arundhati and her brother suffered as children in a house where their mother and her two children were not wanted." Mary Roy, "Three Generations of Indian Women," *Indian Journal of Gender Studies* 6, no. 2 (1999): 215.

34. Arundhati Roy, *The God of Small Things* (New York: Random House, 1997), 215.

35. See Praveena Kodoth, "Gender, Community and Identity in Property Law Reform: The Case of Early Twentieth Century Tiruvitamkoor," *Inter-Asia Cultural Studies* 3, no. 3 (2002): 385, 389.

36. Ammu's family had given her a dowry upon marriage, which her former father-in-law stole, so, under Syrian Christian custom, she has already received her portion of the estate; see Amali Philips, "Rethinking Dowry, Inheritance and Women's Resistance among the Syrian Christians of Kerala," *Anthropologica* 45, no. 2 (2003): 260.

37. Philips, "Rethinking Dowry," 250.

38. Philips, "Rethinking Dowry," 253.

39. Some attention has been paid to Ammu's legislated dispossession; see, for instance, Elizabeth S. Anker, *Fictions of Dignity: Embodying Human Rights in World Literature* (Ithaca, NY: Cornell University Press, 2012), 197–98. Yet, Anker primarily addresses the liberal subject of human rights rather than India's gendered property laws. See also my earlier essay: Rose Casey, "Possessive Politics and Improper Aesthetics: Property Rights and Female Dispossession in Arundhati Roy's *The God of Small Things*," NOVEL: A Forum on Fiction 48, no. 3 (2015): 381–99.

40. Srila Roy, *Changing the Subject*, 1–3, 13–14.

41. Sarah Brouillette discusses Arundhati Roy in relation to Penguin Books's opening a branch office in India in 1985; Sarah Brouillette, *Postcolonial Writers in the Global Literary Marketplace* (Basingstoke: Palgrave, 2007), 57–58. More generally, see Brouillette's analysis of what she terms "market postcolonialism," 56–75.

42. Caste, in common Western consciousness, operates as the same kind of "displaced figuration," in Gayatri Spivak's terms, of the self-immolating widow: Gayatri Chakravorty Spivak, "Can the Subaltern Speak?," in *Marxism and the Interpretation of Culture*, ed. Cary Nelson and Lawrence Grossberg (Basingstoke: Macmillan Education, 1988), 306.

43. For an astute analysis of the relationship between gender and caste in Roy's novel, see Anuradha Dingwaney Needham, "'The Small Voice of History' in Arundhati Roy's *The God of Small Things*," *Interventions: International Journal of Postcolonial Studies* 7, no. 3 (2005). For a discussion of comparativist feminist methodology, see Tracy Lemaster, "Influence and Intertextuality in Arundhati Roy and Harper Lee," *MFS: Modern Fiction Studies* 56, no. 4 (2010). Lemaster argues that intertextual analyses of given literary texts help to clarify significant feminist debates about how to conceptualize gender in relation to race and colonialism. Susan Stanford Friedman similarly offers a transnational feminist analysis of gendered colonial and postcolonial violence in "Feminism, State Fictions and Violence: Gender, Geopolitics and Transnationalism." Friedman's multiple essays on *The God of Small Things* have been influential, especially in North American academe, yet I note her essay's Orientalism, including its assessment of Ammu as "walled up in a form of modern *sati*" and its claim that Syrian Christians are "known

for generations of in-breeding." Susan Stanford Friedman, "Feminism, State Fictions and Violence: Gender, Geopolitics and Transnationalism," *Communal/Plural* 9, no. 1 (2001): 120, 117.

44. Aijaz Ahmad, "Reading Arundhati Roy Politically," *Frontline*, August 8, 1997, 106.

45. Roy, *The God of Small Things*, 56.
46. Roy, *The God of Small Things*, 82.
47. Roy, *The God of Small Things*, 82.
48. Roy, *The God of Small Things*, 154, 155.
49. Roy, *The God of Small Things*, 56.
50. Roy, *The God of Small Things*, 56.
51. Roy, *The God of Small Things*, 55.
52. Roy, *The God of Small Things*, 56.
53. Roy, *The God of Small Things*, 56.
54. Agarwal, *A Field of One's Own*, 12.
55. Roy, *The God of Small Things*, 261.
56. Roy, *The God of Small Things*, 63.
57. Agarwal, *A Field of One's Own*, 30.
58. Roy, *The God of Small Things*, 56.
59. Roy, *The God of Small Things*, 124.

60. Kirti Singh, *Separated and Divorced Women in India: Economic Rights and Entitlements* (Los Angeles: Sage Law, 2013), 7.

61. Agnes, "Women, Marriage, and the Subordination of Rights," 109.

62. Agnes, "Women, Marriage, and the Subordination of Rights," 111–13; Mytheli Sreenivas, "Conjugality and Capital: Gender, Families, and Property under Colonial Law in India," *The Journal of Asian Studies* 63, no. 4 (2004): 939–40.

63. Sreenivas, "Conjugality and Capital," 940.

64. As Philips explains, "Syrian Christian women, like women in other Indian communities, receive inheritance as residual heirs, which might be given entirely as dowry at the time of marriage or given as testamentary inheritance after marriage." Philips, "Rethinking Dowry," 261.

65. Kodoth, "Gender, Community and Identity in Property Law Reform," 385.

66. Michael P. K. Tharakan, "History as Development Experience: Desegregated and Deconstructed Analysis of Kerala," PhD Diss. (Mahatma Gandhi University, Kottayam, India, 1997), 125, quoted in Kodoth, "Gender, Community and Identity in Property Law Reform," 390 footnote 4.

67. Philips, "Rethinking Dowry," 248.

68. Rachel Sturman, *The Government of Social Life in Colonial India: Liberalism, Religious Law, and Women's Rights* (Cambridge: Cambridge University Press, 2012), 3.

69. Singh, *Separated and Divorced Women in India*, esp. 1–37 and 136–64.

70. See the Law Commission of India, "Consultation Paper on Reform of Family Law," 29–31.

71. Singh, *Separated and Divorced Women in India*, 3.
72. Roy, *The God of Small Things*, 160.
73. For a sophisticated theoretical account of how this novel enacts its opposition to capitalist exploitation and patriarchal violence, see John Lutz, "Commodity Fetishism, Patriarchal Repression, and Psychic Deprivation in Arundhati Roy's *The God of Small Things*," *Mosaic* 42, no. 3 (2009).
74. See Sreenivas, "Conjugality and Capital," esp. 938–42.
75. Roy, *The God of Small Things*, 134.
76. Roy, *The God of Small Things*, 104.
77. For a sophisticated and original account of how Roy's novel itself remains trapped inside normative history in its representation of queerness, see Leila Neti, "'The Love Laws': Section 377 and the Politics of Queerness in Arundhati Roy's *The God of Small Things*," *Law & Literature* 29, no. 2 (2017): 236–39.
78. Roy, *The God of Small Things*, 3.
79. Morris R. Cohen and Felix S. Cohen make their claim with regard to US property law, but the statement holds true in other contexts. India has long had a private property system (the Mitakshara, from approximately the eleventh century CE, outlines male private property rights), even when said private property is jointly owned under the rules of male coparcenary. Morris R. Cohen and Felix S. Cohen, *Readings in Jurisprudence and Legal Philosophy* (Frederick, MD: Beard Books, 2002), 26.
80. Gregory S. Alexander, *Commodity and Propriety: Competing Visions of Property in American Legal Thought, 1776–1970* (Chicago: University of Chicago Press, 1997), 2.
81. Roy, *The God of Small Things*, 116.
82. Roy, *The God of Small Things*, 50.
83. Roy, *The God of Small Things*, 167.
84. Roy, *The God of Small Things*, 172, 44.
85. Roy, *The God of Small Things*, 171.
86. Roy, *The God of Small Things*, 142.
87. Roy, *The God of Small Things*, 385.
88. Roy, *The God of Small Things*, 379.
89. Roy, *The God of Small Things*, 19.
90. Roy, *The God of Small Things*, 18 (emphasis in original).
91. Roy, *The God of Small Things*, 5, 8, 14.
92. Roy, *The God of Small Things*, 299.
93. Elizabeth Outka associates the novel's temporally disjunctive narrative organization with its exploration of trauma. Elizabeth Outka, "Trauma and Temporal Hybridity in Arundhati Roy's *The God of Small Things*," *Contemporary Literature* 52, no. 1 (2011).
94. Aarthi Vadde, "The Backwaters Sphere: Ecological Collectivity, Cosmopolitanism, and Arundhati Roy," *MFS: Modern Fiction Studies* 55, no. 3 (2009): 523.

95. Leela Gandhi, *Affective Communities: Anticolonial Thought, Fin-de-Siècle Radicalism, and the Politics of Friendship* (Durham, NC: Duke University Press, 2006), 184.

96. Gandhi, *Affective Communities*, 2, 20.

97. Vadde frames these variant epistemologies in cosmopolitan terms, arguing that Roy's novel advocates an "interdependent rather than ascendant model of the human." Vadde, "The Backwaters Sphere," 536.

98. Roy, *The God of Small Things*, 5, 4.

99. Roy, *The God of Small Things*, 5.

100. Roy, *The God of Small Things*, 309.

101. Roy, *The God of Small Things*, 311.

102. Roy, *The God of Small Things*, 311.

103. Despite my analysis here, I remain convinced by Leila Neti's argument that Estha and Rahel's sexual interaction reveals this novel's confinement in heterosexist logics and its shaping by Section 377, which made sodomy illegal, in India's penal code. Neti, "The Love Laws," 235, 237.

104. On the former, see Needham, "The Small Voice of History," 382–86; on the latter, see Ahmad, "Reading Arundhati Roy Politically," 104–5.

105. David Scott, *Conscripts of Modernity: The Tragedy of Colonial Enlightenment* (Durham, NC: Duke University Press, 2004), 135.

106. Roy, *The God of Small Things*, 218.

107. Roy is fond of such metanarrational directives and employs the same method toward the end of her sprawling second novel, *The Ministry of Utmost Happiness*, in Tilo's poem "How to Tell a Shattered Story?." Arundhati Roy, *The Ministry of Utmost Happiness* (New York: Alfred A. Knopf, 2017), 442.

108. Roy, *The God of Small Things*, 222.

109. Roy, *The God of Small Things*, 221 (emphasis in original).

110. Roy, *The God of Small Things*, 223.

111. Roy, *The God of Small Things*, 223.

112. Roy, *The God of Small Things*, 224.

113. Roy, *The God of Small Things*, 222.

3. Accretion: Decolonizing Intellectual Property Law

1. I am electing to capitalize "Black" in this chapter, even though this orthographic convention applies more to North American and some diasporic contexts than to South African or African circumstances. Capitalizing "Black" signals an identity that is at once cultural and racial as well as registering dignity and pride. The broad public recognition of Black experience that capitalization signifies, especially since the 2020 Black Lives Matter protests, is most welcome, with outlets like the *New York Times* and *Associated Press* adapting their style guides to acknowledge shared cultural histories and experiences of marginalization. Scholarship that has pushed back against such editorial decisions — Fred Moten's is a

thoughtful and compelling example — has done so by reckoning with capitalization's potential for flattening cultural, racial, ethnic, and national differences. As Tsitsi Jaji and Lily Saint explain in a joint essay about African identities, and by way of Sylvia Wynter's scholarship on "genres of human being," capitalization registers "the violences of classification at the core of colonial processes." See Tsitsi Jaji and Lily Saint, "Introduction: Genre in Africa," *The Cambridge Journal of Postcolonial Literary Inquiry* 4, no. 2 (2017): 153.

South Africa's complexities of racialization index the limits, in a postcolonial context, of marking racial categories through capitalization. The apartheid state assigned rigid racial categories to the country's population based on visible markers like facial features and skin color. Enshrined in law, these legal categories functioned to subjugate, diminish, and dispossess the country's majority Black and brown population, whether by allowing differential access to education or denaturalizing residents of the so-called homelands into which many Black communities were forced. It is for this reason that writers like Zoë Wicomb, whose work this chapter discusses at length, reject capitalized racial categories, like the term "coloured," for reproducing the apartheid state's racial essentialism even as the lowercased variant is reclaimed to recognize multiracial heritage. (For more on Wicomb's position, see note 58, below).

Alongside using "Black," which acknowledges African ancestry, and in order to also recognize the limits of this term, especially but not only in a South African context, I also use "brown" to recognize broader global experiences of racialization and multiracial heritage, especially in the context of colonial racial capitalism, which do not necessarily entail cohesive ethnic, racial, or cultural identities. My use of the term "brown" also operates according to Manu Samriti Chander's observation that "brown serves (or can serve, or should serve) as a way of establishing anti-racist solidarities, solidarities that resist those imperial institutions that have divided the globe along racial lines." See "Manu Samriti Chander's Brown Ramblist," *The Rambling*, February 13, 2021, https://the-rambling.com/2021/02/13/ramblist-chander/.

The phrase "Black and brown" is thus useful in multiple ways: it allows for an expansive acknowledgment of shared experiences of racialization for the global majority; it acknowledges significant racial, ethnic, cultural, and national differences; and it articulates modes of solidarity, existent or potential, in the face of colonial racial capitalism's pervasive white supremacy and globalized inequality.

2. For an excellent analysis of the ways in which IP law operates according to the desires of former colonizing countries, see Olufunmilayo B. Arewa, "TRIPs and Traditional Knowledge: Local Communities, Local Knowledge, and Global Intellectual Property Frameworks," *Marquette Intellectual Property Law Review* 10, no. 2 (2006): 163–64. For Arewa, the reason behind the ongoing imbalance of power ultimately lies in Indigenous peoples' and Global South countries' lacking decision-making power at international conventions, whether in the late nineteenth century or in the twenty-first.

3. Paul K. Saint-Amour, *The Copywrights: Intellectual Property and the Literary*

Imagination (Ithaca, NY: Cornell University Press, 2003), 14; Joseph Slaughter, "World Literature as Property," *Alif: Journal of Comparative Poetics* 34 (2014): 60–61.

4. But see Saint-Amour, who argues that European property law actually recognizes that creative work builds on existing ideas: "[B]y creating a terminal property form, they also acknowledge that prior inventions and expressions are at least part of the raw material for future innovation, that creation ex nihilo, if it exists at all, is always compounded with reuse and recombination." Saint-Amour, *The Copywrights*, 3.

5. Slaughter, "World Literature as Property," 41.

6. Peter Drahos wryly "wonders whether Indigenous groups in various developing countries saw any use to them in these rights of the nation state over national folklore." Drahos adroitly recognizes the often-competing interests between postcolonial nation-states and Indigenous peoples in his analysis of how the former pushed for adequate protections for Indigenous knowledge between 1967 and 1976, when the Tunis Model Law was signed in an attempt to stabilize the globalized Berne system. Peter Drahos, *Intellectual Property, Indigenous People and Their Knowledge* (Cambridge: Cambridge University Press, 2014), 80, 79–83.

7. Chidi Oguamanam, "Local Knowledge as Trapped Knowledge: Intellectual Property, Culture, Power and Politics," *The Journal of World Intellectual Property* 11, no. 1 (2008): 31–32.

8. One of the earliest and most comprehensive articles on biopiracy is Naomi Roht-Arriaza's "Of Seeds and Shamans: The Appropriation of the Scientific and Technical Knowledge of Indigenous and Local Communities," *Michigan Journal of International Law* 17, no. 4 (1996): 919–65. See also Chidi Oguamanam, "Beyond Theories: Intellectual Property Dynamics in the Global Knowledge Economy," *Wake Forest Intellectual Property Law Journal* 9, no. 2 (2008): esp. 137–38, and Ikechi Mgbeoji, *Global Biopiracy: Patents, Plants, and Indigenous Knowledge* (Vancouver: University of British Columbia Press, 2006).

9. For extensive coverage, see Susy Frankel, "'Ka Mate Ka Mate' and the Protection of Traditional Knowledge," in *Intellectual Property at the Edge: The Contested Contours of IP*, ed. Rochelle Cooper Dreyfus and Jane C. Ginsburg (Cambridge: Cambridge University Press, 2014), 193–214.

10. In the *Mbube* case, the descendants of Solomon Linda, who had recorded a folk song by this name in 1939, filed suit against Disney and other parties for reversionary copyright. The song had traveled to the United States and, thereafter, a global audience, having been recorded by Pete Seeger in the 1950s as *Wimoweh* and then adapted by Disney for *The Lion King*. Wanjiku Karanja, "The Legitimacy of Indigenous Intellectual Property Rights' Claims," *Strathmore Law Review* 1, no. 1 (2016): 183–85.

11. Boatema Boateng, "The Hand of the Ancestors: Time, Cultural Production, and Intellectual Property Law," *Law & Society Review* 47, no. 4 (2013): 949–51.

12. Elizabeth Sumida Huaman demonstrates that Quecha agricultural practices are part of their *kaymiyatayninchik*, or knowledge system: that is, Indigenous farming

traditions operate not only as knowledge about biodiversity and resource extraction but also as forms of cultural practice. Elizabeth Sumida Huaman, "Indigenous Rights Education (IRE): Indigenous Knowledge Systems and Transformative Human Rights in the Peruvian Andes," *International Journal of Human Rights Education* 1, no. 1 (2017): 12–15.

13. Oguamanam, "Local Knowledge as Trapped Knowledge," 32.

14. Eleni Polymenopoulou identifies the many ways in which current international norms and protocols remain insufficient, arguing that successful protections are usually won at the local level rather than on the international scale: Eleni Polymenopolou, "Indigenous Cultural Heritage and Artistic Expressions: Localizing Intellectual Property Rights and UNESCO Claims," *Canadian Journal of Human Rights* 6 (2017): 112–23.

15. Boateng, "The Hand of the Ancestors," 943.

16. Enyinna S. Nwauche, "The Swakopmund Protocol and the Communal Ownership and Control of Expressions of Folklore in Africa," *The Journal of World Intellectual Property* 17, no. 5–6 (2014): 191–201.

17. Swakopmund Protocol on the Protection of Traditional Knowledge and Expressions of Folklore Within the Framework of the African Regional Intellectual Property Organization (ARIPO) (August 9, 2010), Preamble.

18. World Intellectual Property Organization (WIPO), *Glossary of Key Terms Related to Intellectual Property and Genetic Resources, Traditional Knowledge and Traditional Cultural Expressions*, Intergovernmental Committee on Intellectual Property and Genetic Resources, Traditional Knowledge and Folklore, WIPO/GRTKF/IC/40/INF/7 (April 10, 2019), 22–23. For an overview of the debates, see Oguamanam, "Local Knowledge as Trapped Knowledge," 35–36.

19. For a comprehensive overview of the early stage of this process, up to 2007, see Mogege Mosimege, "The Development of Indigenous Knowledge Systems Policy and Legislation in South Africa: Intellectual Property Implications for Knowledge Holders and Practitioners," in *Indigenous Knowledge System and Intellectual Property Rights in the Twenty-First Century: Perspectives from Southern Africa*, ed. Isaac Mazonde and Thomas Pradip (CODESRIA, 2007), 95–103.

20. For a clear overview, see Andrew van der Vlies, ed., *Print, Text and Book Cultures in South Africa* (Johannesburg: Wits University Press, 2012), esp. 2–48.

21. Anelile Gibixego and Athambile Masola, "South Africa's Trade Publishing Sector: Has There Been Transformation?," in *Mintirho Ya Vulavula: Arts, National Identities and Democracy in South Africa*, ed. Innocentia J. Mhlambi and Sandile Ngidi (Johannesburg: Mapungubwe Institute (Mistra), 2021), 255–86.

22. Matthew Eatough, "Futures, Inc.: Fiction and Intellectual Property in the (South) African Renaissance," in *World Literature, Neoliberalism, and the Culture of Discontent*, ed. Sharae Deckard and Stephen Shapiro (Cham, Switzerland: Palgrave Macmillan, 2019), 228–34; and Joseph Slaughter, "World Literature as Property," 45–49.

23. Aryn Bartley, "The Violence of the Present: David's Story and the Truth and

Reconciliation Commission," *Comparative Literature Studies* 46, no. 1 (2009): 108–9, 115–18.

24. On the masculinist orientation of postapartheid nation-building, see Dina al-Kassim, "Archiving Resistance: Women's Testimony at the Threshold of the State," *Cultural Dynamics* 20, no. 2 (2008): 167–92. On the neglect of women's crucial role in anti-apartheid resistance fighting, see Meg Samuelson, "The Disfigured Body of the Female Guerilla: (De)Militarization, Sexual Violence, and Redomestication in Zoë Wicomb's *David's Story*," *Signs* 32, no. 4 (2007): 833–56.

25. An extensive body of research in law and literature studies identifies IP law's cultural, material, and intellectual history. Most particularly, see Mark Rose, *Authors and Owners: The Invention of Copyright* (Cambridge, MA: Harvard University Press, 1993); Martha Woodmansee and Peter Jaszi, "Introduction," in *The Construction of Authorship: Textual Appropriation in Law and Literature*, ed. Martha Woodmansee and Peter Jaszi (Durham, NC: Duke University Press, 1994), 1–14; and Rosemary Coombe, *The Cultural Life of Intellectual Properties: Authorship, Appropriation, and the Law* (Durham, NC: Duke University Press, 1998).

26. C. B. Macpherson, *The Political Theory of Possessive Individualism: Hobbes to Locke* (Oxford: Oxford University Press, 2011).

27. Woodmansee and Jaszi, "Introduction," 3.

28. Simon Stern, "From Author's Right to Property Right," *University of Toronto Law Journal* 62 (2012): 38–39.

29. Rose, *Authors and Owners*, 1.

30. Rose, *Authors and Owners*, 1.

31. Woodmansee and Jaszi, "Introduction," 6.

32. Woodmansee and Jaszi, "Introduction," 6.

33. Woodmansee and Jaszi, "Introduction," 6–7.

34. Stern, "From Author's Right to Property Right," 59.

35. Stern, "From Author's Right to Property Right," 87.

36. Rose, *Authors and Owners*, 1–9.

37. According to Woodmansee and Jaszi, copyright's "exclusive vision of authorship" is "part of [its] postcolonial legal legacy." "Introduction," 12.

38. Zoë Wicomb, *David's Story* (New York: The Feminist Press at City University of New York, 2001), 1.

39. Wicomb, *David's Story*, 2.

40. Wicomb, *David's Story*, 1.

41. Samuelson, "The Disfigured Body of the Female Guerilla," 835–39.

42. Wicomb, *David's Story*, 2.

43. Wicomb, *David's Story*, 140.

44. Andrew van der Vlies, *Present Imperfect: Contemporary South African Writing* (Oxford: Oxford University Press, 2017), 138.

45. On copyright's paternity clause and the cultural presumptions it encodes, see Rose, *Authors and Owners*, 55.

46. Coombe, *The Cultural Life of Intellectual Properties*, 404.

47. *Letter from an Author to a Member of Parliament*, 1735, quoted in Coombe, *The Cultural Life of Intellectual Properties*, 404.
48. Coombe, *The Cultural Life of Intellectual Properties*, 404.
49. Caroline B. Ncube, "The Creative Industry and South African Intellectual Property Law," *Law and Development Review* 11, no. 2 (2018): 600–601.
50. Wicomb, *David's Story*, 2.
51. Peter D. McDonald, *The Literature Police: Apartheid Censorship and Its Cultural Consequences* (Oxford: Oxford University Press, 2009), 21–82.
52. Wicomb, *David's Story*, 147.
53. Wicomb, *David's Story*, 5.
54. Wicomb, *David's Story*, 7.
55. Wicomb, *David's Story*, 134.
56. Isabel Hofmeyr, "Colonial Copyright, Customs, and Port Cities: Material Histories and Intellectual Property," *Comparative Literature* 70, no. 3 (2018): 272.
57. Hofmeyr, "Colonial Copyright, Customs, and Port Cities," 274.
58. Van der Vlies explains that "Wicomb's own background—born to a family that would have been classified Coloured—and her resistance to the revisionism she has seen at work in the politics of this community (eliding the experience of slavery and miscegenation, for instance, in its drive to claim descent instead from autochthonous communities like the !Xam and the Khoi), drives this critique of . . . a fetishization of ethnicity and origin." Van der Vlies, *Present Imperfect*, 128.
59. Brenna M. Munro, "Queer Family Romance: Writing the 'New' South Africa in the 1990s," *GLQ: A Journal of Lesbian and Gay Studies* 15, no. 3 (2009): 406–7.
60. Wicomb, *David's Story*, 28.
61. Van der Vlies, *Present Imperfect*, 129.
62. Dorothy Driver, "Afterword," in *David's Story* by Zoë Wicomb (New York: The Feminist Press at City University of New York, 2001), 227.
63. WIPO, *Intellectual Property Needs and Expectations of Traditional Knowledge Holders*, WIPO Report on Fact-Finding Missions (FFM) on Intellectual Property and Traditional Knowledge 1998–1999 (April 2001), esp. 62–63, 108–10, 122, 136–37, 174–80. For a concise summary, see Tertia Beharie and Tshepo Shabangu, "Traditional Knowledge, Traditional Cultural Expressions and Folklore" in *Introduction to Intellectual Property Law*, ed. Owen Dean and Alison Dyer (Oxford: Oxford University Press, 2014), 345.
64. Hershini Bhana Young, *Illegible Will: Coercive Spectacles of Labor in South Africa and the Diaspora* (Durham, NC: Duke University Press, 2017), 34–35.
65. Wicomb, *David's Story*, 17.
66. Young, *Illegible Will*, 23.
67. On the Tulalip Tribe's database of traditional knowledge, see Jonathan Curci, *The Protection of Biodiversity and Traditional Knowledge in International Law of Intellectual Property* (Cambridge: Cambridge University Press, 2010), 228–29.
68. Protection, Promotion, Development and Management of Indigenous

Knowledge Act 6 of 2019 (Indigenous Knowledge Act) (Notice 1082, Government Gazette 42647) (19 Aug. 2019) (South Africa), §11.

69. Indigenous Knowledge Act, Preamble.

70. For an overview of these positions, see Mikhalien du Bois, "Recognition and Protection of Traditional Knowledge Interests as Property in South African Law," *European Property Law Journal* 2, no. 2 (2013): 154–55.

71. In her discussion of the Intellectual Property Laws Amendment Act of 2013, which was the precursor to the Indigenous Knowledge Protections Act and which was not signed by the president, Sunelle Geyer uncritically identifies Afrikaner cultural practice as eligible for protection under the 2013 act, at once revealing the limits of that bill and her own failure to recognize that white settler-colonial populations can never claim Indigenous status. Sunelle Geyer, "Copyright in Traditional Works: Unraveling the Intellectual Property Laws Amendment Act of 2013," *South African Mercantile Law Journal* 29, no. 1 (2017): 63–64.

72. Du Bois, "Recognition and Protection of Traditional Knowledge Interests," 155.

73. Copyright Act 98 of 1978 (Notice 1349, Government Gazette 6092) (10 Dec. 1978) (South Africa), §28B(2).

74. ARIPO, Swakopmund Protocol, §4, iii. For an overview of the Protocol and its impact, see Nwauche, "The Swakopmund Protocol," 191–98.

75. Ncube, "The Creative Industry," 603–4.

76. On Eugene de Kock's infamous *Vlakplaas* paramilitary unit, trauma narratives, and the TRC's "onus for reconciliation almost entirely on South Africa's black citizens," see Lily Saint, *Black Cultural Life in South Africa: Reception, Apartheid, and Ethics* (Ann Arbor: University of Michigan Press, 2018), 119–22.

77. Wicomb, *David's Story*, 15.

78. Saint-Amour, *The Copywrights*, 159–98; Ravit Reichman, "Mourning, Owning, Owing," *American Imago* 64, no. 3 (2007): 433–49.

79. Wicomb, *David's Story*, 35.

80. Wicomb, *David's Story*, 8–9.

81. Wicomb, *David's Story*, 81.

82. For a complex account of ethics in Black South African postapartheid writing, see Saint, *Black Cultural Life in South Africa*, 115–50.

83. Margreta De Grazia, "Sanctioning Voice: Quotation Marks, the Abolition of Torture, and the Fifth Amendment," in *The Construction of Authorship: Textual Appropriation in Law and Literature*, ed. Peter Jaszi and Martha Woodmansee (Durham, NC: Duke University Press, 1993), 288.

84. De Grazia, "Sanctioning Voice," 289.

85. Wicomb, *David's Story*, 161.

86. Wicomb, *David's Story*, 162.

87. Nwauche, "The Swakopmund Protocol," 197.

88. Wicomb, *David's Story*, 126.

89. Wicomb, *David's Story*, 126.

90. Beharie and Shabangu, "Traditional Knowledge," 345.

91. Justin Hughes, "Traditional Knowledge, Cultural Expression, and the Siren's Call of Property," *San Diego Law Review* 49, no. 4 (2012): 1249.

92. Wicomb, *David's Story*, 143.

93. Wicomb, *David's Story*, 49.

94. Wicomb, *David's Story*, 61.

95. Wicomb, *David's Story*, 138.

96. Young, *Illegible Will*, 34.

97. Wicomb, *David's Story*, 87.

98. Van der Vlies, *Present Imperfect*, 128–29. See also Zoë Wicomb, "Shame and Identity: The Case of the Coloured in South Africa," in *Writing South Africa: Literature, Apartheid, and Democracy, 1970–1995*, ed. Derek Attridge and Rosemary Jolly (Cambridge: Cambridge University Press, 1998), 91–107.

99. Van der Vlies identifies the rain sisters as "examples of autochthonous queerness that have thus far survived the colonial encounter and the new nation's investment in heritage and authenticity." Van der Vlies, *Present Imperfect*, 135.

100. Wicomb, *David's Story*, 153.

101. Driver, "Afterword," 259.

102. Wicomb, *David's Story*, 2.

103. Wicomb, *David's Story*, 134.

104. Wicomb, *David's Story*, 103.

105. Wicomb, *David's Story*, 3.

4. Dispersal: Admiralty Law and Raising the Dead

1. For an excellent example of this kind of bicentennial scholarly attention to the Zong massacre, see the symposium of seven articles in *The Journal of Legal History* 28, no. 3 (2007): 283–373. For an overview of literary responses to the massacre, see Erin M. Fehskens, "Accounts Unpaid, Accounts Untold: M. NourbeSe Philip's Zong! and the Catalogue," *Callaloo* 35, no. 2 (2012): 408.

2. Katherine McKittrick, "Mathematics of Black Life," *The Black Scholar* 44, no. 2 (2014): 19.

3. Jane Webster, "The Zong in the Context of the Eighteenth-Century Slave Trade," *The Journal of Legal History* 28, no. 3 (2007): 289–90.

4. See London news report of early 1782, reproduced in James Walvin, *The Zong: A Massacre, the Law and the End of Slavery* (New Haven, CT: Yale University Press, 2011).

5. The standard insurance policy issued by Lloyd's of London identified coverage for "Perils, Losses and Misfortunes that have or shall come to the Hurt, Detriment, or Damage of the said Goods and Merchandises and Ship, &c., or any Part thereof." The complete policy, along with variations after *Gilbert v. Gregson*, can be found in James Oldham, "Insurance Litigation Involving the Zong and Other British Slave Ships, 1780–1807," *The Journal of Legal History* 28, no. 3 (2007): 301.

6. Almas Khan, "Poetic Justice: Slavery, Law, and the (Anti-)Elegiac Form in

M. NourBese Philip's Zong!," *The Cambridge Journal of Postcolonial Literary Inquiry* 2, no. 1 (2015): 15–16.

7. Sarah Dowling, *Translingual Poetics: Writing Personhood Under Settler Colonialism* (Iowa City: University of Iowa Press, 2018), 69.

8. Alexandra Schultheis Moore, "'Dispossession within the Law': Human Rights and the Ec-Static Subject in M. NourbeSe Philip's Zong!," *Feminist Formations* 28, no. 1 (2016): 168.

9. Elizabeth S. Anker, "Globalizing Law and Literature," in *New Directions in Law and Literature*, ed. Elizabeth S. Anker and Bernadette Meyler (Oxford: Oxford University Press, 2017), 218.

10. Laurie R. Lambert on Philip's improvisational performance of "Zong! #15" in "Poetics of Reparation in M. NourbeSe Philip's Zong!" *The Global South* 10, no. 1 (2016): 107–08. See also M. NourbeSe Philip, "Defending the Dead, Confronting the Archive: A Conversation with M. NourbeSe Philip," interview by Patricia Saunders, *Small Axe* 26 (2008): 67, 76.

11. Christina Sharpe, *In the Wake: On Blackness and Being* (Durham, NC: Duke University Press, 2016), 26–67.

12. Sharpe, *In the Wake*, 9, 5, 2.

13. Sharpe, *In the Wake*, 18.

14. Tiffany Lethabo King, *The Black Shoals: Offshore Formations of Black and Native Studies* (Durham, NC: Duke University Press, 2019), 24.

15. See, in particular, James Oldham, "Insurance Litigation Involving the Zong and Other British Slave Ships, 1780–1807," *The Journal of Legal History* 28, no. 3 (2007): 299–318. See also Michael Lobban, "Slavery, Insurance and the Law," *The Journal of Legal History* 28, no. 3 (2007): 319–28.

16. Most prominently, Ian Baucom develops an extended analysis of the speculative financial system that provided the epistemological conditions of possibility for the Zong massacre, as well as offering a close reading of Philip's Zong!. Ian Baucom, *Specters of the Atlantic: Finance Capital, Slavery, and the Philosophy of History* (Durham, NC: Duke University Press, 2005). See also Moore, "Dispossession within the Law," 175–78. Analyses of Zong! routinely draw attention to insurance law, perhaps not least because Philip provides this same reading in her afterword, "Notanda": M. NourbeSe Philip, *Zong!* (Middletown, CT: Wesleyan University Press, 2008), 189–207.

17. Baucom, *Specters of the Atlantic*, 3–34, 80–112.

18. Jasper Jolly, "Bank of England Owned 599 Slaves in 1770s, New Exhibition Reveals." *The Guardian*, April 2022. More broadly, see the Commercial Legacies section of University College London's *Legacies of British Slavery* project: "Legacies," on Legacies of British Slavery (website), University College London, 2024, https://www.ucl.ac.uk/lbs/legacies/.

19. Many of the National Trust's historic properties are economically linked to slavery, as revealed in a 2020 report that has since been widely reported on by the British press. Sally-Anne Huxtable, "Interim Report on the Connections between

Colonialism and Properties Now in the Care of the National Trust, Including Links with Historic Slavery," *National Trust*, 2020, www.nationaltrust.org.uk/who-we-are/research/addressing-our-histories-of-colonialism-and-historic-slavery.

20. Lionel H. Laing identifies the slow development of admiralty jurisdiction over the course of the fourteenth and fifteenth centuries: "Institutions are the products of slow growth which must be shaped to time and circumstances. There was a place for an admiralty court in England, but its effective functioning needed particular conditioning. The Fifteenth Century could scarcely be called a propitious time for such development" (171–72). Lionel H. Laing, "Historic Origins of Admiralty Jurisdiction in England," *Michigan Law Review* 45, no. 2 (1946): 167, 171–72, 174.

21. Laing, "Historic Origins of Admiralty Jurisdiction," 174–78.

22. Renisa Mawani, *Across Oceans of Law: The Komagata Maru and Jurisdiction in the Time of Empire* (Durham, NC: Duke University Press, 2018), 80.

23. Mawani, *Across Oceans of Law*, 80.

24. V. C. D. Mtubani, "African Slaves and English Law" (Pula: Michigan State Libraries Digital Repository, 1983), 71.

25. An Act for increase of Shipping, and Encouragement of the Navigation of this Nation (October 1651) (England and Wales) in *Acts and Ordinances of the Interregnum, 1642–1660*, edited by C. H. First and R. S. Rait (London, 1911) 559–62. *British History Online*, https://www.british-history.ac.uk/no-series/acts-ordinances-interregnum/pp559-562.

26. Susan Staves, "Chattel Property Rules and the Construction of Englishness, 1660–1800," *Law and History Review* 12, no. 1 (1994): 124.

27. *Butts v. Penny* (July 1677). 2. Lev. 201, in 83 *English Reports*, 518. Holly Brewer explains that the "Common Pleas' Judge Creswell Levinz took [these] notes, which circulated in manuscript before being published in 1701." Holly Brewer, "Creating a Common Law of Slavery for England and Its New World Empire," *Law and History* 39, no. 4 (2021): 792.

28. Sir Francis Winnington, "America and West Indies: July 1677, 16–31." *Calendar of State Papers Colonial, America and West Indies, vol. 10, 1677–1680*, edited by W. Noel Sainsbury (London: J. W. Fortescue, 1896). *British History Online*, https://www.british-history.ac.uk/cal-state-papers/colonial/america-west-indies/vol10/pp116-138.

29. See also the Charles Talbot and Philip Yorke opinion in 1729, later published in the *Boston Gazette*, which held that "a Slave, by coming from the *West-Indies* to *Great Britain* or *Ireland*, either with or without his Master, doth not become free, and that his Master's Property, or Right in him, is not thereby determined or varied." P. Yorke and C. Talbot, "Advertisement," *Boston Gazette*, no. 561, Sept. 7 (1730): 2.

30. Bryant Smith, "Legal Personality," *Yale Law Journal* 37, no. 3 (1928): 283.

31. Smith, "Legal Personality," 287–89, 296.

32. Mawani, *Across Oceans of Law*, 22, 77.

33. As Mawani explains, "Slaves became legal persons in two interrelated moments: when African captives were transported on ships as cargo and when slaves were accused of committing a crime on land or at sea." *Across Oceans of Law*, 86.

34. Colin Dayan, *The Law Is a White Dog: How Legal Rituals Make and Unmake Persons* (Princeton, NJ: Princeton University Press, 2011), 129.

35. Mtubani, "African Slaves and English Law," 72, 73.

36. On racialized nonpersonhood under anglophone law and in contemporary lyric poetry, including *Zong!*, see Dowling, *Translingual Poetics*, 57–89.

37. Fred Moten, *In the Break: The Aesthetics of the Black Radical Tradition* (Minneapolis: University of Minnesota Press, 2003), 6.

38. Mawani's assessment of anglophone admiralty law and legal personality is extremely useful; note, though, that she examines American maritime law rather than English admiralty law, and the two have a slightly different relationship to the deodand and the associated methods of forcing appearance in court: Mawani, *Across Oceans of Law*, esp. 80–82. On legal personality and its obverse, negative, or retractable personhood, see Colin Dayan; note that she focuses on the relationship between legal personality and anti-Black processes of racialization, not the specific relationship between admiralty law and legal personality. Dayan, *The Law Is a White Dog*, 53–57.

39. Griffith Price, "Statutory Rights in Rem in English Admiralty Law," *Journal of Comparative Legislation and International Law* 27, no. 3–4 (1945): 21–23, 24–25.

40. Mawani, *Across Oceans of Law*, 82.

41. Angela Naimou, *Salvage Work: U.S. And Caribbean Literatures Amid the Debris of Legal Personhood* (New York: Fordham University Press, 2015), 11.

42. Stephen Best, *The Fugitive's Properties: Law and the Poetics of Possession* (Chicago: University of Chicago Press, 2004), 9.

43. Best, *The Fugitive's Properties*, 1–17 and 269–71.

44. Best, *The Fugitive's Properties*, 270.

45. Dayan coined this term in a 2001 essay: Colin Dayan, "Legal Slaves and Civil Bodies," *Nepantla: Views from South* 2, no. 1 (2001): 3–39.

46. Philip, *Zong!*, 16.

47. Mawani, *Across Oceans of Law*, 87.

48. Philip, *Zong!*, 88. Here, as in other in-text quotations from *Zong!*, I employ some transliteration, as is necessary with a poem that is at once visual and aural. I encourage readers to review the original text to see the full effect; recordings of Philip reading *Zong!* also help to understand this poem in its full complexity and impact.

49. Saidiya Hartman, *Lose Your Mother: A Journey Along the Atlantic Slave Route* (New York: Farrar, Strauss & Giroux, 2008), 143.

50. Philip, *Zong!*, 106–7.

51. Philip, *Zong!*, 131.

52. *Gregson v. Gilbert* (1783) *English Reports* 99, 629–30.

53. *Gregson v. Gilbert*, 630.

54. Best, *The Fugitive's Properties*, 52.

55. Smith, "Legal Personality," 293.

56. Dayan, *The Law is a White Dog*, 25.

57. Mawani, *Across Oceans of Law*, 86.

58. Simon Stern, "Legal Fictions and Legal Fabrications," in *Fictional Discourse and the Law*, ed. Hans J. Lind (Abingdon: Routledge, 2020), 196.

59. Stern, "Legal Fictions and Legal Fabrications," 197.

60. Philip, *Zong!*, 115.

61. Dayan, *The Law is a White Dog*, 5.

62. Stambovsky v. Ackley, 169 NY Ct. App. 254 (1991). I owe thanks to Simon Stern for directing me toward this detail.

63. Stambovsky v. Ackley, 572 N.Y.S.2d 672 (1991) (U.S.), §1.

64. Dayan, *The Law is a White Dog*, 3.

65. For a reading of *Zong!*'s deployment and production of pronounced affective states, see Jenny Sharpe, *Immaterial Archives: An African Diaspora Poetics of Loss* (Evanston, IL: Northwestern University Press, 2020), 1956.

66. Hortense Spillers, "Mama's Baby, Papa's Maybe: An American Grammar Book," in "Culture and Countermemory: The 'American' Connection," ed. S. P. Mohanty, special issue, *Diacritics* 17, no. 2 (1987): 79.

67. Philip, *Zong!*, 69.

68. Philip, *Zong!*, 116.

69. Philip, *Zong!*, 27.

70. Philip, *Zong!*, 27.

71. Nathaniel Mackey, "Other: From Noun to Verb," *Representations* 39 (1992): 52.

72. Evie Shockley, "Going Overboard: African American Poetic Innovation and the Middle Passage," *Contemporary Literature* 52, no. 4 (2011): 813.

73. Shockley argues that Philip employs a poetic form of underwriting in *Zong!* that "counters the dehumanization of the African passengers aboard the *Zong*" that is financially enabled through the practice of insuring enslaved people as commodities. Shockley, "Going Overboard," 814.

74. Unlike elsewhere in this book, I use Moten's orthographic decisions in these sentences, which refer directly to his work and ideas, by not capitalizing "black." Fred Moten, *In the Break: The Aesthetics of the Black Radical Tradition* (Minneapolis: University of Minnesota Press, 2003), 1.

75. Moten, *In the Break*, 1.

76. See, for instance, Rachel Galvin's rich essay on "radical reauthoring" in North American literature: Rachel Galvin, "Poetry Is Theft," *Comparative Literature Studies* 51, no. 1 (2014): 21, 34, 45. On fragmentation as symptoms of trauma, see Dawn Lundy Martin, "The Language of Trauma: Faith and Atheism in M. NourbeSe Philip's Poetry," in *Eleven More American Women Poets in the 21st Century: Poetics Across North America*, ed. Claudia Rankine and Lisa Sewell (Middletown, CT: Wesleyan University Press, 2012), 295.

77. Anthony Reed, *Freedom Time: The Poetics and Politics of Black Experimental Writing* (Baltimore, MD: Johns Hopkins University Press, 2016), 28.

78. Reed, *Freedom Time*, 53.

79. Sharpe, *Immaterial Archives*, 474.

80. Walt Hunter, *Forms of a World: Contemporary Poetry and the Making of Globalization* (New York: Fordham University Press, 2019), 1.

81. Sharpe, *In the Wake*, 38.

82. Sharpe, *In the Wake*, 109.

83. Philip, *Zong!*, 168, orthography mine. Quoting from *Zong!* requires some transliteration, as discussed in note 48 above. In this case, I have used periods to identify the sounds of the vowels when spoken rather than read.

84. Jahan Ramazani, *Poetry of Mourning: The Modern Elegy from Hardy to Heaney* (Chicago: University of Chicago Press, 1994), xi.

85. Anne Carson, *Economy of the Unlost: Reading Simonides of Keos with Paul Celan* (Princeton, NJ: Princeton University Press, 2002), 73.

86. Philip, *Zong!*, 63.

87. Philip, *Zong!*, 68.

88. Philip, *Zong!*, 143.

89. Philip, *Zong!*, 135.

90. Philip, *Zong!*, 140.

91. Philip, *Zong!*, 140.

92. In an interview with Patricia Saunders, Philip reflects on the predominance granted to this white sailor in *Zong!*: "[O]ne of the discernible voices in the text is that of a white European male voice, who is confronting his own actions and responsibility in this horrific event, and ordinarily I would never have been interested in that voice, and for good reason. . . . [But] for us—African people—and for the world as a whole, to survive, that person, not to mention the impulse and action he represents, has to die. Had I excised the voice, that death would not have happened." Philip, "Defending the Dead, Confronting the Archive," 75.

93. Lambert, "Poetics of Reparation," 119; Moore, "Dispossession within the Law," 184.

94. Philip, *Zong!*, 61.

95. Philip, *Zong!*, 85.

96. Philip, *Zong!*, 170.

97. Philip, *Zong!*, 152.

98. Philip, *Zong!*, 128.

99. Neil Adkin, "On a New Virgil Acrostic: Aeneid 6.77–84," *Mnemosyne* 68 (2015): 1018.

100. Adkin, "On a New Virgil Acrostic," 2018.

101. Oliver Wendell Holmes Jr., "The Path of the Law," *Harvard Law Review* 10, no. 8 (1897): 461.

102. Holmes, "The Path of the Law," 457.

103. In the very first book of Grotius's *The Free Sea*, he quotes twice from Virgil, including lines from Book I of *The Aeneid*: "What race of men, and what land is so barbarous as to permit this custom? We are debarred the welcome of the beach": Virgil, *Aeneid I*, 539–40, quoted in Hugo Grotius, *The Free Sea*, ed. David Armitage, trans. Richard Hakluyt (Liberty Fund, 2004).

104. Thomas Dikant offers a rich analysis of the rhetorical and legal history of the figure of the oracle in US common law and on Holmes's assessment of a judge's authority. As Dikant observes, the *Libri Syballini* that the Romans used extensively to produce knowledge in the face of crisis were substantially incomplete: only three of the original nine Greek books remained. "[T]o describe the common law as sybilline books, as 'scattered prophecies,' is to align the task of the late nineteenth-century American lawyer to those Romans who used fragmentary and incomplete books to interpret ominous events." Thomas Dikant, "'Oracles of the Law:' Oliver Wendell Holmes Jr.'s Legal Futurism," *Law and Literature*, 36, no. 3 (2024): 470.

105. Vergil, *The Aeneid*, trans. Shadi Bartsch (Modern Library, 2021), VI, 71–76.

106. The connection that I am drawing between Virgil's Sybil and Oliver Wendell Holmes Jr.'s theory of law's predictive capacities is built upon a 1922 analysis in *The Michigan Law Review*: "according to Vergil (*Aeneid*, III, 452), the Sibyl wrote her prophecies on the leaves of trees and so arranged them within the cave that the approach of inquirers blew them into such confusion that their meaning became incomprehensible." "Maritime Law: Personality of Ship: Immunity of Government Property," *Michigan Law Review* 20, no. 5 (1922): 534.

107. Holmes, "The Path of the Law," 433.

Conclusion: Hope's Impropriety

1. Kandice Chuh, *The Difference Aesthetics Makes: On the Humanities "After Man"* (Durham, NC: Duke University Press, 2019), 122–25.

2. Anna Kornbluh, *The Order of Forms: Realism, Formalism, and Social Space* (Chicago: University of Chicago Press, 2019), 157.

3. On jurisprudence and the relationship between the general and the specific, see Oliver Wendell Holmes Jr., for whom "[j]urisprudence . . . is simply law in its most generalized part." Oliver Wendell Holmes Jr., "The Path of the Law," *Harvard Law Review* 10, no. 8 (1897): 474.

4. On July 23, 2019, Jamaican Culture Minister Olivia Grange declared in Parliament her government's intentions to see Taíno artifacts returned from the British Museum. "Jamaica Going After Artefacts," *The Gleaner*, July 24, 2019, https://jamaica-gleaner.com/article/news/20190724/jamaica-going-after-artefacts. See also Mark Brown, "Jamaica Seeks Return of Artefacts from the British Museum," *The Guardian*, August 7, 2019. For the catalog entry in the British Museum, see Taíno-Arawak, *Figure*, 1500 800, Wood, 1500 800, Am1977, The British Museum, www.britishmuseum.org/collection/object/E_Am1977-Q-2.

5. John Singleton Copley, *The Death of Major Peirson*, January 6, 1781.

6. For a discussion of Locke's use of cardboard, see Hew Locke, "Let's Make Something Positive," *YouTube*, n.d., https://www.youtube.com/watch?v=11d64_f-m6U, 00:05:42–00:06:11.

7. Locke, "Let's Make Something Positive," 00:06:12–00:06:34.

8. A few examples of the many other identifiable shares include those belonging to the West India Improvement Company, an American syndicate that ran Jamaica's railway system between 1889 and 1898; the Société Commerciale et Industrielle de l'Afrique Occidentale (the West African Commercial and Industrial Society/ SCIAO), a French company that invested significantly in Nigerian trade, especially kapok, in the early 1900s; and the Compagnie Universelle du Canal Interocéanique de Panama (the Global Company of the Interoceanic Panama Canal), which funded France's attempt to construct the Central American waterway, a project that was ultimately commandeered by the United States in what was seemingly a well-planned imperialist strategy to seize political and economic control of the region. For the West India Improvement Company, see Veront M. Satchell and Cezley Sampson, "The Rise and Fall of Railways in Jamaica, 1845–1975," *The Journal of Transport History* 24, no. 1 (2003): 8. For SCIAO, see Peter J. Yearwood, *Nigeria and the Death of Liberal England: Palm Nuts and Prime Ministers, 1914–1916* (Cham, Switzerland: Palgrave Macmillan, 2018), 246–47. For the Global Company, see Richard W. Alstyne, "The Panama Canal: A Classic Case of an Imperial Hangover," *Journal of Contemporary History* 15, no. 2 (1980): 299–303.

9. Castara Estates was owned by first Patrick Ferguson and then George Ferguson of Scotland, and in May 1836, the younger Ferguson filed a claim for the value of 299 enslaved people after Britain's Slavery Abolition Act (1834) had come into force: "Tobago 67 (Castara and Englishman's Bay)," Legacies of British Slavery database (University College London, n.d.), www.ucl.ac.uk/lbs/claim/view/27741.

10. Hollis Urban Liverpool, "Origins of Rituals and Customs in the Trinidad Carnival: African or European?" in "Trinidad and Tobago Carnival," ed. Milla C. Riggio, special issue, *The Drama Review (TDR)* 42, no. 3 (1998): 24–27.

11. Many of these figures can be found in Carol Martin's "Trinidad Carnival Glossary," part of the same special issue as Liverpool's article, supra note 10: Carol Martin, "Trinidad Carnival Glossary," in "Trinidad and Tobago Carnival," ed. Milla C. Riggio, special issue, *The Drama Review (TDR)* 42, no. 3 (1998): 220–35.

Works Cited

Legal Works

Cases

Amodu Tijani v. the Secretary, Southern Provinces. Nigeria Supreme Court (1921) (Nigeria).

Bahadur v. Bratiya & Others, HP 1555 High Court of Himachal Pradesh (2015) (India), https://highcourt.hp.gov.in/viewojpdf/viewtext.php?path=2003&fname=202300000082003_2.pdf&smflag=N.

Butts v. Penny [July 1677] 2 Lev. 201, in 83 English Reports 518 (Eng. & Wales).

D. Chelliah Nadar & Anr. v. G. Lalita Bai And Anr, All India Reporter (AIR) (1978) 66 (1976) (India), *Indian Kanoon*, https://indiankanoon.org/doc/1113433.

Four Nigerian Farmers and Milieudefensie v. Shell. The Hague Court of Appeal, 29 Jan. 2021, 32–134, ECLI:NL:GHDHA:2021:132 (Oruma), ECLI:NL:GHDHA:2021:133 (Goi), ECLI:NL:GHDHA:2021:134 (Ikot Ada Udo), https://uitspraken.rechtspraak.nl/#!/details?id=ECLI:NL:GHDHA:2021:1825 (English version).

Gregson v. Gilbert [1783] English Reports 99 629–630 (Gr. Brit.), http://www.commonlii.org/uk/cases/EngR/1783/85.pdf.

Madhu Kishwar v. State of Bihar, AIR 1826 SCC (3) 644 (1996) (India) https://main.sci.gov.in/jonew/judis/15684.pdf.

Mohd. Ahmed Khan v. Shah Bano Begum & Ors, AIR 945 SCR 3–844 (1985) (India), *Indian Kanoon*, https://indiankanoon.org/doc/823221.

Mrs. Mary Roy Etc. Etc v. State of Kerala & Ors, AIR 101 SCR 1–371 (1986) (India), *Indian Kanoon*, https://indiankanoon.org/doc/1143189.

Okpabi & Ors. v. Royal Dutch Shell Plc & Anor. [2021] UKSC 3 (appeal taken from [2018] EWCA Civ 191) (UK), https://www.supremecourt.uk/cases/uksc-2018-0068.html.

Pope v. Currl [1741] Reports of Cases Argued and Determined in the High Court of Chancery, in the time of Lord Chancellor Hardwicke: collected and methodized by John Tracy Atkyns 2 356 (1781) (Gr. Brit.).

Solomon & Ors. v. Muthiah & Ors, Madras Law Journal 1–53 (1974) (India), *Indian Kanoon*, https://indiankanoon.org/doc/1822174.

Stambovsky v. Ackley, 572 N.Y.S.2d 672 (1991) (U.S.).

Vedanta Resources PLC and another (Apellants) v. Lungowe and others (Respondents) (2019) UKSC 20 [EWCA Civ 1528] [UKSC 2017/0185] (UK), www.supremecourt.uk/cases/uksc-2017-0185.html.

Western Maid v. United States, 257 U.S., 419 (1922).

Statutes

An Act for increase of Shipping, and Encouragement of the Navigation of this Nation (October 1651) (England and Wales) in *Acts and Ordinances of the Interregnum, 1642–1660*, edited by C. H. First and R. S. Rait (London, 1911) 559–62. *British History Online*, accessed May 10, 2022, https://www.british-history.ac.uk/no-series/acts-ordinances-interregnum/pp559-562.

Chota Nagpur Tenancy Act (Bengal Act 6 of 1908), 1908 (India). *India Code: Digital Repository of State Acts, State Government of Jharkhand*, www.indiacode.nic.in/handle/123456789/12219?view_type=search&sam_handle=123456789/2488.

Christian Succession Act (Repeal) Bill, 1958 (Kerala State, India).

Copyright Act 98 of 1978 (Notice 1349, Government Gazette 6092) (10 Dec. 1978) (South Africa).

Environmental Impact Assessment Decree No. (86) (1992). (Nigeria).

Hindu Marriage Act, 1955 (India). *India Code: Digital Repository of Laws*, https://www.indiacode.nic.in/handle/123456789/1560.

Hindu Succession (Amendment) Act, 2005 (Act No. 39 of 2005) (India). *Indian Kanoon*, https://indiankanoon.org/doc/1291956/.

Hindu Succession Act, 1956 (Act. No. 38 of 1956) (India). *India Code: Digital Repository of Laws*, https://www.indiacode.nic.in/handle/123456789/1713?locale=en.

Indian Succession (Amendment) Act, 2002 (Act No. 26 of 2002) (India). *Indian Kanoon*, https://indiankanoon.org/doc/1529594/.

Indian Succession Act, 1925, (Act No. 39 of 1925) (India). *India Code*, https://www.indiacode.nic.in/bitstream/123456789/2385/1/a1925-39.pdf.

Intellectual Property Laws Amendment Act 28 of 2013 (Notice 5820, Government Gazette 37148) (10 December 2013) (South Africa).

Land Use Act (1978) Cap. L5, Laws of the Federation of Nigeria 2004 (Nigeria).

Marriage Laws Amendment Bill, 2010 (Bill No. 41 of 2010) (lapsed) (India). *PRS Legislative Research*, https://prsindia.org/billtrack/the-marriage-laws-amendment-bill-2010.

Marriage Laws Amendment Bill, 2013 (Bill No. 41 of 2010 as passed by Rajya Sabha)

(lapsed) (India). *PRS Legislative Research*, https://prsindia.org/files/bills_acts/bills_parliament/2010/Marriage_Laws_Bill_as_passed_by_RS.pdf.
Mineral Oils Ordinance (1914). Federal Government of Nigeria.
Minerals Act (1946) Cap. 121. *Federal Republic of Nigeria: Mines Manual*, 9th ed. (Govt. of Nigeria 1965), 39–103.
Muslim Women (Protection on Divorce) Act, 1986 (Act No. 26 of 1986) (India). *India Code*, https://www.indiacode.nic.in/handle/123456789/1873?view_type=search&col=123456789/1362.
Part B States (Laws) Act, 1951 (Act No. 3 of 1951) (India). *Indian Kanoon*, https://indiankanoon.org/doc/54974890/.
Petroleum Act (1969) Cap. P10 (Cap. 350, Laws of the Federation of Nigeria, 1990).
Protection of Traditional Knowledge and Traditional Cultural Expressions Act No. 33 (2016) Cap. 218 (Act No. 28 2018). *Kenya Law*. http://kenyalaw.org:8181/exist/kenyalex/actview.xql?actid=CAP.%20218A.
Protection, Promotion, Development and Management of Indigenous Knowledge Act 6 of 2019 (Notice 1082, Government Gazette 42647) (19 Aug. 2019) (South Africa).
Travancore Christian Succession Act, 1916, Abstract Proceedings of the Travancore Legislative Council (TLC) (9), December 20, 1916 (Travancore State, India). *Kerala Legislative Assembly: Proceedings*, http://klaproceedings.niyamasabha.org/index.php.

Other Legal

Blair, Peter. "Legal Directions: Judge's Handout, R. v Milo Ponsford, Sage Willoughby, Rhian Graham & Jake Skuse." Hodge Jones & Allen. January 5, 2022. https://www.hja.net/wp-content/uploads/2022/01/R-v-Milo-Ponsford-Sage-Willoughby-Rhian-Graham-Jake-Skuse-Legal-Directions-Judges-Handout.pdf.
Colston Four, Attorney General's Reference on a Point of Law [2022] No. 1 of 2022 (EWCA Crim 1259) (appeal taken from Bristol Crown Court 202201151 B3) (England and Wales). *Courts and Tribunals Judiciary*. www.judiciary.uk/wp-content/uploads/2022/09/AG-Ref-Colston-Four-judgment-280922.pdf.
Constitution of India, 1950. https://www.indiacode.nic.in/handle/123456789/10231?view_type=search&col=123456789/1362.
Constitution of Nigeria (1999), http://www.nigeria-law.org/ConstitutionOfTheFederalRepublicOfNigeria.htm.
Law Commission of India. Consultation Paper on Reform of Family Law (August 31, 2018). https://archive.pib.gov.in/documents/rlink/2018/aug/p201883101.pdf
Swakopmund Protocol on the Protection of Traditional Knowledge and Expressions of Folklore Within the Framework of the African Regional Intellectual Property Organization (ARIPO) (August 9, 2010). https://www.wipo.int/tk/en/databases/tklaws/articles/article_0044.html.
UN G.A. Res. 61/295, Declaration on the Rights of Indigenous Peoples (Sept. 13,

2007), https://www.ohchr.org/en/indigenous-peoples/un-declaration-rights-indigenous-peoples.

World Intellectual Property Organization (WIPO). *Glossary of Key Terms Related to Intellectual Property and Genetic Resources, Traditional Knowledge and Traditional Cultural Expressions*. Intergovernmental Committee on Intellectual Property and Genetic Resources, Traditional Knowledge and Folklore. WIPO/GRTKF/IC/40/INF/7 (April 10, 2019).

Intellectual Property Needs and Expectations of Traditional Knowledge Holders. WIPO Report on Fact-Finding Missions (FFM) on Intellectual Property and Traditional Knowledge 1998–1999 (April 2001).

Works Cited: Primary and Secondary Sources

Adkin, Neil. "On a New Virgil Acrostic: Aeneid 6.77–84." *Mnemosyne* 68 (2015): 1018–19.

Adunbi, Omolade. *Oil Wealth and Insurgency in Nigeria*. Bloomington: Indiana University Press, 2015.

Agarwal, Bina. *A Field of One's Own: Gender and Land Rights in South Asia*. Cambridge: Cambridge University Press, 1994.

Agathangelous, Anna M., and Kyle D. Killian, eds. *Time, Climate Change, Global Racial Capitalism and Decolonial Planetary Ecologies*. London: Routledge, 2022.

Agathocleous, Tanya. *Disaffected: Emotion, Sedition, and Colonial Law in the Anglosphere*. Ithaca: Cornell University Press, 2021.

Agnes, Flavia. "From Shah Bano to Kausar Bano: Contextualizing the 'Muslim Woman' within a Communalised Polity." In *South Asian Feminisms*, edited by Ania Loomba and Ritty A. Lukose, 33–53. Durham, NC: Duke University Press, 2012.

———. *Law and Gender Inequality: The Politics of Women's Rights in India*. Oxford: Oxford University Press, 1999.

———. "Women, Marriage, and the Subordination of Rights." In *Community, Gender and Violence: Subaltern Studies XI*, edited by Partha Chatterjee and Pradeep Jeganathan, 106–37. London: Hurst, 2000.

Ahmad, Aijaz. "Reading Arundhati Roy Politically." *Frontline*, August 8, 1997, 103–8.

Ako, Rhuks T. "Nigeria's Land Use Act: An Anti-Thesis to Environmental Justice." *Journal of African Law* 53, no. 2 (2009): 289–304.

Ako, Rhuks T., and Patrick Okonmah. "Minority Rights Issues in Nigeria: A Theoretical Analysis of Historical and Contemporary Conflicts in the Oil-Rich Niger Delta Region." *International Journal on Minority and Group Rights* 16, no. 1 (2009): 53–65.

Alexander, Gregory S. *Commodity and Propriety: Competing Visions of Property in American Legal Thought, 1776–1970*. Chicago: University of Chicago Press, 1997.

Al-Kassim, Dina. "Archiving Resistance: Women's Testimony at the Threshold of the State." *Cultural Dynamics* 20, no. 2 (2008): 167–92.

Alstyne, Richard W. "The Panama Canal: A Classic Case of an Imperial Hangover." *Journal of Contemporary History* 15, no. 2 (1980): 299–316.

Anker, Elizabeth S. *Fictions of Dignity: Embodying Human Rights in World Literature*. Ithaca, NY: Cornell University Press, 2012.

———. "Globalizing Law and Literature." In *New Directions in Law and Literature*, edited by Elizabeth S. Anker and Bernadette Meyler, 210–26. Oxford: Oxford University Press, 2017.

Apter, Andrew. *The Pan-African Nation: Oil and the Spectacle of Culture in Nigeria*. Chicago: University of Chicago Press, 2014.

Arewa, Olufunmilayo B. "TRIPs and Traditional Knowledge: Local Communities, Local Knowledge, and Global Intellectual Property Frameworks." *Marquette Intellectual Property Law Review* 10, no. 2 (2006): 155–80.

Baker, Sir John. *Introduction to English Legal History*. 5th ed. Oxford: Oxford University Press, 2019.

Bartley, Aryn. "The Violence of the Present: David's Story and the Truth and Reconciliation Commission." *Comparative Literature Studies* 46, no. 1 (2009): 103–24.

Bassey, Nnimmo. *Oil Politics: Echoes of Ecological Wars*. Montréal: Daraja Press, 2016.

———. *The Secure and the Dispossessed: How the Military and Corporations Are Shaping a Climate-Changed World*. London: Pluto Press, 2015.

Baucom, Ian. *Specters of the Atlantic: Finance Capital, Slavery, and the Philosophy of History*. Durham, NC: Duke University Press, 2005.

Beharie, Tertia, and Tshepo Shabangu. "Traditional Knowledge, Traditional Cultural Expressions and Folklore." In *Introduction to Intellectual Property Law*, edited by Owen Dean and Alison Dyer, 331–59. Oxford: Oxford University Press, 2014.

Benn, Alex. "Criminal Damage: The 'Colston Four,' Proportionality and the Concerns That Linger." *The Journal of Criminal Law* 87, no. 1 (2023): 61–64.

Benton, Lauren A. *Law and Colonial Cultures: Legal Regimes in World History, 1400–1900*. Cambridge: Cambridge University Press, 2002.

Best, Stephen. *The Fugitive's Properties: Law and the Poetics of Possession*. Chicago: University of Chicago Press, 2004.

Bhandar, Brenna. *Colonial Lives of Property: Law, Land, and Racial Regimes of Ownership*. Durham, NC: Duke University Press, 2018.

Blackstone, William. "Commentaries of the Laws of England." In *Book II: Of the Rights of Things*, edited by Simon Stern. Oxford: Oxford University Press, 2016.

Blalock, Corinne. "Introduction: Law and the Critique of Capitalism." *South Atlantic Quarterly* 121, no. 2 (2022): 223–37.

Boateng, Boatema. "The Hand of the Ancestors: Time, Cultural Production, and Intellectual Property Law." *Law & Society Review* 47, no. 4 (2013): 943–73.

Boehmer, Elleke. *Indian Arrivals, 1870–1915: Networks of British Empire*. Oxford: Oxford University Press, 2015.

Bois, Mikhalien du. "Recognition and Protection of Traditional Knowledge Interests as Property in South African Law." *European Property Law Journal* 2, no. 2 (2013): 144–70.

Brewer, Holly. "Creating a Common Law of Slavery for England and Its New World Empire." *Law and History* 39, no. 4 (2021): 765–834.

Brouillette, Sarah. *Postcolonial Writers in the Global Literary Marketplace*. Basingstoke, Hampshire: Palgrave Macmillan, 2007.

Brown, Mark. "Jamaica Seeks Return of Artefacts from the British Museum." *The Guardian*, August 7, 2019.

Butler, Judith, and Athena Athanasiou. *Dispossession: The Performative in the Political: Conversations with Athena Athanasiou*. New York: Polity Press, 2013.

Carpenter, Kristen A., Sonia K. Katyal, and Angela R. Riley. "In Defense of Property." *The Yale Law Journal* 118, no. 6 (2009): 1022–1124.

Carson, Anne. *Economy of the Unlost: (Reading Simonides of Keos with Paul Celan)*. Princeton, NJ: Princeton University Press, 2002.

Casey, Rose. "Possessive Politics and Improper Aesthetics: Property Rights and Female Dispossession in Arundhati Roy's *The God of Small Things*." *NOVEL: A Forum on Fiction* 48, no. 3 (2015): 381–99.

Chander, Manu Samriti. "Manu Samriti Chander's Brown Ramblist." *The Rambling*. February 13, 2021. https://the-rambling.com/2021/02/13/ramblist-chander/.

Chandler, David, and Julian Reid. "Becoming Indigenous: The 'Speculative Turn' in Anthropology and the (Re)Colonization of Indigeneity." *Postcolonial Studies: Culture* 23, no. 4 (2020): 485–504.

Cheah, Pheng. *What Is a World? On Postcolonial Literature as World Literature*. Durham, NC: Duke University Press, 2016.

Chuh, Kandice. *The Difference Aesthetics Makes: On the Humanities "After Man."* Durham, NC: Duke University Press, 2019.

Cohen, Morris R., and Felix S. Cohen. *Readings in Jurisprudence and Legal Philosophy*. Frederick, MD: Beard Books, 2002.

Colvin, Christopher J. "Trafficking Trauma: Intellectual Property Rights and the Political Economy of Traumatic Storytelling." *Critical Arts* 20, no. 1 (2006): 171–82.

Coombe, Rosemary J. *The Cultural Life of Intellectual Properties: Authorship, Appropriation, and the Law*. Durham, NC: Duke University Press, 1998.

Cooper, Frederick. *Colonialism in Question: Theory, Knowledge, History*. Berkeley: University of California Press, 2005.

Copley, John Singleton. *The Death of Major Peirson*, January 6, 1781.

Cork, Tristan, and Estel Farell Roig. "The Bristol Things Named After Edward Colston That Have Changed Their Name in the Past Year," n.d. https://www.bristolpost.co.uk/news/bristol-news/bristol-things-named-after-5486550.

Curci, Jonathan. *The Protection of Biodiversity and Traditional Knowledge in International Law of Intellectual Property*. Cambridge: Cambridge University Press, 2010.

Dango, Michael. *Crisis Style: The Aesthetics of Repair*. Stanford, CA: Stanford University Press, 2022.

Dayan, Colin. *The Law Is a White Dog: How Legal Rituals Make and Unmake Persons*. Princeton, NJ: Princeton University Press, 2011.

———. "Legal Slaves and Civil Bodies." *Nepantla: Views from South* 2, no. 1 (2001): 3–39.

De, Rohit. *A People's Constitution: The Everyday Life of Law in the Indian Republic*. Princeton, NJ: Princeton University Press, 2018.

Dedering, Tilman. "'We Are Only Humble People and Poor': A.A.S. Le Fleur and the Power of Petitions." *South African Historical Journal* 2, no. 1 (2010): 121–42.

Derrida, Jacques. "Force of Law: The 'Mystical Foundation of Authority.'" In *Acts of Religion*, edited by Gil Anidjar, 230–98. New York: Routledge, 2002.

Dikant, Thomas. "'Oracles of the Law:' Oliver Wendell Holmes Jr.'s Legal Futurism." *Law and Literature* 36, no. 3 (2024): 465–80.

Dowling, Sarah. *Translingual Poetics: Writing Personhood Under Settler Colonialism*. Iowa City: University of Iowa Press, 2018.

Drahos, Peter. *Intellectual Property, Indigenous People and Their Knowledge*. Cambridge: Cambridge University Press, 2014.

Driver, Dorothy, and Zoë Wicomb. "Afterword." In *David's Story*, 215–71. New York: The Feminist Press at City University of New York, 2001.

Eatough, Matthew. "Futures, Inc.: Fiction and Intellectual Property in the (South) African Renaissance." In *World Literature, Neoliberalism, and the Culture of Discontent*, edited by Sharae Deckard and Stephen Shapiro, 215–38. Cham, Switzerland: Palgrave Macmillan, 2019.

Elam, Daniel. *World Literature for the Wretched of the Earth: Anticolonial Aesthetics, Postcolonial Politics*. New York: Fordham University Press, 2020.

Elias, T.O. *Nigerian Land Law*. 4th ed. London: Sweet & Maxwell, 1971.

Evans, Mel. *Art Wash: Big Oil and the Arts*. London: Pluto Press, 2015.

Falola, Toyin, and Matthew Heaton. *A History of Nigeria*. Cambridge: Cambridge University Press, 2008.

Fanon, Frantz. *The Wretched of the Earth*. Translated by Richard Philcox. New York: Grove Press, 2011.

Fehskens, Erin M. "Accounts Unpaid, Accounts Untold: M. NourbeSe Philip's *Zong!* and the Catalogue." *Callaloo* 35, no. 2 (2012): 407–24.

Frankel, Susy. "'Ka Mate Ka Mate' and the Protection of Traditional Knowledge." In *Intellectual Property at the Edge: The Contested Contours of IP*, edited by Rochelle Cooper Dreyfus and Jane C. Ginsburg, 193–214. Cambridge: Cambridge University Press, 2014.

Fretwell, Erica. *Sensory Experiments: Psychophysics, Race, and the Aesthetics of Feeling*. Durham, NC: Duke University Press, 2022.

Friedman, Susan Stanford. "Feminism, State Fictions and Violence: Gender, Geopolitics and Transnationalism." *Communal/Plural* 9, no. 1 (2001): 111–29.

Galvin, Rachel. "Poetry Is Theft." *Comparative Literature Studies* 51, no. 1 (2014): 18–54.
Gandhi, Leela. *Affective Communities: Anticolonial Thought, Fin-de-Siècle Radicalism, and the Politics of Friendship*. Durham, NC: Duke University Press, 2006.
Geyer, Sunelle. "Copyright in Traditional Works: Unraveling the Intellectual Property Laws Amendment Act of 2013." *South African Mercantile Law Journal* 29, no. 1 (2017): 43–65.
Ghosh, Amitav. *The Great Derangement: Climate Change and the Unthinkable*. Chicago: University of Chicago Press, 2016.
——. "Petrofiction." *The New Republic*, March 2, 1992.
Gibixego, Anelile, and Athambile Masola. "South Africa's Trade Publishing Sector: Has There Been Transformation?" In *Mintirho Ya Vulavula: Arts, National Identities and Democracy*, edited by Innocentia J. Mhlambi and Sandile Ngidi, 255–86. Johannesburg: Mapungubwe Institute (Mistra), 2021.
Gikandi, Simon. "Introduction: Africa, Diaspora, and the Discourse of Modernity." *Research in African Literatures* 27, no. 4 (1996): 1–6.
Gilroy, Paul. *The Black Atlantic: Modernity and Double Consciousness*. Cambridge, MA: Harvard University Press, 1993.
"Global Gas Flaring Tracker Report." World Bank, 2023. www.worldbank.org/en/programs/gasflaringreduction/global-flaring-data.
Goyal, Yogita. "Africa and the Black Atlantic." *Research in African Literatures* 45, no. 3 (2014).
Grazia, Margreta De. "Sanctioning Voice: Quotation Marks, the Abolition of Torture, and the Fifth Amendment." In *The Construction of Authorship: Textual Appropriation in Law and Literature*, edited by Peter Jaszi and Martha Woodmansee, 281–302. Durham, NC: Duke University Press, 1993.
Grotius, Hugo. *Mare Liberum or The Free Sea*. Edited by David Armitage. Translated by Richard Hakluyt. Liberty Fund, 2004.
Habila, Helon. *Oil on Water*. London: Penguin, 2011.
Haksar, Nandita. "Human Rights Lawyering: A Feminist Perspective." In *Women's Studies in India: A Reader*, edited by Mary E. John, 278–85. New Delhi: Penguin, 2008.
Haraway, Donna J. *Staying with the Trouble: Making Kin in the Chthulucene*. Durham, NC: Duke University Press, 2016.
Harlin, Kate. "'How Can a River Be Red?' Violent Petroculture in Chigozie Obioma's *The Fishermen*." *Journal of Postcolonial Writing* 55, no. 5 (2019): 685–97.
Harris, Cheryl I. "Whiteness as Property." *Harvard Law Review* 106, no. 8 (1993): 1707–91.
Hartman, Saidiya. *Lose Your Mother: A Journey Along the Atlantic Slave Route*. New York: Farrar, Straus & Giroux, 2008.
Hensley, Nathan. *Forms of Empire: The Poetics of Victorian Sovereignty*. Oxford: Oxford University Press, 2018.

"Hew Locke: Restoration." Spike Island. www.spikeisland.org.uk/programme/exhibitions/hew-locke-restoration, July 2023.
Hofmeyr, Isabel. "Colonial Copyright, Customs, and Port Cities: Material Histories and Intellectual Property." *Comparative Literature* 70, no. 3 (2018): 264–77.
Holmes, Oliver Wendell, Jr. "The Path of the Law." *Harvard Law Review* 10, no. 8 (1897): 457–78.
Hopkins, Samantha, Ciarán O'Kelly, Ciara Hackett, and Clare Patton. "Okpabi and Others v Royal Dutch Shell Plc and Another [2021] UKSC 3." *Northern Ireland Legal Quarterly* 72, no. 1 (2021): 148–59.
"How Statues Are Falling Around the World." *New York Times*. June 24, 2020.
Huaman, Elizabeth Sumida. "Indigenous Rights Education (IRE): Indigenous Knowledge Systems and Transformative Human Rights in the Peruvian Andes." *International Journal of Human Rights Education* 1, no. 1 (2017): 1–34.
Hughes, Justin. "Traditional Knowledge, Cultural Expression, and the Siren's Call of Property." *San Diego Law Review* 49, no. 4 (2012): 1215–66.
Hunter, Walt. *Forms of a World: Contemporary Poetry and the Making of Globalization*. New York: Fordham University Press, 2019.
Hussain, Nasser. *The Jurisprudence of Emergency: Colonialism and the Rule of Law*. Ann Arbor: University of Michigan Press, 2003.
Huxtable, Sally-Anne. "Interim Report on the Connections between Colonialism and Properties Now in the Care of the National Trust, Including Links with Historic Slavery." *National Trust*, 2020. www.nationaltrust.org.uk/who-we-are/research/addressing-our-histories-of-colonialism-and-historic-slavery.
Iheka, Cajetan. *Naturalizing Africa: Ecological Violence, Agency, and Postcolonial Resistance in African Literature*. Cambridge: Cambridge University Press, 2018.
"Impropriety, (n.1)." In *Oxford English Dictionary*. Oxford: Oxford University Press, September 2023.
Irele, Abiola. *The African Experience in Literature and Ideology*. London: Heinemann, 1981.
Jack-Osimiri, Uche. "Repeal Land Use Act 1978 or Amendment of Its Provisions Governing Compensation for Compulsory Acquisition?" In *Critical Issues in Nigerian Property Law*, edited by Agbe Utuama, 135–54. Lagos, Nigeria: Malthouse Press, 2016.
Jaji, Tsitsi, and Lily Saint. "Introduction: Genre in Africa." *The Cambridge Journal of Postcolonial Literary Inquiry* 4, no. 2 (2017): 151–58.
"Jamaica Going After Artefacts." *The Gleaner*. July 24, 2019. https://jamaica-gleaner.com/article/news/20190724/jamaica-going-after-artefacts.
James, C. L. R. *The Black Jacobins: Toussaint L'Ouverture and the San Domingo Revolution*. 2nd edition. New York: Vintage, 1989.
John, Thomas. "Succession Law in India and Obstacles in the Road to Gender Equality: The Experience of Mary Roy v. State of Kerala." *Student Bar Review* 18, no. 2 (2006): 38–58.

Jolly, Jasper. "Bank of England Owned 599 Slaves in 1770s, New Exhibition Reveals." *The Guardian*, April 2022.

Kalliney, Peter. *The Aesthetic Cold War: Decolonization and Global Literature*. Princeton, NJ: Princeton University Press, 2022.

Kapur, Ratna. "Hecklers to Power? The Waning of Liberal Rights and Challenges to Feminism in India." In *South Asian Feminisms*, edited by Ania Loomba and Ritty A. Lukose, 333–55. Durham, NC: Duke University Press, 2012.

Karanja, Wanjiku. "The Legitimacy of Indigenous Intellectual Property Rights' Claims." *Strathmore Law Review* 1, no. 1 (2016): 165–90.

Khan, Almas. "Poetic Justice: Slavery, Law, and the (Anti-)Elegiac Form in M. NourBese Philip's *Zong!*" *The Cambridge Journal of Postcolonial Literary Inquiry* 2, no. 1 (2015): 5–32.

King, Tiffany Lethabo. *The Black Shoals: Offshore Formations of Black and Native Studies*. Durham, NC: Duke University Press, 2019.

Kitchen, Stephanie, and Mary Jay. "Decolonisation and Co-Publishing." *African Books Collective*. www.Readafricanbooks.Com/Conferences-and-Workshops/Decolonisation-and-Co-Publishing/.

Kodoth, Praveena. "Gender, Community and Identity in Property Law Reform: The Case of Early Twentieth Century Tiruvitamkoor." *Inter-Asia Cultural Studies* 3, no. 3 (2002): 383–93.

Konne, Barisere Rachel. "Inadequate Monitoring and Enforcement in the Nigerian Oil Industry: The Case of Shell and Ogoniland." *Cornell International Law Journal* 47, no. 1 (2014): 181–204.

Kornbluh, Anna. *The Order of Forms: Realism, Formalism, and Social Space*. Chicago: University of Chicago Press, 2019.

Koshy, Susan, Lisa Marie Cacho, Jodi A. Byrd, and Brian Jordan Jefferson, eds. *Colonial Racial Capitalism*. Durham, NC: Duke University Press, 2022.

Ladan, Muhammed Tawfiq. "Status of Environmental Law and Sustainable Land Use in Nigeria." In *Land Use Law for Sustainable Development*, edited by Natalie J. Chalifour, Patricia Kameri-Mbote, Lin Heng Lye, and John R. Nolon, 240–52. Cambridge: Cambridge University Press, 2007.

Laing, Lionel H. "Historic Origins of Admiralty Jurisdiction in England." *Michigan Law Review* 45, no. 2 (1946): 163–82.

Lambert, Laurie. "Poetics of Reparation in M. NourbeSe Philip's *Zong!*" *The Global South* 10, no. 1 (2016): 107–29.

Legacies of British Slavery database. "Tobago 67 (Castara and Englishman's Bay)." University College London, n.d. www.ucl.ac.uk/lbs/claim/view/27741.

Leman, Peter. *Singing the Law: Oral Jurisprudence and the Crisis of Colonial Modernity in East African Literature*. Liverpool: Liverpool University Press, 2020.

Lemaster, Tracy. "Influence and Intertextuality in Arundhati Roy and Harper Lee." *MFS: Modern Fiction Studies* 56, no. 4 (2010): 788–814.

LeMenager, Stephanie. *Living Oil: Petroleum Culture in the American Century*. Oxford: Oxford University Press, 2014.

Levine, Caroline. *Forms: Whole, Rhythm, Hierarchy, Network*. Princeton, NJ: Princeton University Press, 2015.
Liberty. "Colston Four Ruling 'Puts a Threshold on Our Human Rights' Liberty Warns." Liberty. September 28, 2022. https://www.libertyhumanrights.org.uk/issue/colston-four-ruling-puts-a-threshold-on-our-human-rights-liberty-warns/.
Liverpool, Hollis Urban. "Origins of Rituals and Customs in the Trinidad Carnival: African or European?" in "Trinidad and Tobago Carnival," edited by Milla C. Riggio, special issue, *The Drama Review (TDR)* 42, no. 3 (1998): 24–37.
Lloyd, David. *Under Representation: The Racial Regime of Aesthetics*. New York: Fordham University Press, 2019.
Lobban, Michael. "Slavery, Insurance and the Law." *The Journal of Legal History* 28, no. 3 (2007): 319–28.
Locke, Hew. *Castara Estates*. 2012. Acrylic and ink. *Hales Gallery*. https://privateviews.artlogic.net/2/dd6c8bb2ef64ca2d2b56ee/3398/1.
———. *Hinterland*. 2013. Acrylic on chromogenic print. *Hales Gallery*. https://halesgallery.com/artists/15-hew-locke/works/3817-hew-locke-hinterland-2013/.
———. "Let's Make Something Positive." Tate, May 3, 2022. YouTube video. https://www.youtube.com/watch?v=11d64_f-m6U.
———. *The Procession*. 2022. Installation of 129 figures: plastic, cardboard, fabric, wood, paper, metal, and mixed media. *Hales Gallery*. https://halesgallery.com/artists/15-hew-locke/works/14644-hew-locke-the-procession-2022/.
———. *Sovereign with Spider Monkeys*. 2016. Watercolor on paper. *Art Image*. https://artimage.org.uk/17455/hew-locke/sovereign-with-spider-monkeys--2016.
Locke, Hew, Stephanie James, and Peter Bonnell. *Strangers in Paradise*. London: Black Dog Publishing, 2011.
Loomba, Ania, and Ritty A. Lukose, eds. *South Asian Feminisms*. Durham, NC: Duke University Press, 2012.
Lutz, John. "Commodity Fetishism, Patriarchal Repression, and Psychic Deprivation in Arundhati Roy's *The God of Small Things*." *Mosaic* 42, no. 3 (2009): 57–74.
Lye, Lin Heng. "Land Law and the Environment: Re-Examining the Concept of Ownership and Forging New Rights and Obligations in a Changed World." *Land Law and the Environment* 22 (2010): 189–228.
Mackey, Nathaniel. "Other: From Noun to Verb." *Representations* 39 (1992): 51–70.
Macpherson, C. B. *The Political Theory of Possessive Individualism: Hobbes to Locke*. Oxford: Oxford University Press, 2011.
"Maritime Law: Personality of Ship: Immunity of Government Property." *Michigan Law Review* 20, no. 5 (1922): 533–35.
Martin, Carol. "Trinidad Carnival Glossary." *Trinidad and Tobago Carnival, Special Issue of The Drama Review (TDR)* 42, no. 3 (1998): 220–35.
Martin, Dawn Lundy. "The Language of Trauma: Faith and Atheism in M. NourbeSe Philip's Poetry." In *Eleven More American Women Poets in the 21st Century: Poetics Across North America*, edited by Claudia Rankine and Lisa Sewell, 283–307. Middletown, CT: Wesleyan University Press, 2012.

Mawani, Renisa. *Across Oceans of Law: The Komagata Maru and Jurisdiction in the Time of Empire*. Durham, NC: Duke University Press, 2018.

McDonald, Peter D. *The Literature Police: Apartheid Censorship and Its Cultural Consequences*. Oxford: Oxford University Press, 2009.

McKittrick, Katherine. "Mathematics of Black Life." *The Black Scholar* 44, no. 2 (2014): 16–28.

Menon, Nivedita. "A Uniform Civil Code in India: The State of the Debate in 2014." *Feminist Studies* 40, no. 2 (2014): 480–86.

Mgbeoji, Ikechi. *Global Biopiracy: Patents, Plants, and Indigenous Knowledge*. Vancouver: University of British Columbia Press, 2006.

Mintz, Sidney. *Sweetness and Power: The Place of Sugar in Modern History*. New York: Viking, 1985.

Mishra, Archana. "Towards Women's Equal Right to Property." *Property Law Review* 5, no. 3 (2016): 161–75.

Mohanty, Chandra Talpade. "Cartographies of Struggle: Third World Women and the Politics of Feminism." In *Feminism without Borders: Decolonizing Theory, Practicing Solidarity*. Durham, NC: Duke University Press, 2003.

Moore, Alexandra Schultheis. "'Dispossession within the Law': Human Rights and the Ec-Static Subject in M. NourbeSe Philip's Zong!" *Feminist Formations* 28, no. 1 (2016): 166–89.

Moreton-Robinson, Aileen. *The White Possessive: Property, Power, and Indigenous Sovereignty*. Minneapolis: University of Minnesota Press, 2015.

Morton, Stephen. *States of Emergency: Colonialism, Literature and Law*. Liverpool: Liverpool University Press, 2013.

Mosimege, Mogege. "The Development of Indigenous Knowledge Systems Policy and Legislation in South Africa: Intellectual Property Implications for Knowledge Holders and Practitioners." In *Indigenous Knowledge Systems and Intellectual Property Rights in the Twenty-First Century: Perspectives from Southern Africa*, edited by Isaac Mazonde and Thomas Pradip, 95–103. CODESRIA, 2007.

Moten, Fred. *In the Break: The Aesthetics of the Black Radical Tradition*. Minneapolis: University of Minnesota Press, 2003.

Mtubani, V. C. D. "African Slaves and English Law." Pula: Michigan State Libraries Digital Repository, 1983. https://n2t.net/ark:/85335/m53b5xn59.

Munro, Brenna M. "Queer Family Romance: Writing the 'New' South Africa in the 1990s." *GLQ: A Journal of Lesbian and Gay Studies* 15, no. 3 (2009): 397–439.

Naimou, Angela. *Salvage Work: U.S. and Caribbean Literatures Amid the Debris of Legal Personhood*. New York: Fordham University Press, 2015.

Nair, Janaki. *Women and Law in Colonial India: A Social History*, New Delhi: Kali for Women in collaboration with the National Law School of India University, 1996.

Ncube, Caroline B. "The Creative Industry and South African Intellectual Property Law." *Law and Development Review* 11, no. 2 (2018): 589–607.

Needham, Anuradha Dingwaney. "'The Small Voice of History' in Arundhati Roy's *The God of Small Things*." *Interventions: International Journal of Postcolonial Studies* 7, no. 3 (2005): 369–91.

Neti, Leila. "Imperial Inheritances: Lapses, Loves and Laws in the Colonial Machine." *Interventions: International Journal of Postcolonial Studies* 16, no. 2 (2014): 197–214.

——. "'The Love Laws': Section 377 and the Politics of Queerness in Arundhati Roy's *The God of Small Things*." *Law & Literature* 29, no. 2 (2017): 223–46.

Ngai, Sianne. *Our Aesthetic Categories: Zany, Cute, Interesting*. Cambridge, MA: Harvard University Press, 2012.

Nichols, Robert. *Theft Is Property!: Dispossession & Critical Theory*. Durham, NC: Duke University Press, 2020.

Nixon, Rob. *Slow Violence and the Environmentalism of the Poor*. Cambridge, MA: Harvard University Press, 2011.

NOSDRA. "Nigerian Oil Spill Monitor. NOSDRA, National Oil Spill Detection and Response Agency," n.d. https://nosdra.oilspillmonitor.ng/.

Nwapi, Chilenye. "A Legislative Proposal for Public Participation in Oil and Gas Decision-Making in Nigeria." *Journal of African Law* 54, no. 2 (2010): 184–211.

Nwauche, Enyinna S. "The Constitutional Challenge of the Integration and Interaction of Customary and the Received English Common Law in Nigeria and Ghana." *Tulane European & Civil Law Forum* 25, no. 4 (2010): 37–63.

——. "The Swakopmund Protocol and the Communal Ownership and Control of Expressions of Folklore in Africa." *The Journal of World Intellectual Property* 17, no. 5–6 (2014): 191–201.

Obi, Cyril. "The Geopolitical Consequences of Oil in Africa: The Case of Nigeria." *The Brown Journal of World Affairs* 26, no. 2 (2020): 1–18.

Obioma, Chigozie. *The Fishermen*. London: Little, Brown & Company, 2016.

Oguamanam, Chidi. "Beyond Theories: Intellectual Property Dynamics in the Global Knowledge Economy." *Wake Forest Intellectual Property Law Journal* 9, no. 2 (2008): 104–54.

——. "Local Knowledge as Trapped Knowledge: Intellectual Property, Culture, Power and Politics." *The Journal of World Intellectual Property* 11, no. 1 (2008): 29–57.

Okonkwo, Chidumeje Ndidi Patience, Lalit Kumar, and Subhashni Taylor. "The Niger Delta Wetland Ecosystem: What Threatens It and Why Should We Protect It?" *African Journal of Environmental Science and Technology* 9, no. 5 (2015): 451–63.

Okri, Ben. "What the Tapster Saw." In *Stars of the New Curfew*, 183–94. London: Vintage, 1999.

Oldham, James. "Insurance Litigation Involving the *Zong* and Other British Slave Ships, 1780–1807." *The Journal of Legal History* 28, no. 3 (2007): 299–318.

Olong, Adefi. *Land Law in Nigeria*. 2nd ed. Lagos, Nigeria: Malthouse Press, 2012.

Olumide, Ekanade. "Minorities and Resource Allocation in a Transitional State: The Nigerian Experience." In *Horror in Paradise: Frameworks for Understanding* the Crises of the Niger Delta Region of Nigeria, edited by Christopher LaMonica and J. Shola Omotola, 67–84. Durham, NC: Carolina Academic Press, 2014.

Outka, Elizabeth. "Trauma and Temporal Hybridity in Arundhati Roy's The God of Small Things." Contemporary Literature 52, no. 1 (2011): 21–53.

Philip, M. NourbeSe. "Defending the Dead, Confronting the Archive: A Conversation with M. NourbeSe Philip." By Patricia Saunders. Small Axe 26 (2008): 63–79.

———. Zong! Middletown, CT: Wesleyan University Press, 2008.

Philips, Amali. "Rethinking Dowry, Inheritance and Women's Resistance among the Syrian Christians of Kerala." Anthropologica 45, no. 2 (2003): 245–63.

Polymenopolou, Eleni. "Indigenous Cultural Heritage and Artistic Expressions: Localizing Intellectual Property Rights and UNESCO Claims." Canadian Journal of Human Rights 6 (2017): 87–126.

Price, Griffith. "Statutory Rights in Rem in English Admiralty Law." Journal of Comparative Legislation and International Law 27, no. 3–4 (1945): 21–31.

"Proprietary (n. & Adj.)." In Oxford English Dictionary. Oxford: Oxford University Press, March 2024. https://doi.org/10.1093/OED/1922005579.

Quayson, Ato. Strategic Transformations: Orality and History in the Work of Rev. Samuel Johnson, Amos Tutuola, Wole Soyinka, and Ben Okri. Oxford: Currey, 1997.

Rajan, Rajeswari Sunder. The Scandal of the State: Women, Law, and Citizenship in Postcolonial India. Durham, NC: Duke University Press, 2003.

Ramazani, Jahan. Poetry of Mourning: The Modern Elegy from Hardy to Heaney. Chicago: University of Chicago Press, 1994.

Rancière, Jacques. "The Distribution of the Sensible: Politics and Aesthetics." In The Politics of Aesthetics, edited by Gabriel Rockhill, 7–14. London: Bloomsbury, 2004.

Reed, Anthony. Freedom Time: The Poetics and Politics of Black Experimental Writing. Baltimore. MD: Johns Hopkins University Press, 2016.

Reeder, Jessie. The Forms of Informal Empire: Britain, Latin America, and Nineteenth-Century Literature. Baltimore, MD: Johns Hopkins University Press, 2020.

Reichman, Ravit. "Mourning, Owning, Owing." American Imago 64, no. 3 (2007): 433–49.

Riley, Christopher, and Oludara Akanmi. "Examining and Evaluating Transnational Tortious Actions Against Parent Companies: Lessons from Shell and Nigeria." African Journal of International and Comparative Law 30, no. 2 (2022): 229–51.

Robinson, Cedric J. Black Marxism: The Making of the Black Radical Tradition. 3rd ed. Chapel Hill: University of North Carolina Press, 2020.

Roht-Arriaza, Naomi. "Of Seeds and Shamans: The Appropriation of the Scientific and Technical Knowledge of Indigenous and Local Communities." Michigan Journal of International Law 17, no. 4 (1996): 919–65.

Roorda, Lucas. "Broken English: A Critique of the Dutch Court of Appeal Decision in Four Nigerian Farmers and Milieudefensie v Shell." *Transnational Legal Theory* 12, no. 1 (2021): 144–50.

Roorda, Lucas, and Daniel Leader. "Okpabi v. Shell and Four Nigerian Farmers v Shell: Parent Company Liability Back in Court." *Business and Human Rights Journal*, no. 6 (2021): 368–76.

Rose, Mark. *Authors and Owners: The Invention of Copyright*. Cambridge, MA: Harvard University Press, 1993.

Roy, Arundhati. *The God of Small Things*. New York: Random House, 1997.

———. *The Ministry of Utmost Happiness*. New York: Alfred A. Knopf, 2017.

Roy, Mary. "Three Generations of Indian Women." *Indian Journal of Gender Studies* 6, no. 2 (1999): 203–19.

Roy, Srila. *Changing the Subject: Feminist and Queer Politics in Neoliberal India*. Durham, NC: Duke University Press, 2022.

Said, Edward W. *The Question of Palestine*. London: Vintage Books, 1992.

Saint, Lily. *Black Cultural Life in South Africa: Reception, Apartheid, and Ethics*. Ann Arbor: University of Michigan Press, 2018.

Saint-Amour, Paul K. *The Copywrights: Intellectual Property and the Literary Imagination*. Ithaca, NY: Cornell University Press, 2003.

Samuelson, Meg. "The Disfigured Body of the Female Guerilla: (De)Militarization, Sexual Violence, and Redomestication in Zoë Wicomb's *David's Story*." *Signs* 32, no. 4 (2007): 833–56.

Sarkar, Lotika. "Women's Movement and the Legal Process." *CWDS: Occasional Paper*, no. 24 (1995): 1–29.

Satchell, Veront M., and Cezley Sampson. "The Rise and Fall of Railways in Jamaica, 1845–1975." *The Journal of Transport History* 24, no. 1 (2003): 1–21.

Schorr, David B. "How Blackstone Became a Blackstonian." *Theoretical Inquiries in Law* 10 (2009): 103–26.

Scott, David. *Conscripts of Modernity: The Tragedy of Colonial Enlightenment*. Durham, NC: Duke University Press, 2004.

Seshu, Meena Sarawathi. "Women in Sex Work." In *Negotiating Spaces: Legal Domains, Gender Concerns, and Community Constructs*, edited by Flavia Agnes and Shoba Venkatesh Ghosh, 29–58. Delhi: Oxford University Press, 2012.

Sharafi, Mitra. "South Asian Legal History." *Annual Review of Law and Social Science* 11 (2015): 309–36.

Sharpe, Christina. *In the Wake: On Blackness and Being*. Durham, NC: Duke University Press, 2016.

Sharpe, Jenny. *Immaterial Archives: An African Diaspora Poetics of Loss*. Evanston, IL: Northwestern University Press, 2020.

Shockley, Evie. "Going Overboard: African American Poetic Innovation and the Middle Passage." *Contemporary Literature* 52, no. 4 (2011): 791–817.

Singh, Kirti. *Separated and Divorced Women in India: Economic Rights and Entitlements*. Los Angeles; New Delhi: Sage Law, 2013.

Slaughter, Joseph. *Human Rights, Inc: The World Novel, Narrative Form, and International Law*. New York: Fordham University Press, 2007.
———. "World Literature as Property." *Alif: Journal of Comparative Poetics* 34 (2014): 39–73.
Smith, Bryant. "Legal Personality." *Yale Law Journal* 37, no. 3 (1928): 283–99.
Spillers, Hortense. "Mama's Baby, Papa's Maybe: An American Grammar Book." *Culture and Countermemory: The "American" Connection, Special Issue of Diacritics* 17, no. 2 (1987): 64–81.
Spivak, Gayatri Chakravorty. "Can the Subaltern Speak?" In *Marxism and the Interpretation of Culture*, edited by Cary Nelson and Lawrence Grossberg, 271–313. Basingstoke: Macmillan Education, 1988.
Sreenivas, Mytheli. "Conjugality and Capital: Gender, Families, and Property under Colonial Law in India." *The Journal of Asian Studies* 63, no. 4 (2004): 937–60.
Staves, Susan. "Chattel Property Rules and the Construction of Englishness, 1660–1800." *Law and History Review* 12, no. 1 (1994): 123–54.
Stephens, Lisa. "The Illusion of Sustainable Development: How Nigeria's Environmental Laws Are Failing the Niger Delta." *Vermont Law Review* 36, no. 2 (2011): 387–407.
Stern, Simon. "From Author's Right to Property Right." *University of Toronto Law Journal* 62 (2012): 29–91.
———. "Legal Fictions and Legal Fabrications." In *Fictional Discourse and the Law*, edited by Hans J. Lind, 191–99. Abingdon, Oxon: Routledge, 2020.
Steyn, Phia. "Oil Exploration in Colonial Nigeria, c. 1903–58." *The Journal of Imperial and Commonwealth History* 37, no. 2 (2009): 249–74.
Stoler, Ann Laura. *Duress: Imperial Durability in Our Times*. Durham, NC: Duke University Press, 2016.
Sturman, Rachel. *The Government of Social Life in Colonial India: Liberalism, Religious Law, and Women's Rights*. Cambridge: Cambridge University Press, 2012.
Taíno-Arawak. *Figure*. 1500 800. Wood. Am1977. The British Museum. www.britishmuseum.org/collection/object/E_Am1977-Q-2.
Tate Museum. "Tate." *Hew Locke*, June 12, 2023.
Tharakan, Michael P. K. "History as Development Experience: Desegregated and Deconstructed Analysis of Kerala." PhD diss., Mahatma Gandhi University, Kottayam, India, 1997.
Tremblay, Jean-Thomas. *Breathing Aesthetics*. Durham, NC: Duke University Press, 2022.
Udo, R. K. *The National Land Policy of Nigeria*. Ibadan, Nigeria:: Development Policy Center, 1999.
Vadde, Aarthi. "The Backwaters Sphere: Ecological Collectivity, Cosmopolitanism, and Arundhati Roy." *MFS: Modern Fiction Studies* 55, no. 3 (2009): 522–44.

Van der Vlies, Andrew. *Present Imperfect: Contemporary South African Writing*. Oxford: Oxford University Press, 2017.
Van der Vlies, Andrew, ed. *Print, Text and Book Cultures in South Africa*. Johannesburg: Wits University Press, 2012.
Van Ho, Tara. "Vedanta Resources Plc and Another v. Lungowe and Others." *American Journal of International Law* 114, no. 1 (2020): 110–16.
Van Hulle, Inge. *Britain and International Law in West Africa*. Oxford: Oxford University Press, 2020.
Vergès, Françoise. "Racial Capitalocene." In *Futures of Black Radicalism*, edited by Gaye Theresa Johnson and Alex Lubin, 72–82. New York: Verso, 2017.
Vergil. *The Aeneid*. Translated by Shadi Bartsch. Modern Library, 2021.
Walvin, James. *The Zong: A Massacre, the Law and the End of Slavery*. New Haven, CT: Yale University Press, 2011.
Watts, Michael. "Resource Curse? Governmentality, Oil and Power in the Niger Delta, Nigeria." *Geopolitics* 9, no. 1 (2004): 50–80.
Webster, Jane. "The Zong in the Context of the Eighteenth-Century Slave Trade." *The Journal of Legal History* 28, no. 3 (2007): 285–98.
Wenzel, Jennifer. "Petro-Magic-Realism: Toward a Political Ecology of Nigerian Literature." *Postcolonial Studies* 9, no. 4 (2006): 449–64.
———. *The Disposition of Nature: Environmental Crisis and World Literature*. New York: Fordham University Press, 2019.
Wenzel, Jennifer, and Patricia Yaeger. "Introduction." In *Fueling Culture: 101 Words for Energy and Environment*, edited by Imre Szeman. New York: Fordham University Press, 2017.
Whyte, Kyle. "Settler Colonialism, Ecology, and Environmental Justice." *Environment and Society: Advances in Research* 9 (2018): 125–44.
Wicomb, Zoë. *David's Story*. New York: The Feminist Press at City University of New York, 2001.
———. "Shame and Identity: The Case of the Coloured in South Africa." In *Writing South Africa: Literature, Apartheid, and Democracy, 1970–1995*, edited by Derek Attridge and Rosemary Jolly, 91–107. Cambridge: Cambridge University Press, 1998.
Williams, Eric Eustace. *Capitalism & Slavery*. 3rd ed. Chapel Hill: University of North Carolina Press, 2021.
Williams, Raymond. *Marxism and Literature*. Oxford: Oxford University Press, 1977.
Wilson, Sheena, Imre Szeman, and Adam Carlson. "On Petrocultures: Or, Why We Need to Understand Oil to Understand Everything Else." In *Petrocultures: Oil, Politics, Culture*, edited by Sheena Wilson, Imre Szeman, and Adam Carlson, 3–19. Montréal: McGill-Queen's University Press, 2017.
Winnington, Sir Francis. "America and West Indies: July 1677, 16–31." *Calendar of State Papers Colonial, America and West Indies, vol. 10, 1677–1680*. Edited by W. Noel Sainsbury. London: J. W. Fortescue, 1896. *British History Online*. https://

www.british-history.ac.uk/cal-state-papers/colonial/america-west-indies/vol10/pp116-138.

Wood, Jon. "Photography, Painting and Impossible Sculpture: Hew Locke's Natives and Colonials: Jon Wood in Conversation with Hew Locke." *Sculpture Journal* 15, no. 2 (2006): 282–86.

Woodmansee, Martha. "On the Author Effect: Recovering Collectivity." In *The Construction of Authorship: Textual Appropriation in Law and Literature*, edited by Martha Woodmansee and Peter Jaszi, 15–28. Durham, NC: Duke University Press, 1993.

Woodmansee, Martha, and Peter Jaszi. "Introduction." In *The Construction of Authorship: Textual Appropriation in Law and Literature*, edited by Martha Woodmansee and Peter Jaszi, 1–14. Durham, NC: Duke University Press, 1994.

Woodmansee, Martha, and Peter Jaszi, eds. *The Construction of Authorship: Textual Appropriation in Law and Literature*. Durham, NC: Durham University Press, 1994.

World Bank, The. "Nigeria Economic Report: Report no. 101751." *Nigeria Economic Report*, no. 3 (November 2015). http://documents.worldbank.org/curated/en/684961468197340692/Nigeria-economic-report.

Wynter, Sylvia. "Unsettling the Coloniality of Being/Power/Truth/Freedom: Towards the Human After Man, Its Overrepresentation: An Argument." *The New Centennial Review* 3, no. 3 (2003): 257–337.

Yearwood, Peter J. *Nigeria and the Death of Liberal England: Palm Nuts and Prime Ministers, 1914–1916*. Cham, Switzerland: Palgrave Macmillan, 2018.

Yeats, W. B. *The Collected Poems of W. B. Yeats*. 2nd ed. Edited by Richard J. Finneran. New York: Scribner, 1996.

Yorke, P., and C. Talbot. "Advertisement." *Boston Gazette*, no. 561, September 7, 1730: 2.

Young, Hershini Bhana. *Illegible Will: Coercive Spectacles of Labor in South Africa and the Diaspora*. Durham, NC: Duke University Press, 2017.

Index

Abani, Chris, *Graceland*, 96
Adivasi, 66, 179n5
Adkin, Neil, 151
admiralty law, 6–7, 120, 123–28, 131, 134–36, 140, 153
Adunbi, Omolade, 171n5
aesthetic impropriety: accretion as variant of, 26, 92–95, 107, 112, 115; as anticolonial, 6, 17, 25, 27; definition of, 7, 21–25; dispersal as variant of, 120–23, 137–38, 142, 148, 153; hopefulness and, 24, 122, 157; legal transformation, 24, 80, 122, 156–60; logics of, 14, 16, 21, 54; narrative structure of, 46; openness and, 42, 53, 80, 112; propulsion and, 24, 120, 157; reciprocity as variant of, 68, 77–82; as response to proprietary property laws, 17, 21–22, 25, 34, 41–44, 47–48, 52, 136, 156; symbiosis as variant of, 48, 52, 54, 56–59; as theoretical framework, 17, 25–28
aesthetics: as compositional, 14, 16, 19, 100, 102, 110–112, 114; as sense-making, 15–20, 111, 118, 159; as sensory 14–20, 144; spatialization and, 15, 18, 138, 142–43; theories of, 13–21
Agarwal, Bina, 72–73, 179n1
Agary, Kaine, *Yellow-Yellow*, 33
Agathocleous, Tanya, 168–69n46
Agnes, Flavia, 181n21, 181n22, 181–82n23
Ahmad, Aijaz, 70
Akínwándé, Ayò, "Ogoni Cleanup," 45
Ako, Rhuks T., 43

Ako, Rhuks T., and Patrick Okonmah, 36, 173n27
Al-Kassim, Dina, 97
Alexander, Gregory S., 79
Americas, the, 6, 13, 124–25, 128, 135, 140
Amodu Tijani v. the Secretary, Southern Provinces, 56
animism, 25, 34, 45, 52–54, 60
Anker, Elizabeth S., 122, 183n29
anti-colonialism: and aesthetic theory, 17, 169n51; coalitional forms, 83; in creative practice, 32; as critical approach, 11, 20, 22; legal reforms and, 5–7, 12–13, 20, 24, 109; and liberation, 9; politics, 13; property law, approaches to, 5, 14, 21, 24, 26, 94–95, 97, 109, 117–119, 133
apartheid: atrocities, 93, 97; *David's Story* and, 26, 94; ending of, 90, 101–4, 112; state, 101, 110; racial domination, 95, 102, 105, 108, 114; resistance to, 96–97, 103, 105, 111
appeal (legal), 99, 136, 152
appellate, 133, 182n31
Apter, Andrew, 40
Arewa, Olufunmilayo B., 187n2
Art Not Oil, 29, 59
Atlantic, the, 1, 5, 120–22, 124–25, 150
Australia, 9–11, 51

Baartman, Sarah, 96, 106–7
Bahadur v. Bratiya, 63, 180n8
Bartley, Aryn, 96
Bassey, Nnimmo, 29, 46

Baucom, Ian, 124, 195n16
Beharie, Tertia, and Tshepo Shabangu, 191n63
Benton, Lauren, 12, 167n22, 168n43
Best, Stephen, 129, 134
Bhandar, Brenna, 9–11
biopiracy, 92, 188n8
Black Atlantic, the, 5, 148, 153, 166n12
Black epic, *Zong!* as, 123–42
Black Lives Matter, 1, 3, 186n1
black radical tradition, the, 128, 142
Black studies, 8, 17
Black voices, 26, 90, 95–97, 140
Blalock, Corinne, 166n14, 169n48
Bois, Mikhalien du, 108, 192n70
breath, 27, 120, 123, 144–45, 150, 153. *See also* oratory
Bristol, 1–2, 4, 14, 165n2
British Museum, the, 59, 157, 199n4
British Petroleum (BP), 30, 59, 175n69
Brouillette, Sarah, 183n41
Butler, Judith, and Athena Athanasiou, 11
Butts v. Penny, 27, 126–27, 133, 195n27

capitalist colonialism, 3–4, 8, 11–12, 26, 31, 47–48, 91, 95, 99, 104, 106, 114, 126, 128, 157, 159. *See also* colonial racial capitalism
Caribbean, 124, 135, 159
Carnival, 157–59
Carpenter, Kristen A., Sonia K. Katyal, and Angela R. Riley, 50–51, 177n105
Carson, Anne, 146
caste, 65, 68–70, 73, 77–82, 84–85, 87, 183n42
Chander, Manu Samriti, 187n1
chattel slavery. *See under* slavery: chattel
Cheah, Pheng, 18–19
Chota Nagpur Tenancy Act, 63, 179n5
Christian Succession Act (Repeal) Bill, 63
Chuh, Kandice, 17–18, 20, 169–70n53
circulation: of aesthetic works, 5, 14–15; of ideas, discursively, 15, 18, 20–21, 27, 95, 137, 155
Cohen, Morris R., and Felix S. Cohen, 79, 185n29
collaboration: cultural and knowledge production, 91–93, 104, 109, 112, 115; Indigenous and anti-colonial challenges to intellectual property (IP) law, 93, 98, 104, 114–115; narration of *David's Story*, 99, 222; scholarship, 49–50

colonial racial capitalism, 21–22, 122, 142, 187n1. *See also* racial capitalism
colonialism: British, 2–5, 8, 21–22, 37, 62, 67, 69, 71, 83, 97, 110, 157; European, 8, 49–50, 91, 107, 159
Colston Four, Attorney General's Reference, 165n1, 165n3–5
Colston Four, the, 1–2, 4
Colvin, Christopher J., 97
commodification: aesthetic reversal of, 140, 151; African literature's commodity value, 96; commodification and race, 10 (Cheryl Harris on), 104 (Isabel Hofmeyr on), 128–29 (Stephen Best on), 173n25 (Jennifer Wenzel on); enslavement as, 121, 134, 127–28, 131–134; literary work as commodity, 98
common law, 31, 33, 37, 51, 172n9, 177n105, 199n104
Constitution, the: of India 23, 63, 65, 67–68, 77–79, 85, 182n28; of the Federal Republic of Nigeria, 38, 42
Coombe, Rosemary J., 100–101
Cooper, Frederick, 167n17
Copley, John Singleton, 157
Copyright Act, South Africa, 101
copyright, 12, 91, 97–102, 104, 109, 111–113, 188n10, 190n37, 190n45
Court of Appeal, 1–2, 30
Criminal Damage Act, 1–2, 165n2

D. Chelliah Nadar v. G. Lalita Bai, 64
David's Story, 7, 21, 26, 94–107, 109–19, 155
Dayan, Colin, 127,134–36, 196n38
De, Rohit, 67, 182n31
decision (legal): aesthetic dismantling of, 142, 144; enslaved person's status in eighteenth-century English law, addressing, 130–31, 133, 153; *Gregson v. Gilbert*, regarding the *Zong* massacre, 123, 137, 142, 149; juridical norms built through, 134; pertaining to Nigerian oil extraction, 30–31, 56; regarding Indian divorce law, 63; *Stambovsky v. Ackley*, on ghosts in NY law, 136
Derrida, Jacques, 19–20
Dikant, Thomas, 199n104
discourse (discursive): circulation, 14, 18, 21, 27, 95, 137, 155; impact, 3, 14, 32, 60–61, 67, 110, 113, 117–118, 134, 138; process, 9, 28,

53, 78, 89–90, 99. *See also under* circulation: of ideas
dispersal: aural poetics of, 23, 27, 137–38, 141–42, 144, 148–51, 196n48; visual poetics of, 23, 27, 123, 133, 137–39, 141–45, 148–51, 157, 196n48
dispossession: colonial, 7, 9–10, 24, 71, 107, 155, 158; ecological, 30, 43–44; economic, female: 26, 66, 70, 73–74, 155; of land, 9, 97, 110, 116; legislated, 72, 72, 77, 79l; sovereign, 11, 40, 43
divorce law, 6, 11–13, 21, 26, 62, 64–76, 70, 73–77, 79, 83–85, 87, 89, 155–56, 180–81n13, 181n21
doctrine: deodand as, 128; of formal equality, 129; of habeas corpus, 127; as imaginative or fictional, 135; of legal personality, 128; of land in Nigerian customary law, overturned, 37; literature's influence on legal, and vice-versa, 27, 113; of originality, 109–10; racialized legal personality, 6; transforming, potential for, 24
Dowling, Sarah, 196n36
dowry, 74–76, 183n36, 184n64
Drahos, Peter, 188n6
Driver, Dorothy, 106

Eatough, Matthew, 95–96
ecology: extraction, contrasted to, 23, 50–54, 61; harms to, 23, 25, 29–34, 36–44, 46–47, 50, 52, 61; and Indigenous philosophies, 25, 34, 52–60; legal protections for, 23, 61; literary representations of, 33–34, 43, 45–50, 52–60; sustainability and, 21, 34, 61; as symbiotic, 6, 25, 34, 52–54, 56, 61
Ehikhamenor, Victor, 34
Elam, Daniel, 169n51
elegy, 123, 137–138, 145–46, 150
Emecheta, Buchi, *Destination Biafra*, 29, 33
England, 1, 5, 11, 33, 68, 71, 91, 97–98, 124–27, 130–31, 141–42, 155, 195n20
enjambment, 138, 141, 144–45
enslavement. *See* slavery, chattel
Environmental Impact Assessment Decree, 42
environmental law, 11, 34, 42–44, 51, 176n72
epic, 27, 87, 111–112, 120, 123, 147–49, 151, 153
ethnonationalism, 54, 64–66, 126
Europe: colonial rule by, 8, 49, 91, 98, 121; colonial wealth accumulation by, 35–36, 91, 98, 106, 157–59; cultural supremacy, assumed by, 147; ideas from, 8, 11, 50, 91, 93, 98–99; laws originating in, 30, 90, 98, 104, 107, 128; misogyny and, 106–7; multinationals headquartered in, 31; racism and, 17, 97, 107, 121–22, 128, 132
Evans, Mel, 178n42
experimentation: as aesthetic approach, 3, 5, 20–21, 138, 142, 151, 157

Falola, Toyin, and Matthew Heaton, 43, 174n42, 175n69
Fanon, Frantz, 9
Fehskens, Erin M., 193n1
feminism: activism, based in, 62, 65–66, 78; and aesthetic theory, 17; as critique of colonialism, 9; and economics, 72–73; in India, 62, 64–65, 179n5, 181n18, 181n20, 181–82n23, 182n29; and the law, 26, 65–67, 101; and legal reform, 21, 67, 74–75, 78, 85, 89, 155, 181n14; literary approaches to, 68, 70, 72, 79, 83–84, 89, 183n43; and racism, critique of, 101–2; in South Africa, 101–2; and socialism, 23, 68, 78, 83. *See also* gender
figuration, 15, 27, 43, 55, 129, 131–35, 137
Fishermen, The (Obioma), 25, 33, 39, 44–48, 53–59, 79, 107, 156
focalization, 23, 40, 44, 95, 102–3, 109, 112, 115, 148
force (aesthetic), 14, 16, 18–20, 22, 24–25, 27–28, 33, 60–61, 143, 154, 156, 160
form (literary), 15–16, 129
Four Nigerian Farmers and Milieudefensie v. Shell (2021), 30–31, 59, 172n8
Friedman, Susan Stanford, 183–84n43

Galvin, Rachel, 197n76
Gandhi, Leela, 83
gender: and enslaved African women's subjection to sexual violence, 132–33; inequality in Indian inheritance and laws, 6–7, 26, 62–89; in South African intellectual property law, 90, 113, 119; and labor exploitation, 97–103; as pressing social issue in present, 27–28
Ghana, 93
Ghosh, Amitav, 172–73n18, 174n50
Gilroy, Paul, 166n12
Global North, 26, 30–31, 41, 59–60, 90–92, 98, 106, 154
Global South, 30, 38, 59–60, 90–95, 101, 109–10, 112, 115, 187n2

God of Small Things, The (Roy), 7, 21, 26, 62, 66–89, 107, 155–56
Grazia, Margreta De, 113
Gregson v. Gilbert, 121, 123, 131, 133, 137, 140–42, 148, 152, 193n5
Griqua, 96–97, 102, 104–7, 110–117
Grotius, Hugo, 125, 152, 198n103

Habila, Helon, 29, 34
Haraway, Donna J., 177n94
Harlin, Kate, 45
Harris, Cheryl I., 9–10, 168n42
Hartman, Saidiya, 122, 132
Hindu Succession (Amendment) Act, 85
Hindu Succession Act, 64, 180n8
Hofmeyr, Isabel, 104
Holmes, Oliver Wendell, Jr., 151–53, 199n106
hope, 23–25, 34, 122, 138, 154–57, 159–60, 169n50
Hopkins, Samantha et al., 172n8
Huaman, Elizabeth Sumida, 188–89n12
Hunter, Walt, 144, 169n2
Hussain, Nasser, 168n46

Ifowodo, Ogaga, *The Oil Lamp* 34
Iheka, Cajetan, 29, 49–50, 60
imagination, 27, 54, 66–67, 82, 85, 123, 127, 134–36, 148, 151, 153
impropriety: anticolonial property law reform, in, 14; characteristics of, 22; as not contrarian, 22; logical structure of, 54; as rejection of proprietary property law, 22. *See also* aesthetic impropriety
in personam, 128
in rem, 128
India, 5–7, 12–13, 21, 23, 26, 51, 62–89, 92, 107, 117, 155–56
Indian Succession (Amendment) Act, 64, 85, 180n12
Indian Succession Act, 63, 180n9, 180n12
Indigenous: cultural production, 7, 112–114, 23, 26, 92–95; dispossession, 6, 9–11, 90–92, 97, 117; intellectual property law reforms, 90–94, 96, 101, 104, 107–9, 117–119, 155; land, philosophies of, 8–9, 25, 48, 51–52. *See also* Whyte, Kyle
Indigenous Knowledge Act (2019), South Africa, 14, 93–95, 108–9, 115, 117–118, 155, 192n71
Indigenous peoples: Anishinaabe, 49; Goenpul, 9; Griqua, 96, 104; Ijaw, 46; Ogoni, 29, 34, 46; in the Niger Delta, 36, 39–40, 50; in South Africa; 96–97
inheritance law, 6, 11, 24, 26, 62–70, 72–75, 77, 84–85, 107, 155, 179n5, 180n8, 184n64
innovation (literary), 5–6, 13, 123
instrument (legal), 5, 10, 14, 16, 42, 63, 155
intellectual property law 11–13, 21–23, 26–27, 90–104, 106–12, 114, 117–119, 133, 155
Intellectual Property Laws Amendment Act, 192n71

Jack-Osimiri, Uche, 174n48
Jaji, Tsitsi, and Lily Saint, 186–7n1
Jamaica, 121, 199n4, 200n8
James, C. L. R., 86, 167n18
Jaszi, Peter, and Martha Woodmansee, 98–9, 190n25
Joyce, James, *Ulysses*, 111–112
justice: criminal, 125; environmental, 31, 49, 61; ex post facto, 120; gender, 62–65, 86; in legal thought, 13, 20, 24, 86, 118, 122–23, 155–57; literary approaches to, 27, 118, 141; literature's role in producing, 27, 61, 141–43, 145–47, 151, 155; messianic, 24; poetic, 69; racial, 2, 4, 14, 122, 135, 138, 142–43; restorative, 93; social, 64, 73, 180n8; symbolic, 46; Virgil and, 152–53

Kalliney, Peter, 170n53
Kapur, Ratna, 64, 179n1, 181n18, 182n28
Kathakali, 86–89
Kenya, 114
Kerala, 64, 68, 74, 78, 86, 179n6, 180n12
King, Tiffany Lethabo, 122–23
Konne, Barisere Rachel, 176n72, 177n103
Kornbluh, Anna, 15–16

labor, 9, 12, 35, 66, 71–73, 77, 82, 91, 96–100, 102–3, 109, 114–116, 122, 127, 168n43, 182n27. *See also under* gender: labor exploitation
Laing, Lionel H., 195n20
Lambert, Laurie, 122
land law, 24–25, 30, 32–37, 40–41, 43–45, 47, 49–51, 56–57, 59–60
Land Use Act, 25, 36, 38, 42–43, 56, 59
Legacies of British Slavery database, 194n18
legal personality, 6–7, 27, 88, 120, 122, 125–28, 134–37, 139–41, 149, 151, 153, 155, 196n38. *See also* personhood
Leman, Peter, 169n47

INDEX

Lemaster, Tracy, 183n43
LeMenager, Stephanie, 174n51
Levine, Caroline, 15–16
Liberate Tate, 29, 59
lineation, 131, 144, 146, 148, 151
litigation, 30, 32, 60, 75–76, 99, 120
Lloyd, David, 17
Lobban, Michael, 194n15
Locke, Hew: 2–5, 14, 157–160; *Sovereign with Spider Monkeys*, 158; *Castara Estates*, 158, 200n9; *Hinterland*, 158; *The Procession*, 157–160
Locke, John, 5, 98
Lye, Lin Heng, 51

Mackey, Nathaniel, 140
Macpherson, C. B., 11
Madhu Kishwar v. State of Bihar, 63, 179n5
Marriage Laws Amendment Bill, 2010, 64, 76, 180–81n13
Marriage Laws Amendment Bill, 2013, 26, 156, 180–81n13
Martin, Dawn Lundy, 197n76
Marxism, 6, 8, 15, 66, 128, 167n19, 169n48
materialism, 16, 27, 40, 43, 45, 60
Mawani, Renisa, 125, 127–28, 134–5, 167n22
McKittrick, Katherine, 121
Mda, Zakes, *Heart of Redness*, 96
Menon, Nivedita, 66, 181n20
metaphor, 22, 40, 44, 47, 50, 71, 81, 83, 100–101, 128–29, 134, 137–38, 145, 150–51
metonymy, 4, 34, 41, 46–47, 55, 105, 139
Mgbeoji, Ikechi, 188n8
Mineral Oils Ordinance, 25, 33, 36–37
Minerals Act, 37, 56
Mintz, Sidney, 167n18
Mishra, Archana, 66
Mohanty, Chandra Talpade, 166n15
Mohd. Ahmed Khan v. Shah Bano Begum & Ors, 65
monument, 2–4
Moreton-Robinson, Aileen, 9, 11, 167n20
Morton, Stephen, 168n46
Mosimege, Mogege, 189n19
Moten, Fred, 128, 142, 187–87n1, 197n74
Mrs. Mary Roy Etc. Etc v. State of Kerala & Ors, 26, 63, 65–67, 72–73, 85, 180n9
Mtubani, V. C. D., 125, 128
Munro, Brenna M., 105
Muslim Women (Protection on Divorce) Act, 65, 181n25

Naimou, Angela, 129, 169n50
narrative: collective production of, 7, 51, 93, 95, 98, 109, 113–117, 119; labor, 96–100, 102–3; oral, 7, 54, 58, 92–94, 109, 116–117, 122, 137, 148; about origins, 92, 96–100, 104–6, 110–112, 115, 117; recursive, 47, 57, 79, 81–82, 86, 138; temporality, 19, 46, 57–58, 68, 83, 87, 95, 100, 103–106, 110–111; trajectory, 84, 89, 142
nationalism, 104–105, 110, 114
Navigation Acts, 27, 125–27, 133
Ncube, Caroline B., 101, 109
Needham, Anuradha Dingwaney, 80–81, 183n43, 186n104
Neti, Leila, 185n77
Ngai, Sianne, 169n53
Nichols, Robert, 10, 167n20
Niger Delta, the, 13, 20, 25, 39–36, 38–46, 50, 52–53, 55–57, 59, 61, 120, 171n2, 173n26, 175n6, 103n177
Nigeria, 5–6, 12, 23, 25, 29–30, 33–47, 49–61, 96, 107, 155, 157, 200n8
Nixon, Rob, 29–30, 42, 171n2, 171n7, 175n64, 176n74

Obi, Cyril, 36
Obioma, Chigozie, 7, 20, 23, 25, 33–34, 44–48, 52–58, 79, 107, 123, 156
Oguamanam, Chidi, 92
Okpabi & Ors. v. Royal Dutch Shell Plc, 25, 31, 33, 59–60, 172n15
Okpewho, Isidore, *Tides*, 29, 34, 49–50
Okri, Ben, 7, 20, 23, 25, 29, 33–34, 39–45, 47–50, 52–54, 56–59, 79, 107, 123, 156
Oldham, James, 193n15, 194n15
Olunide, Ekanade, 37, 173n26, 176n77
oral narrative. *See* narrative: oral
oratory, 145, 147–49, 151–53; incantatory form, 27, 123, 137, 144, 149–51, 153
Outka, Elizabeth, 185n93
Oxford English Dictionary, 12, 22

Part B States (Laws) Act, 63
patriarchy: authorial authority as, 100–101; and domination, 72–73, 78; in Indian inheritance and divorce laws, 23, 26, 62, 65, 700, 76–77, 85, 89; social norms shaped by, 64, 68–70, 76–77, 80–81, 181n18; and white supremacy, 168
personhood: legal, 11, 133, 23–24, 88, 121–23, 128, 134–35, 151, 155, 167n22; negated, 122,

personhood (continued)
   149; negative, 127, 196n38; retractable, 129, 137, 139, 196n38; spectral, 27, 123, 151. See also legal personality
petro: -activism, 46; -aesthetics, 29, 47; -fiction, 38; -magic-realism, 38–39; -violence, 43
Petroleum Act, 37–38, 42–43
Philip, M. NourbeSe, 7, 21, 23, 27, 120–21, 123–24, 129–33, 139–53, 155–56, 194n16
Philips, Amali, 69, 76, 183n36, 184n64
Platform London, 29, 59
plot, 15, 23, 47; in *David's Story*, 95–97, 100, 104–6, 109–14; in *The Fishermen*, 34, 44; in *The God of Small Things*, 26, 67–68, 77–78, 81–84; 87–89; in "What the Tapster Saw," 39; in *Zong!*, 138
Pope v. Currl, 98
possession, 9–12, 21–22, 50–51, 79, 115, 123, 126, 134, 137–39, 143
postcolonial studies, 7, 13–14, 18, 24, 49–50, 64, 86, 156–57
privation: as consequence of English-derived property law: 6, 21, 23, 38, 56; racialized, 3
property: as alienable, 8, 10, 35, 37, 43, 48, 56; exclusion from, 23, 40, 51, 67–69, 72–73, 79–85, 89–91, 94, 99, 105, 108–9, 113, 119–20, 128, 132, 153; as immoveable, 6, 8, 26, 30, 38, 62, 72, 73, 166n3; as inalienable, 36; marital, 64, 75–76; as moveable, 6, 26, 62, 74, 127, 166n3; patriarchal approaches to, 26, 62, 72, 77, 85; personal, 90, 126, 166n13, 188n6; private, 38, 40, 66, 79, 99, 113, 179n5, 185n79; protections, 12, 26, 65–66, 68, 73–74, 76, 78, 85–86, 90, 94, 107–10, 112, 115, 179n1, 179n5; public, 1–3; theft of, 75, 92, 106, 158; theories of, 3, 5–12, 21–27. See also admiralty law; divorce law; environmental law; inheritance law; intellectual property law; legal personality; personhood
proprietariness: as analytically generative framework, 11–12, 21–23; anti-colonial rejection of, Hew Locke's, 156, 158; of colonial land law as enabling petroleum extraction, 30, 32–34, 37–44, 48–49, 52, 54, 67; emergent anti-colonial challenge to, 6–7, 17; in English-derived property law, 5, 11–12, 25–26; in intellectual property law, 90–91, 93–94, 97–101, 103, 107, 109–10, 113–114, 119; and patriarchal property ownership, 60, 68, 72; and racialized legal personality, 3, 131, 136, 142, 144, 148; and racial separatism of apartheid, 114; and whiteness as property (Harris), 10
protocol (legal), 30, 91, 93, 109, 155, 189n14, 192n74

racial capitalism, 31, 139, 167n19, 172n18. See also colonial racial capitalism
racial justice. See under justice: racial
racial violence, 2, 4, 27, 132, 142, 157, 167n18, 169n50
racialized: dispossession, 8, 90–91, 155, 158; distribution of ecological harms, 31–36, 47; imaginative survival of, 17; labor exploitation, 97–98, 101–4, 119, 157; ownership of land, 9, 11; ownership of people, 2–3, 12, 117, 130–31, 133, 137–39; ship as juridical form (Mawani), 125; subordination, redressing, 94, 117, 139
Rajan, Rajeswari Sunder, 64–65, 182n29
Ramazani, Jahan, 146
Rancière, Jacques, 19–20, 118, 169n53
ratio decidendi: as trope, 133–134. See also under trope: as legal principle
Reed, Anthony, 143
Reichman, Ravit, 111
resource extraction, 8, 23, 26, 31–33, 35–38, 42–43, 47, 49, 43–54, 61
rhetoric: as aesthetic element, 15; in legal thinking, 129, 134, 199n104; as literary figuration, 40–42, 58, 78, 99, 137, 140, 149
Riley, Christopher, and Oludara Akanmi, 60, 172n13
Robinson, Cedric J., 167n19, 172n18
Roht-Arriaza, Naomi, 188n8
Roorda, Lucas, and Daniel Leader, 30–31, 172n9
Rose, Mark, 98, 101, 190n25
Roy, Arundhati, 7, 23, 26, 62, 67–68, 70, 72–73, 75, 77–89, 107, 123, 155
Roy, Mary, 63, 67–68, 72–73, 155, 182n33
Roy, Srila, 70, 179n2
Royal Dutch Shell (RDS), 13, 30–33, 41, 59, 171n2, 175n69

Said, Edward W., 9
Saint-Amour, Paul K., 111, 188n4
Saint, Lily, 192n76
Samuelson, Meg, 97, 100, 190n24
Sarkar, Lotika, 181n14

INDEX

Schorr, David B., 177n105
Scott, David, 86
settler colonialism, 9–11, 48–49, 51, 95, 105, 108, 110, 192n71
Sharpe, Christina, 122, 144
Sharpe, Jenny, 143, 197n65
Shell Plc, 13, 30–33, 41, 59, 171n2, 175n69
Shockley, Evie, 140, 197n73
Singh, Kirti, 74, 76
Slaughter, Joseph, 14, 96, 170n54
slave ship, 27, 120, 128. *See also* Zong (ship)
slave trader, 1, 3–4, 35, 121, 124, 126
slavery, chattel: 1, 8–12, 121–49; *passim*, 157, 191n58, 194–95n19, 200n9
Smith, Bryant, 127, 134
Solomon v. Muthiah, 64, 180n9
South Africa, 5–7, 12–14, 21, 23, 26–27, 90–97, 101–2, 104–11, 114, 116–117, 155, 186–87n1, 192n76
Spike Island (Bristol), 2
Spillers, Hortense, 138
Spivak, Gayatri Chakravorty, 183n42
Stambovsky v. Ackley, 135–136, 197n62
statue, 1–5, 13, 157–58
Staves, Susan, 126
Stephens, Lisa, 176n72, 176n74
Stern, Simon, 99, 135
Stoler, Ann Laura, 166–67n16
structures of thought: aesthetic impropriety as model to identify, 96; and aesthetic involvement in legal transformation, 119, 160; as aesthetically encoded, 5, 95; as affective, aesthetic, and epistemological, 16; art's power to slowly shift, 25, 32, 34, 61, 110, 118, 115; circulation of, 15, 21; as epistemological condition, 143; registering and producing, process of 14, 16; syntactical interventions in, as grammar (Spillers), 138; in relation to Raymond Williams, structures of feeling, 16, 19. *See also* Williams, Raymond
Sturman, Rachel, 76
style, 3, 7, 15–16, 19, 22–23, 25, 34, 39, 45, 67–68, 79, 83, 86, 89, 115
succession law. *See* inheritance law
Swakopmund Protocol, 93, 109, 155
symbolism, 40, 45–47, 56–57, 69, 71, 75, 80, 83, 136, 141–42, 150, 158

Taíno-Arawak, 157, 159n4
Tate Britain, 157–158

The National Trust, 124, 194–195n19
Traditional Knowledge and Traditional Cultural Expressions Act, Kenya, 114
tragedy, 44–45, 47, 55, 57, 68–69, 79, 82, 86–89, 123–24, 137, 148
transatlantic, 134, 143, 153, 166n12
transformation: aesthetic, 2, 16, 81, 117, 141, 144, 148, 151, 155–57; of ideas, 4, 10, 14, 20, 86; legal (contemporary), anti-colonial potential, 2, 13, 25, 60, 64, 85, 110, 113, 118, 135–37, 160; legal (historical), effecting racial domination, 121, 125, 128, 133–34
Travancore Christian Succession Act (1916), 63–64, 67–69, 72–73, 75, 85, 179n6, 180n9
TRC. *See* Truth and Reconciliation Commission (TRC)
Tremblay, Jean-Thomas, 169n53
trope: of author as patriarchal in Zoë Wicomb's work, 100; of enclosure in *The God of Small Things*, 78–79, 86; as legal principle, 133–34; of mouth in *Zong!*, 151; affirming multiracial identity, 111; of national family in South African literature, 105; racialized ownership (*Zong!*), 131–32, 137–39; of reciprocal relationship in *The God of Small Things*, 81, 83
Truth and Reconciliation Commission (TRC), 93–94, 96–97, 192n76

Udo, R. K., 35–37
UN Declaration on the Rights of Indigenous Peoples, 92
United Kingdom, 2, 4, 31, 33, 59, 154, 156, 166n13
United States, 9–19, 27, 39, 50–51, 74, 91, 128–29, 135, 154, 157

Vadde, Aarthi, 82, 186n97
Van der Vlies, Andrew, 100, 105, 189n20, 191n58, 193n99
Van Hulle, Inge, 35
Vedanta Resources PLC v. Lungowe, 31–33, 59
Vergès, Françoise, 172n18
Virgil, *The Aeneid*, 123, 150–53, 199n106
visual art, 4, 32, 34, 59, 157
visual poetics. *See under* dispersal: visual poetics of

Watts, Michael, 174n42
Wenzel, Jennifer, 29, 38, 43, 47, 53–54, 175n52

West Africa, 3, 25, 34–35, 49, 56–57, 59, 132, 138–39, 147–48
West Indies, 71, 157
Western Maid v. United States, 153
"What the Tapster Saw," 25, 33, 39–43, 52–54, 56–59, 72, 79, 107, 156
Whyte, Kyle, 49–50
Wicomb, Zoë, 7, 21, 23, 26–27, 94–97, 100–107, 109–19, 123, 155, 187n1
Williams, Raymond, 16, 19–20
Wilson, Sheena, Imre Szeman, and Adam Carlson, 173n19
Winnington, Sir Francis, 126–27
Woodmansee, Martha, 98–99, 190n25, 190n37
World Intellectual Property Organization (WIPO), 92–93, 106–7
Wynter, Sylvia, 167n19

Yeats, W. B., "The Second Coming," 47
Yorke, P., and C. Talbot, 195n29
Young, Hershini Bhana, 106–7

Zambia, 31–32
Zong (ship), 7, 13, 27, 120–152, *passim*
Zong! (work of poetry), 7, 21, 27, 120–53, *passim*, 155

Rose Casey is Assistant Professor of English at West Virginia University.

www.ingramcontent.com/pod-product-compliance
Lightning Source LLC
Chambersburg PA
CBHW020406080526
44584CB00014B/1193